international
DESIGN
yearbook

1997

farra

First published in the United States of America in 1997
by Abbeville Press, 488 Madison Avenue, New York,
N.Y. 10022.

First published in Great Britain in 1997 by Laurence King
Publishing, an imprint of Calmann & King Ltd.,
71 Great Russell Street, London WC1B 3BN.

The text of this book was set in Myriad.
Printed and bound in Hong Kong.

First edition
10 9 8 7 6 5 4 3 2 1

ISBN 0-7892-0292-1

Based on an original idea by Stuart Durant
Designed by Michael Phillips, Archetype

Photographic Credits

Åke E:Son Lindman 1.115. Jean-François Aloisi page 13, no. 13. Roberto Angelotti 5.61.
Gianni Antoniali 1.2. Ole Arkhog 1.30, 121; 4.39. Jan Armgardt 1.87, 94. Daniel Aubry
4.42. Maria Vittoria Bäckhaus and Luciano Soave 1.22. Baleri Italia 1.16, 100. Daniela
Beranek 2.61; 5.73. Thomas Bialek 5.71. Morten Bjarnhof 5.10, 14. Industrial Bohner &
Lippert/D. Gallo, M. Krohn 5.83. Paolo Bolzoni 3.35. Philippa Brock 4.13, 14. Feddow
Claassen 2.45. David Cripps 3.4–7, 59. Kari Decock 3.47. R. Diehl 5.99. Deltaprint 5.15.
Christian Duchet 2.3, 21. Edelkoort Agency page 11, nos 5, 7; page 12 no. 8. Rick English
5.1, 17–19, 90. Carlo Fei 1.92. Alberto Ferrero 1.18. Siggi Fischer 2.75. Frogdesign/
Steven Moeder 5.11, 86–88. Mr Furlà, Milan 1.93. Gaspar Glusberg 2.78. Deborah Goletz
5.85, 103. Sam Griffiths 5.13. Thomas Grothmann 5.81. Léon Gulikers 3.16, 17, 24.
Darrin Haddad 4.38. Hans Hansen 1.114. Eric Hanson 5.6. Simon Harper 1.4. Sven
Heestermann 5.82. Jochen Henkels Büro für Produktgestaltung 5.47, 98. Osiris Hertman
3.60. Ian Hobbs 3.26. Yoichi Horimoto 2.26, 28, 29. B. Hubschmid 1.42. Setsu Ito and
Bruno Gregori 5.32. Markus Jans 1.52. José King 5.66. Paul Kozlowsky 2.86. Dan Kramer
3.42. Sigurd Kranendonk 5.65. Thomas Krause 5.64. Dorte Krogh 2.44; 3.30. Hisashi
Kudohu 5.89. Lydia Kümel 2.2, 66. Maurizio Lamponi 5.80. Per Larsson 3.57. Carlo
Lavatori 1.77; 2.11; 3.66. Tom Lee 4.26. Salvatore Licitra 5.95. Ernesto Martens 5.2.
Sue McNab 4.15–19. Tsuneo Miyagima 3.48. Hirofumi Miyamoto 5.37–39. Hiroyuki
Murakami 5.20. Louise Murray 3.39. Nacása & Partners Inc. 5.74. James Newell 4.21, 22.
Guido A. Niest 3.32. Bart Nieuwenhuijs 4.35–37. Jürgen Nogai 3.8; 5.67. Andrés Otero
1.73–75; 2.20. Keith Parry 5.48. Jim Pascoe 4.20. Kostas Pasvantis 1.80; 3.55. Tommaso
Pellegrini 5.21. Andrew Penketh 2.52. Photostudio D.S.P. 4.31. Mario Pignata-Monti 2.1,
38. Jan Pohribny 5.105. Nick Pope 1.76; 2.31. Porsche Design GmbH 5.9. Walter Prina
5.92. Marino Ramazzotti 1.49, 62. Johnny Ricci 3.15. Ann Richards 4.23–25. Markus
Richter 3.53, 58; 5.27, 68, 107. Doug Rosa 1.64. Katsuji Sato 4.11, 12. Pietro Savorelli
5.60. Rudi Schmutz 4.32–34; 5.106. Schnakenburg & Brahl 1.86, 108. Frank Schreiner
1.37; 5.75. Jan-Chr. Schultchen 1.1. Uffe Schultz 2.6. Bob Shimer © Hedrich Blessing
2.4. Sauro Sorana 5.78. Stan Stansfield 5.53. Jasper Startup 1.65; 5.49. Studio ABCDE
1.90. Studio Forma 3 2.62. Studio Rusch 3.10. Studio Serrapica/Stefano Stagni 1.27.
Nobuo Tanaka 2.87. Hervé Ternisien 1.59; 2.82. Stefano Topuntoli 1.118, 122. Leo Torri
1.20; 3.19–21, 23. Jason Tozer 2.12; 3.31; 5.72, 108–10. Emilio Tremolada 1.40, 44.
Tom Vack 3.37, 63; 5.23, 24, 104. Jacqueline van den Boom 5.16. Jan van Deuren 1.120.
Albert van Rosendaal 1.12, 83; 2.64. Tom Wedel 5.35, 36. Kersten Weichbrot 5.76. Chas
Wilder 3.64. Jens Willebrand 2.55; 3.29. Miro Zagnoli 1.50, 79. Andrea Zani 5.29.

editor

general editor

assistant editor

international design

Yearbook 1997

Philippe Starck

Conway Lloyd Morgan

Jennifer Hudson

Abbeville Press Publishers

New York   London   Paris

CONTENTS

Manifeste pour

Philippe Starck

Pendant light, *Romeo Moon*

Steel, glass, 150w halogen bulb

h 22.5cm max. l of cable 400cm

h 8 ⅞ in max. l of cable 157 ½ in

Flos, Italy

or an Autocracy of Design

une Dictature d' Autarchie

Philippe Starck

Today, we have a global need to

catch up on the evolutionary

process in design. Some might

see this as a need for revolution,

but we would be far better

thinking about an ongoing,

permanent and intelligent

evolution of design. This would

be preferable to the archaic

system of ebb and flow, rise and

fall we have had to date, which is

essentially non-evolution, merely

spasmodic revolution. And

revolutions take more energy –

and waste more energy – than

evolution.

Le temps de combat est revenu

If we consider that civilization and the human societies it produces follow a quasi-biological rhythm of cycles of development, then we can say that Western society is now emerging from a short, fifteen-year period of occasional brightness, and is about to pass, for an indeterminate time, into darkness. In retrospect, this fifteen-year term was a moment of indulgence, when surplus, luxury and fantasy reigned over what designers did. This period is now over and the times call for urgency, for political awareness, for social intervention, for militantism. The days of struggle are back. This change has an immediate effect on those involved in creating the forms and signs that define our social environment: architects, interior designers and designers. We cannot afford the indulgence of relaxing our concerns with the global sources of raw materials, with the industrial process. To do so would condemn our profession to obsolescence – and an immoral obsolescence at that. Immoral because we must face up to the social obligations of our profession and act according to them.

La reinvention d'une morale est le retour à un civisme moderne

By morality I don't mean the old, stifling and regulated morality of the past. I am calling for a new morality. We must reinvent morality. Today, too many societies are tipping too easily into antisocial forms. Under respectable pretexts of liberty, some social movements are advocating antisocial actions, which will ineluctably lead to repression, and to a partial or total loss of individual liberty. This tide must be changed, by urgently reinventing new codes of social life that will redefine the extent of both our individual liberty and our social duty. The reinvention of morality is a return to a modern civics. Without such individual decisions of conscience, there is no way forward for today's society. It is out of the question to imagine that a modern society, in which so many have a participatory role, can survive in a state of anarchy. A humane, intelligent, responsible social order, in which generosity and mutual respect are the rule, is the only path to freedom.

Le design ne doit pas être compris comme une aide à la consommation, mais comme une service envers la société

With such a society as ours, design is the victim of paradox, for example the paradoxes between art and industry, between conservation and consumption. But the apparently central paradox stems from the confusion between design and production. Design must ask itself questions in order to find a new role and a new legitimacy. It must not be seen as the tool of consumerism, but as a service to society. Once we see design in such terms, the paradox is resolved. Design as a social service, as a way of improving the life of others in society, creates a different program and different results. In particular, the design result need not involve production at all. In the re-evolution of design that is needed today, challenging the necessity to produce at all must be the first step. The designer's duty, because of past links to the production system, must now be to be the first to ask the user 'Is consumption necessary?' No is the best answer, but if it has to be yes, the finished design must involve the minimum use of raw materials, and contain a maximum of human values.

Le designer morale de demain a une role beaucoup plus large envers la société

The old idea of the designer as a mediator is also wholly wrong. A designer as mediator is inevitably involved in the process of production. The designer should be a doctor, listening to the patient, seeking out the best cure for the condition. In some cases where the illness is serious, a medicine of extreme sophistication is required; in some a traditional remedy suffices; in others good advice is all that is needed. So the new, moral designer of tomorrow has a much wider role in and towards society, and designís means of expression are not limited to production systems. Production is only one means of expression, and it should be the last resort. All the other possible solutions, not involving material consumption, should be explored first. And if production is necessary, that production should be ethical. For example, reorganizing a bus timetable to reduce city-centre pollution is design – it is honest work that serves social ends. It is 'design production' even though no consumption of material is involved. It is pure design.

Aujourd'hui apparaît – avec plaisir – une mouvement plus politique, plus rigoureuse, et plus pragmatique

This book by its nature excludes non-material design. But after the different formalisms of design in recent years, I am now pleased to perceive a tendency towards more political, more rigorous and more pragmatic design. Unfortunately, alas, we live in a mediated world, where ideas spread quickly, but are picked up, copied and imitated equally quickly. And in recent years design has also been very much – too much – a paradigm of fashion, and has pulled along in its train too many people who had nothing to offer, but were always willing to jump on any passing fad or idea as a source of inspiration. Already the *rigor mortis* of style has appeared in minimalist design, in ethical design and in recycled design. Ludicrously this leads to styles appearing in those very areas where style has no place at all! This is one of the misfortunes of modern society, which through the media seeks to dump work in categories or stick labels on to it. In fact once the label is in place, imitation starts, and the death of the idea begins. No sooner does a concept swim into life than its obituary can be written.

Ce qui est néfaste est généralement la forme

Most human ideas have a basic kernel of correctness. This is true at all times, as most ideas arise either from the unconscious, or from external basic necessities. What degrades ideas, what is their downfall, is often the form that they take. Consider the ideas in Jules Verne, or in *Tintin*, or any of the images of the future from the last fifty or one hundred years. There you see that the ideas were right, and have been achieved, but not in the form originally depicted. So it is that intuition proves almost always to be right, and the expression of it wrong! This wider, more political and more involved role must lead to the designer having a wider social understanding, so as to create answers with a wider reach. But at the same time we should not lose sight of the specific nature of design activities. Design is a vocation linked to certain abilities, which the designer has to learn to use. So while the designer's understanding of society must be as general and broad-based as possible, the design solution must be within the designer's capacity and technical understanding. It's tragic to see some designers establishing intelligently and rightfully their competence in one area, then trying their hand at another, not appropriate to their skills, and falling into ridicule. Losing sight completely of the duty they have to society and to design in this way, and doing quite the opposite of what they should be doing as designers, ruins their worth.

L'appel aux designers est d'avoir une vie riche

If I am making an appeal to designers, it is for them to have a full and rich life. To ask questions, and not to be too concentrated on their profession but to look around them, at civilization, at society and at themselves. Design must be led by passion, not by fear. Designers must use the unconscious rather than the conscious, think in terms of semantics not aesthetics, and not lose sight of the political ends of their work. They must always listen to the world around them, and never fall into the perversity of listening to the design profession. Trying to follow and answer criticism blow-by-blow is the best way to take a fall on a road you never had to travel! A good designer should never have to read a design magazine! Read fiction and literature, read science – but only be vaguely aware of what is going on in design. We must avoid formulating movements in design. For myself, I've always tried – and managed – to keep out of any design movement. Some might say that I have, unfortunately, become a one-man movement. But that way I have also kept my freedom. There is a caricature view of me and my work, in which some have tried to crystallize me, make me into a living statue. But I have my freedom, because I have the power to break out of the mould.

La notoriété exige de vous-même une grande vigilance, anxiété, honnêteté et moralité

Today's media society offers both advantages and disadvantages to a designer, as I have learnt myself. One advantage is that a certain reputation – even notoriety – is a source of power, and so of freedom. But remember, whatever others say (and have said about me) that you can never create your own public image. I have never tried to, because there is a functional analysis, real to me, of the surface elements of my media image. Not to construct a public image of oneself is a necessary honesty. The public image of a designer exists, I believe, in two forms. There is the caricature created by the media: it has a life of its own and you can do nothing about it, for or against. Such an image is as valuable as it is dangerous. Valuable, because of the power it confers, and the public recognition it offers. Dangerous, because such an image gets tied down to a period (media people love to think in decades) and nailed down to a style. I have always worked against those two ideas. Then there is the true public image. This consists of what people really think of you, as opposed to the media image. One cannot fabricate this either. It comes spontaneously from the quality of the service you have given. The more honest, respectful and passionate you are, the more gratitude you will create, and it is that gratitude which carries you forward in the long term. A media image can be knocked up in six months (and down in the next), while the true public image takes fifteen years to build up. That's the time necessary to form a clear and true view of a designer, unlike the media habit of playing with their toy images, now in favour, now out, now praised, now condemned.

The sum of these two images is in fact logical and practical; firstly because we live in a world of communication; secondly because design is communication. I am not interested in the object as a thing in itself, but as communicating the sum of its signs, even though this communication takes, for the moment, a wholly material form. The total image also allows people to understand their own position, their way of life and their modes of thought. It helps them to identify themselves. The image and the work of a designer empowers people to define themselves, by accepting or rejecting what is offered, and so deciding which groups or tendencies they are linked to. The image is practical in the context of an industrial society, in which a designer's reputation can be the basis for justifying investment and getting a return. It offers a guarantee to the industrialist, giving him confidence to invest more in technology and so creating progress. And finally, the industrialist has to take the project on trust from the designer, so reducing the risk of bastardizing the final design.

L'obligation à la qualité

The corollary of this, of course, is that the designer bears the sole responsibility for the success or failure of the product. In sum, the more reputation you have as a designer, the more you must question your work in terms of vigilance, concern, humility and ethics. And the greatest obligation that brings is for quality. It is the quality and not the quantity of a reputation that counts. A reputation is a communication tool like any other, except that it is not one that you can create for yourself: it is created by the society in which you live. In this sense, a creative person is only the representative of the expression of a group, a 'tribe'. Every creative person is carried forward and supported by such a tribe. It can be a cultural tribe, a generational one, even both. So there is no such thing as a solitary creator – that's a false notion, even for artists. It's élitist, artificial and catastrophic to think that creative people rely solely on inspiration. A designer's worth lies in what the work reveals about society – the designer cannot be detached from society.

Conway Lloyd Morgan

'If I wear boots it's because I ride a motorbike, if I dress in black it's because I'm overweight, if I have a beard it's because of my double chin, if I don't go to cocktail parties it's because I'm too busy.' Philippe Starck's definition of himself was made in answer to a question about his public image, often a contested one. No-one could disagree with the last part of his remark. Over the last two years he has had complete design direction of domestic electronic products for the whole Thomson Group (including Telefunken, RCA and other *marques*) in one of the most ambitious design appointments of the decade. He has designed and advised for Kartell and other furniture manufacturers, and is

submarine carrot and the French Olympic Committee to choose a torch based on a burning arm? 'Is Starck a Designer?' was the title of a London Design Museum exhibition of his work in those heady days of the young genius; he gleefully admits now that he chose the provocative title himself. A monk, he told an audience at the Salon du Meuble in 1996, advised his mother to put her son into design: a pious start, save that the monk was a Catharist, a sect that always rejected dogma. From such heady ambiguities design history is fabricated and design media reputation made.

One way to get to ground level with Starck is to start with his office. It is in Issy les Moulineaux, an

1

2

3

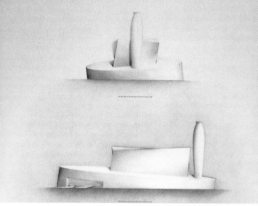

completing the interiors of three hotels and negotiating several others. As well as producing a series of lighting designs. And a motorcycle and a car. In the course of an afternoon's discussion of the contents of this *Design Yearbook*, he also laid the plans for a potential design retail centre in an American city, refused an invitation to lecture in Korea, organized a nursery school for his new child, and supervised the electricians working on the top storey of his office building.

Where in all this is the Starck of the 1980s, designing the interiors of the Elysée Palace for Mitterrand by day and hanging out in his own-designed clubs at night? Persuading a Japanese company to top their building with an immense

island quarter in unfashionable south-western Paris oddly ravaged by the tides of the century's urbanism. On one side of the Seine is a roaring motorway linking to the périphérique, below that abandoned barges and depressed houseboats echo a past industrial highway. Across the road stand pretentious suburban villas and a semi-derelict clapboard chalet. A hundred yards away in one direction a scrap metal dealer's *cimetière de bagnoles*, in the other a pristine office block in sub-post-Modern steel and glass. Next to the office on one side is the concrete templum Starck designed for one of his first clients, and just down from that Nouvel's *fausse péniche* for the advertising agency BBDO, complete with fake rust paintmarks. So is

Issy les Moulineaux somewhere to be now, or somewhere to have been? The Agence Starck building offers no evident answer. It is cased in pistachio metal siding, blank to the street but with louvred windows on the canal side. On the ground floor a salon that borders on the kitsch without tipping into it, replete with wood-burning stoves, African figures and flower lamps. Upstairs is Starck's own office – a large desk, no filing cabinets, just a double bed and a cradle for the baby; no floor full of designers and AppleMacs, conference areas or executive offices. The ambiguities of the interior reflect the ambiguities of the exterior setting: is this Madison Avenue, Paris? Is Starck a designer?

to them – and to many commentators – the greatest indulger of all time. They expected, even awaited eagerly, the bizarre and offbeat solution from their beatnik protégé. What they got was often *outré*, but was accompanied by serious questions about what design was for, and serious thought about what the corporation was doing and should be doing. In the early 1990s, chastened (and post-recession impoverished) clients expected designers to be bitten by humility, and accept such crumbs – and diktats – that fell their way. Starck was not subdued by that either, and transcendentally continued to deliver designs full of intelligence and replete with surprise. But the

5

Portable beam television and video projector, *Vertigo*
Bronze, glass
h 55cm w 21cm l 41cm
h 21 ⅝ in w 8 ¼ in l 16 ⅛ in
Saba, France

6

Armchair, *Monsieur X*
Beechwood, cotton
h 86cm w 54cm d 48cm
h 33 ⅞ in w 21 ¼ in d 18 ⅞ in
XO, France

4   **5**   **6**   **7**

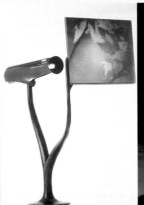
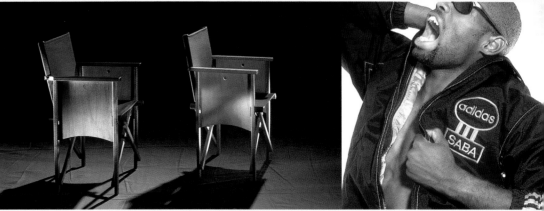

The answer perhaps is that Starck was a designer in the 1980s (but more than in 1980s terms), and is a designer in the 1990s (and still in more than 1990s terms). The meaning of the word has changed with the decades, while Starck remains. Just as the interior design of Starck's offices plays on the ambiguity of home and office (reducing the much-touted management concept of homeworking to semantic pulp in the process), so his tactics as a designer have been cloaked in the ambivalences of recent definitions of design. In the 1980s a designer added flair to a product, in the 1990s value. True design is about neither. In the 1980s it was fashionable (and affordable) for large corporations to indulge in design: Starck seemed

surprise was always linked to the intelligence.
    'Starck', said the commentators, 'has grown up: the enfant terrible is now an adult!' Not so. Starck has neither become grown up nor been ground down. Rather, he has assiduously maintained the barrier between the image of design and the reality of design, and between the exteriority and interiority of the designer. In public, Starck can play the clown: he enjoys doing it, and likes the perplexities caused by his verbal ambiguities, animal noises and *non sequiturs*. But the *non sequiturs* do make sense, the noises off do herald the arrival of the right idea. Like a conjuror, he enjoys getting the rabbit out of the hat: and he is not, acording to the best traditions of the Magic

7

Rhythm jacket, *Krazy Jacket*
Nylon, separate bass and treble stereo speakers
Saba–Adidas

Circle, going to tell us how it comes out. But because he is honest, he does tell us how it gets in. His analysis of the design situation of a company, of how and why his solution is going to achieve the needed results, is framed as accurately as any analysis by the men in suits.

This ability to see design functionally, to look beyond the brief into the management issues, is one key to Starck's enduring success. It is also, as he suggests in his introduction to this book, a technique every designer must learn, in order to meet the designer's duty towards society as a whole. The other key is his resolute refusal to play the game of design, to listen to the immediate

platitude must have a B face, after all) is that over-managed design is at risk of producing reduced and stultified design, in which objectives (management) become substituted for solutions (design). The designer does not just have a duty to the client, but a wider duty to society, which at all times is more important and more relevant than the duty to the client. The designer should – quixotically – take a stand outside the industrial process. Starck's refusal to conform on the inside, while being ready to play to the gallery on the outside, has allowed him to maintain such an inner/outer vision of social design, to establish his own certainties about what he is doing and why.

8

Portable television with integrated satellite antenna, *Partoo*
h 40.8cm w 34.8cm d 44cm
h 16 ⅛in w 13 ¾in d 17 ¼in
Saba, France

9

Chair, *Dr No*
Extruded aluminium, polypropylene
h 80cm w 54cm d 51.5cm
h 31 ½in w 21 ¼in d 20 ¼in
Kartell, Italy

8   **9**   **10**   **11**

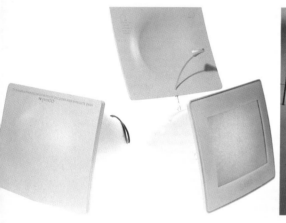

views of contemporaries, to hear the approving roar of the mob. When he has to hear it, of course, he doesn't mind, and even plays up to it. To make a long simile, a Starck lecture is as good an entertainment as a Crazy Gang concert, but also Bud Flannagan's battered boater there becomes as weird as Joseph Beuys's favourite hat. Starck challenges the commonplace, partly by wit – a *reductio ad absurdum* – but mainly by sheer thought – a true logician's ostensive reduction.

To equate good design with good design management is a common mid-1990s trope. Seen positively, it suggests that design for its own sake is now past and irrelevant, and so, barring a few special cases, it should be. But the downside (every

And to deliver design solutions, not management ones, which go beyond the obvious into a true understanding of the nature of design as a social implement. Thus it is that we now see him taking up the responsible role of serious design. But in fact that is what he has been doing all along. To achieve this he has had to resist the blandishments of easy notoriety, while also using – knowingly – that notoriety to establish his own individuality and presence. The temptations to glibness – to produce another *Starckerie* (one of his own terms) – must have been as endless as inviting, yet his own exhortation to designers – and to himself – is always to be modest, always to think. For Starck to have resisted that public clamour is not merely

10

Table lamp, *OA*
Murano glass
35w 12v bulb
h, w & d 50cm
h, w & d 19 ⅝in
Flos, Italy

11

Sunglasses, *Mikli*
Mikli, France

a measure of his achievement, but of the rational gulf he has fixed between the public and the private designer. As he himself puts it, 'the media are forever creating and destroying images of people. What the designer has to understand is that honest and passionate work creates its own consensus – a consensus that takes longer than the timetables of the media – and it is that consensus, that tribe, which supports and nourishes the true designer.' The photographs of Starck's tribe hang on the wall outside his office, like an early Daniel Buren in appearance but for the designer more a *memento vivere* than a *memento mori*, a continuing reminder of his serious and

media and yet independent of them. But I quoted to Starck T.E. Lawrence's comment about two types of dreamer: those who dream with their eyes closed, and those who dream with their eyes open – only the latter could change the world. Starck replied that what Lawrence meant was that only those who dreamt with their eyes open of changing the world could change it. A necessary pretension for designers. Dick's hero tells the truth about the present. Starck, with wit, assiduity and, at times, buffoonery, and from a hidden, private space, offers the truth about the future.

Starck's future is, with appropriate ambiguity, a void. In January 1998, he has announced, he is

12

Asahi Beer Hall, Tokyo (1989)

13

14" portable television,
Jim Nature
Wood, plastics
h 37.5cm w 38.5cm d 37cm
h 14 ⅞ in w 15 ¼ in d 14 ⅝ in
Saba, France

12

13

14

personal duty as a designer, a special kind of social human, with a special duty. For Starck, the object in itself is nothing. It has to have relevance, and content beyond its own material. The process of design, for Starck, is essentially a semantic and purposive one, in which the first question is not what but why.

In Philip K. Dick's novel *The Man in the High Castle* the eponymous hero is the only voice of truth and reason in a world tribalized and divided by ideology and propaganda. Given Starck's well-known liking for Dick's writing (a number of his designs carry names from Dick's science fiction stories), this might be the appropriate role for him – the last voice of sanity for design, using the

giving up design. This is to give himself more time to choose what he wants to do, whether in design or some other field: to dream eyes wide. It is also a decision linked to his conviction of the eventual futility of the object in a fragile world, and his belief that new modes of communication, virtual rather than material, must and will oblige humankind to look at itself anew, defining new ways of thinking, new ways of interacting with the world. 'The twenty-first century', he said recently, 'has to be immaterial and human. It is an absolute priority. If humankind remains stuck with the idea of possessing the material object, if the idea of material is not replaced by the concept of love, how will we survive?'

14

Bathroom designed for Duravit
Bath:
h 59cm l 180cm
h 23 ¼ in l 70 ⅞ in

f u r n i t u r e

Starck's selection of furniture for this Yearbook emphasizes the
need to reinvent design highlighted in his introduction. His choices could
be grouped under different headings: the artists, such as Ron Arad or Patrick
Chia, who pursue an individual vision; those interested in recycling and
reuse, for example Niels Hvass; the technologists such as Andrea Ponsi or Jan
Armgardt; the naturalists interested in the honest treatment of materials,
such as Natanel Gluska; and the minimalists, for example Konstantin Grcic or
that long-established and highly original designer Enzo Mari, for whom
reductionism is the aim. But apart from these his choice includes a large
number of designs he termed 'les anonymes plus', what might be called
'anonymity with attitude'. By this he means designs that take a minimal form,
have a general lack of decoration, and use materials, both natural and
artificial, sparingly and with care. They are often intended for the mass
market, as with Design Studio Copenhagen's work for IKEA. Figures as diverse
as Vico Magistretti, Antonio Citterio and Josep Lluscà come into this broad
category of designers who are seeking to meet the needs of society, rather
than following an independent, other voice. Such work is particularly
relevant today, at a time when design, for Starck, has to be led not by
aesthetics but by content.
    The anonymity of such design means that it will fit with any
interior, traditional or modern, and also emphasizes the mobility of the
consumer: living spaces today are occupied for shorter periods, people move
house more often, and virtual space, through the World Wide Web and the
Internet, offers an alternative to real space as a social and informational
environment.
    The 'anonymes plus' also reflect a more general trend in
commercial contemporary furniture design, away from the bold statements
of some years ago and towards a measured statement of needs, materials
and processes. This is in part the cautious response of an industry putting its
head over the parapet of recession, and in part a genuine professional
reaction against design extremes and indulgence. It is also a reflection of
the growing presence of what might be termed 'Northern design', from the
UK, Scandinavia, Germany and The Netherlands, in a market long dominated
by Italian designers.

Why pass someone a book when you can pass the bookshelf? Ron Arad's new pieces roll forwards and back, but while the outer flange turns, the inner wheel, mounted on ball-bearings, remains level and immobile. Not content to reinvent the wheel, Arad makes wheels within wheels as well. The result is an ur-wheel, which has the fascination of a huge toy, with its invisible forces and grand scale. It is also an ironical comment on those less adventurous designers who have timidly put standard furniture on castors in the last few years. The practicality of a seven-foot-high freely mobile set of shelving weighing 300 kilos is not the point: echoes of Ixion, the treadmill and even that fabled wartime invention, the Great Panjandarum, make this an iconic work.

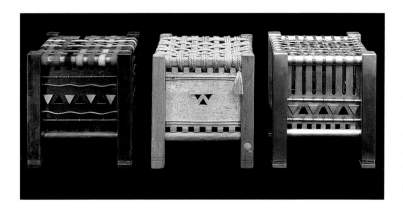

4

Diana Firth

Stools, *Moon, Whittle, Drum*

Moon: aluminium plate, brass wire, woven
aluminium wire

Whittle: demolition rimu, bamboo, inlaid paua,
shells, greenstone, woven muka (flax)

Drum: steel, copper, woven copper wire

h 30cm w 28cm l 28cm

h 11 ⅞ in w 11in l 11in

(Limited batch production)

5

Benny Mosimann

Container, *Ellipse Tower*

Aluminium, birch plywood,
polycarbonate sheet

h 43–148cm di 50–65cm

h 16 ⅞–58 ⅓ in di 19 ¾–25 ⅝ in

Wogg AG Möbelideen, Switzerland

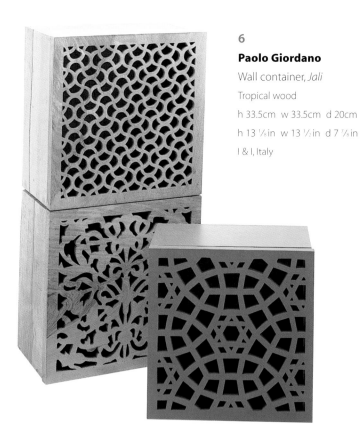

6

Paolo Giordano

Wall container, *Jali*

Tropical wood

h 33.5cm w 33.5cm d 20cm

h 13 ⅛ in w 13 ½ in d 7 ⅞ in

I & I, Italy

8
Gentelle Pedescleaux
Table, *Red Beans 'n Rice*
Wood, beans, rice
h 29.2cm di 17.7cm
h 11 ½ in di 7in
YA/YA, USA
(One-off)

7
Caprica Joseph
Chair, *Fire and Storm*
Wood
h 26.6cm w 15.2cm d 11.4cm
h 10 ½ in w 6in d 4 ½ in
YA/YA, USA
(One-off)

9
Ricardo Paul
Chair, *Jazzy Fingers*
Wood
h 17.7cm w 10cm d 10cm
h 7in w 4in d 4 in
YA/YA, USA
(One-off)

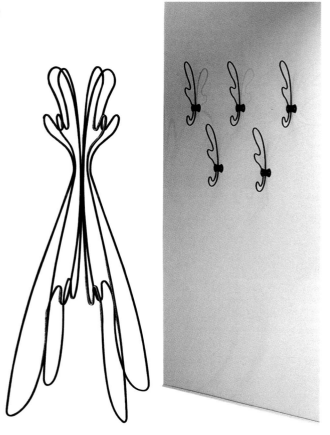

10
Daniel Rode
Coat stand and wall hanger, *Malaika*
Steel wire, baked epoxy
Coat stand:
h 180cm di 93cm
h 70 ⅞ in di 36 ⅛ in
Hanger:
h 27cm d 6.3cm
h 10 ⅝ in d 2 ½ in
Bieffe SpA, Italy

11
Ron Arad
Show-case, *Cler*
Glass
h 176cm w 52cm d 48cm
h 69 ¼ in w 20 ½ in d 18 ⅞ in
Fiam Italia SpA, Italy

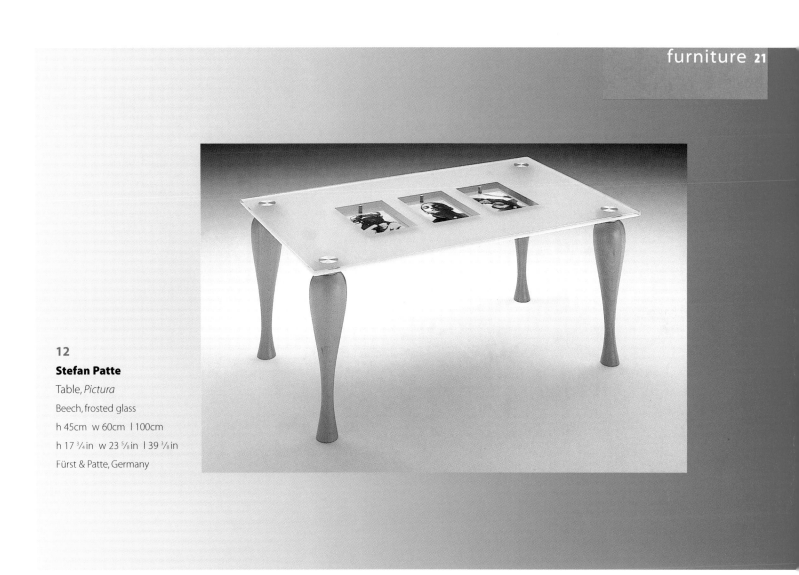

12

Stefan Patte

Table, *Pictura*

Beech, frosted glass

h 45cm w 60cm l 100cm

h 17 ¾ in w 23 ⅝ in l 39 ⅜ in

Fürst & Patte, Germany

13

Ron Arad

Table, *Boat Eye*

Marble, corrugated aluminium,

marble paste

High version:

h 73cm l 218cm d 118cm

h 28 ¾ in l 85 ¾ in d 46 ½ in

Low version:

h 41cm l 118cm d 63cm

h 16 ⅛ in l 46 ½ in d 24 ¾ in

Bigelli Marmi srl, Italy

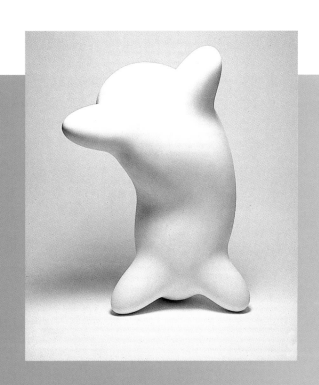

14
Patrick Chia
Seat, *Squeeze*
Resin, onyx, fibreglass
h 45cm w 45cm l 135cm
h 17 ¾in w 17 ¾in l 53 ⅛in
Squeeze Design, Singapore
(Limited batch production)

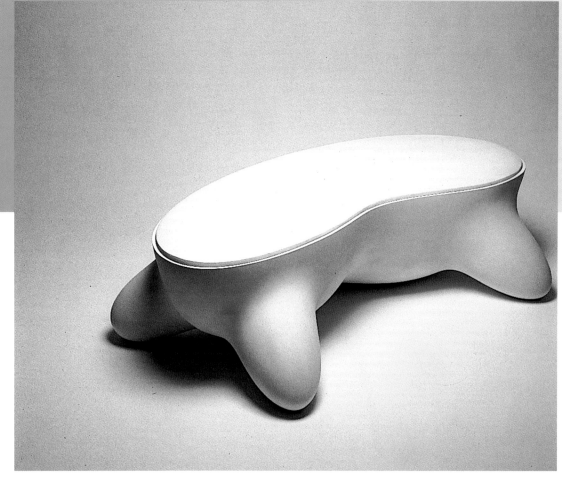

Patrick Chia's amorphous object *Squeeze* is

multipurpose furniture. It can stand vertically or

horizontally, and in horizontal mode with the

protrusions as legs (to create a flat upper surface) or as

arms (so it functions as a couch). The use of fibreglass

and resin as materials means this prototype does not

have to follow a single structural dynamic. It is an

attempt to evolve theoretically new forms of furniture

that both exploit technology and defy convention.

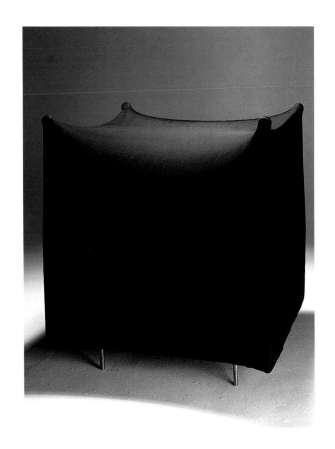

15

**Luciana Martins and
Gerson de Oliveira**

Armchair, *Cadê*

Steel, stainless steel, elastic

h 75cm w 66cm d 66cm

h 29 ¹/₂ in w 25 ⅞ in d 25 ⅞ in

Probjeto, Brazil

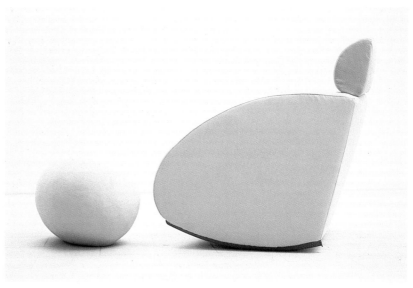

16

Denis Santachiara
Rocking armchair and footrest,
Mama and *Tato*
Steel tubing, polyurethane
Mama:
h 73cm w 77cm d 93cm
h 28 ¾in w 30 ⅛in d 36 ⅝in
Tato:
h 41.5cm w 65cm d 44cm
h 16 ¼in w 25 ½in d 17 ¼in
Baleri Italia, Italy

This chair for Baleri is called *Mama*:
'I conceived this object as a cradle for adults,
a means of rediscovering relaxation through
rocking.' *Mama* is an armchair that animates
domestic space, and involves the whole
body. Unlike a frame rocker, which has a
single plane of motion, this chair has a
separate rocker system for the headpiece,
and a separate, egg-like footrest that can
move independently.

17
Andrea Salvetti
Chair, *Tonzo*
Aluminium
h 75cm l 83cm d 56cm
h 29 ½ in l 32 ⅝ in d 22in
(Limited batch production)

18
Antonio Cagianelli
Suspension table,
Né in Cielo, né in Terra
Crystal, resin
h 70cm di 50cm
h 27 ½ in di 19 ⅝ in
Edizioni Galleria Colombari,
Italy

19
Rene Wansdronk
Table, *Abracadabra*
Glass, aluminium
h 73cm di 120–130cm
h 28 ⅛ in di 47 ⅛–51 ⅛ in
Punt Mobles SL, Spain

20
Marcello Cuneo
Table, *Giano*
Beech, aluminium
Closed:
h 75cm w 128cm d 90cm
h 29 ½ in w 50 ⅜ in d 35 ⅜ in
Open:
h 75cm w 200cm d 95cm
h 29 ½ in w 78 ¾ in d 37 ⅜ in
Cassina SpA, Italy

21
Franco di Bartolomei
Table, *Partner*
h 77cm l 140–226cm d 90cm
h 30 ⅜ in l 55 ⅛–89in d 35 ⅜ in
Cidue, Italy

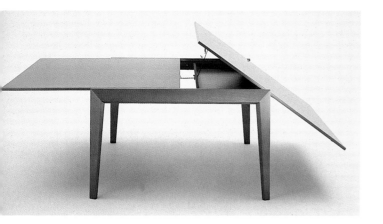 

22
Achille Castiglioni
Table, *Tavolo '95*
Beech, marble, laminate
h 73cm   w & d 140cm
h 28 ¼ in   w & d 55 ⅛ in
e DePadova, Italy

23
Achille Castiglioni
Writing desk, *Scrittarello*
Plywood, beech
h 72cm l 129cm d 65cm
h 28 ⅜in l 50 ¾in d 25 ½in
e DePadova, Italy

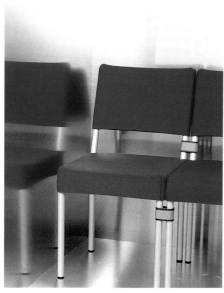

25

Edward van Vliet

Chair, *Yokoo*

Neoprene, metal

h 84cm w 45cm d 45cm

h 33in w 17 ¾in d 17 ¾in

Edward van Vliet, The Netherlands

24

Edward van Vliet

Chair, *Juju*

Metal, plywood

h 86cm w 40cm d 40cm

h 33 ⅞in w 15 ¾in d 15 ¾in

Edward van Vliet, The Netherlands

26

Paolo Rizzato

Chair

Fabric, leather, steel

h 79cm w 56cm d 52cm

h 31 ⅛in w 22in d 20 ½in

Cassina SpA, Italy

28
Francesco Binfare

Bed, *Tangeri*

Wood, metal, chrome plate,
expanded polyurethane

h 100cm l 298cm

h 39 ³/₈ in l 117in

Edra Mazzei, Italy

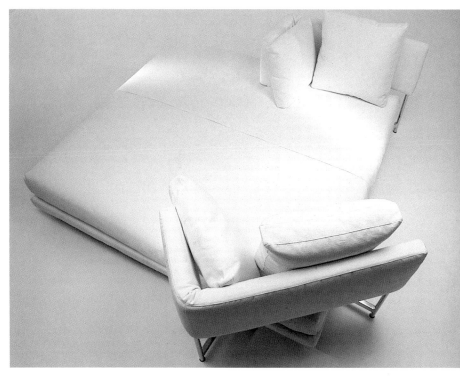

27
Paola Palma and Carlo Vannicola

Armchair, *Ciak*

Fabric, polyurethane

h 90cm w 80cm l 120cm

h 35 ³/₈ in w 31 ½ in l 47 ¼ in

Nuova Metalmobile, Italy

29
**Walter Becchelli and
Stefano Maffei**
Flexible table, *Leaf*
Poplar listel boards
h 74cm l 146cm d 70cm
h 29 ½ in l 57 ½ in d 27 ½ in
(Prototype)

30
Hans Jakobsen
Screen, *Transforma*
Recycled paper
h 160cm w 3cm l 300cm
h 63in w 1 ⅛ in l 118 ⅛ in
Art Andersen & Copenhagen,
Denmark
(Prototype)

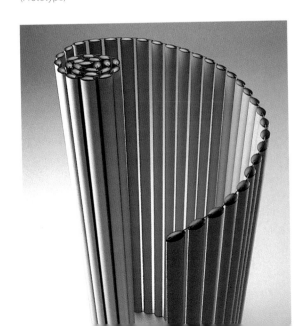

The sinuous form of Hans Jakobsen's
screen is a complement to its material,
recycled paper. The flexible links between
the vertical slats allow for an infinite
range of positions, while the screen rolls
into an elegant trunk shape when not in
use. The curves of the slats also allow
for an interesting play of light across
the object. Jakobsen here exploits the
material simply and directly.

For the 1996 Milan *Salone*, Opos arranged

an opportunity for designers under the

age of 35 to design an independent

piece of furniture. This is an unusual

focus, though more relevant to the

development of feasible design than the

usual approach of a student competition.

Over thirty designs were shown, ranging

from a coatrack made with scrunched up

mineral water bottles to pack-flat

furniture.

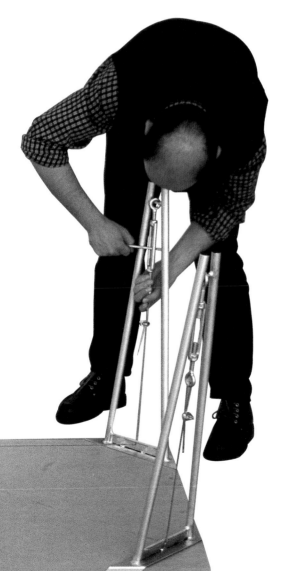

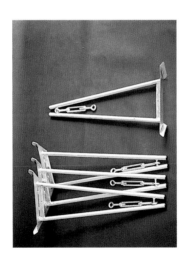

31
Tiziano Bono
Table-leg system, *Tenso*
Steel
Various sizes
(Prototype)

Tom Dixon's jokey chair

uses a traffic bollard as a

frame, cutting in behind

the directional arrow to

make the seat. It offers

the user a one-person

sit-down protest against

car culture: not necessarily

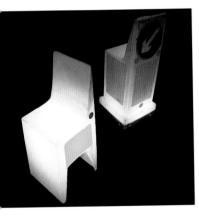

a comfortable one, but

more dignified than on

the tarmac itself.

32
Tom Dixon
Bollard Chair
PEHD, recycled traffic bollard
h 92cm w 37.5cm d 37.5cm
h 36 ⅛in w 14 ¼in d 14 ¼in
(One-off)

34
**Beata Bär, Gerhard Bär
and Hartmut Knell**
Chair
Post-consumer waste plastics
h 80cm w 50cm d 50cm
h 31 ½in w 19 ⅝in d 19 ⅝in
Bär & Knell Design, Germany

33
**Morten Kjeldstrup and
Allan Östgaard**
Child's chair, *Mammut*
Wood, polystyrene, fibreboard
h 58cm d 29cm
h 22in d 11 ⅜in
IKEA, Sweden

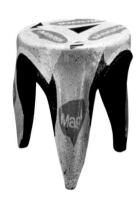

35
Beata Bär, Gerhard Bär
and Hartmut Knell
Table and chair
Post-consumer waste plastics
Table: h 75cm di 70cm
h 29 ½ in di 27 ½ in
Bär & Knell Design, Germany

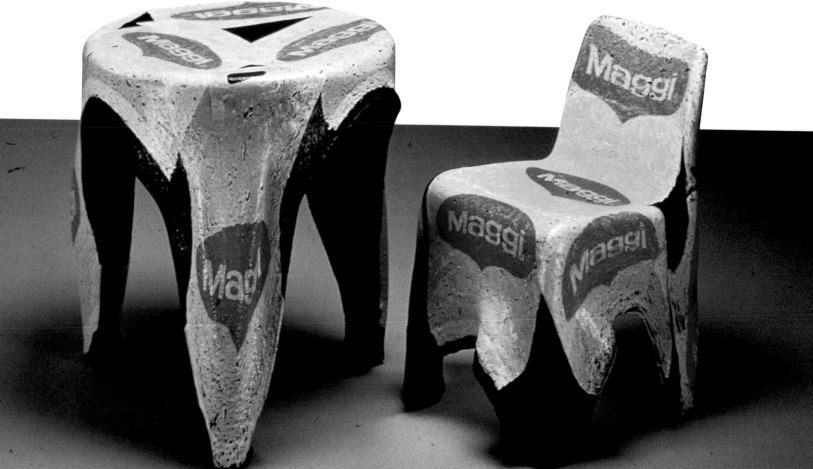

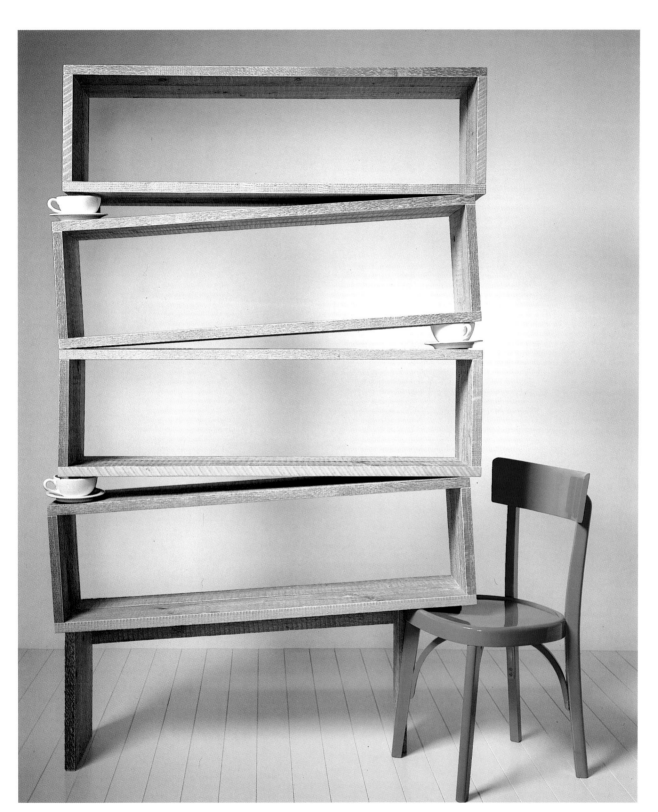

36

Köbi Wiesendanger

Bookshelf, *I Just Moved In*

Pinewood, ceramics

h 193cm w 148cm d 57cm

h 76in w 58 ¼in d 22 ⅜in

Avant de Dormir, Italy

(Limited batch production)

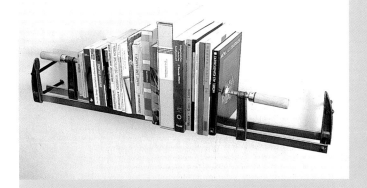

7

Karsten Weigel

Bookshelf, *Viceversa*

screwclamps

h 10cm d 16cm

h 3 ¼in d 6 ¼in

Designvertrieb, Germany

Karsten Weigel's bookshelf has the punning title *Viceversa*, since it not only functions like a vice or screw clamp, but actually uses a pair of them to hold the books in place. Starck distinguishes between recycling and reuse. Reuse involves using existing materials again, in a new role, as here. Recycling is for him a more suspect process, running the risk of becoming fashion rather than commitment.

Niels Hvass's *Newspaper chair*, for Octo in Denmark, reuses stacked, taped and cut newspapers to make a chair. The designer claims that only newspapers with headlines on major events have been used, so as to give this entertaining example of reuse the necessary gravitas.

38

Niels Hvass

Newspaper chair

Newspapers

h 70cm w 86cm d 70cm

h 27 ½in w 33 ⅞in d 27 ½in

Octo Corporation, Denmark

(Limited batch production)

39

Mario Mazzer

Multi-purpose tables, *Basic*

Wood, lacquer

h 44/70cm w 65/90cm d 45/50cm

h 17 ⅜/27 ½in w 25 ⅝/35 ⅜in d 17 ¾/19 ⅜in

Acerbis International SpA, Italy

40

Walter Becchelli, Fabio Bortolani and Stefano Maffei

Step-ladder, *Segreta*

Multi-layered birch

h 57cm w 40cm d 19–51.5cm

h 22 ⅜in w 15 ¼in d 7 ½–20 ¼in

Driade SpA, Italy

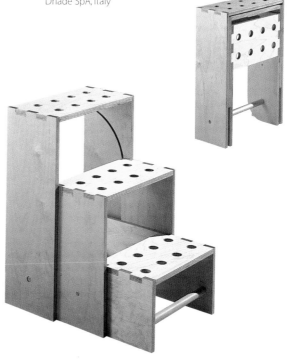

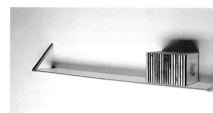

43
Christopher Deam and Tim Power
Stackable shelf, *Tier*
Steel, wood, MDF
h 39cm w 100cm
h 15 ³/₈ in w 39 ¼ in
David Design, Sweden

45
Bruno Anderle
CD shelf, *Andes - 'Darius'*
Glass, foil, chromed steel
h 12.5cm l 100cm d 14.5cm
h 4 ⁷/₈ in l 39 ³/₈ in d 5 ¼ in
Werkstatt, Switzerland

42
Svitalia
Shelving unit, *Endlos*
Aluminium
h 72cm d 10cm
h 28 ³/₈ in d 3 ⁷/₈ in
Svitalia, Switzerland

41
Lloyd Schwan
Bookshelf, *Balance Beam*
Brushed metal, stained white beech
h 180cm w 90cm d 45cm
h 70 ⁷/₈ in w 35 ³/₈ in d 17 ¾ in
Cappellini, Italy

44
Enzo Mari
Chair, *Box*
Tubular steel, polypropylene
h 81.5cm w 43cm d 45.5cm
h 32in w 16 ⁷/₈ in d 17 ⁷/₈ in
Driade SpA, Italy

46
Pete Sans
Shelf, *Phantasma*
Extruded anodized aluminium,
chrome-plated brass
l 300cm d 16.5cm
l 118 ⅛in d 6 ½in
Bd Ediciones de Diseño, Spain

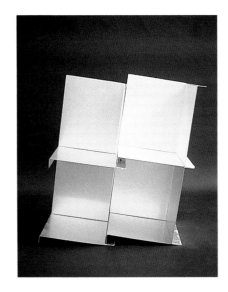

47
Pietro Silva
Shelves, *P*
Aluminium
h, w & d 30cm
h, w & d 11 ⅞in
(Prototype)

For Starck, Enzo Mari is *the* minimalist. He is

certainly no stranger to extremism. In the

seminal catalogue *Italy: The New Domestic*

Landscape shown at the Museum of Modern

Art, New York, in 1972, he took four pages to

explain why he was not going to create an

environment for the exhibition. The same

artful vigour underpins this kit chair for

Driade, consisting of simple components

sold packed in the box that gives the chair

its name.

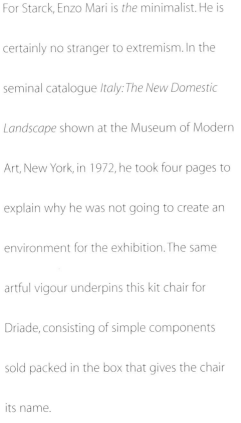

48
Venturi and Bortolani
Furniture series, *Boxes*
Plastic sheets
h 50cm l 90cm d 40cm
h 19 ⅝in l 35 ⅜in d 15 ¾in
(Prototype)

49
Prospero Rasulo
Table, *Texo*
Steel, leather
h 45cm di 60cm
h 17 ¾ in di 23 ¼ in
Zanotta SpA, Italy

50
Carlo Bartoli
Armchair, *Breeze*
Aluminium, polypropylene
h 70cm w 57cm d 48cm
h 27 ½ in w 22 ¾ in d 18 ⅞ in
Segis SpA, Italy

51
Daniel Rode
Chair, *Margot*
Steel tube, baked epoxy, fabric
h 80cm w 38cm d 49cm
h 31 ½ in w 15in d 19 ¼ in
Bieffe SpA, Italy

52

Werner Aisslinger

Armchair, *Juli Chair*

Polyurethane, steel

h 85cm w 55cm l 60cm

h 33 ½ in w 21 ⅝ in l 23 ⅝ in

Cappellini, Italy

53

Antonio Citterio

Chair, *Minni*

Aluminium, wood, plastic

h 78cm w 52cm d 48cm

h 30 ¾ in w 20 ½ in d 18 ⅞ in

Halifax srl, Italy

54

Vico Magistretti

Chair, *Maui*

Coloured polyurethane, chromed
tubular steel

h 79cm w 50.5cm d 46cm

h 31 ⅛in w 19 ⅞in d 18 ⅛in

Kartell SpA, Italy

55

**Uwe Fischer and Klaus-
Achim Heine for Ginbande**

Folding table, *Wogg 16 system*

Laminate, aluminium

Various sizes

Wogg AG Möbelideen, Switzerland

56

**Dante Donegani and
Giovanni Lauda**

Home office furniture, *Quant*

Metal, wood, fabric

Various sizes

Radice snc, Italy

57

Miki Astori

Trolley, *Galoppino*

Chrome-plated tubular steel, translucent plastic

h 48.5/63.5/94/110/140cm w 59cm d 44cm

h 19/25/37/43 1/4/55 1/8 in w 27 1/8 in d 17 3/8 in

Driade, Italy

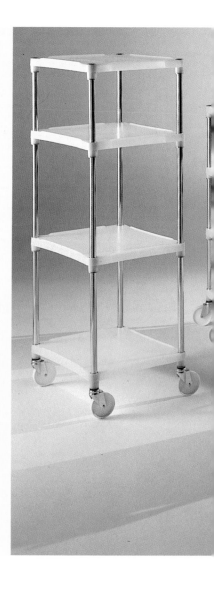

58
Giovanni d'Ambrosio
Trolley, *Mate*
Steel
h 63cm w 75cm d 75cm
h 24 ¾in w 29 ½in d 29 ½in
Bieffe SpA, Italy

59
Andrew Martin
Outdoor chair, *Rib*
Aluminium
h 80cm w 42cm d 50cm
h 31 ½ in w 16 ½ in d 19 ⅛ in
(Limited batch production)

60
Jasper Morrison
Stackable chair, *Lima*
Anodized or varnished aluminium,
coloured polypropylene
h 67cm w 60cm d 80cm
h 26in w 23 ⅝ in d 31 ½ in
Cappellini SpA, Italy

62

Patrizia Scarzella

Stacking chair, *Ginestra*

Aluminium alloy, natural fibres

h 82cm w 45cm d 52cm

h 32 ¼ in w 17 ¼ in d 20 ½ in

Zanotta SpA, Italy

63

Kasper Salto

Chair

Maple

h 75cm w 48cm d 45cm

h 29 ½ in w 18 ⅞ in d 17 ¾ in

Botium, Denmark

64

Brian Kane

Chair, *Xorel Chair*

Rigid and moulded Xorel fabric

h 79cm w 64cm d 56cm

h 31in w 25in d 22in

Carnegie, USA

65

Jasper Startup

Conference Chair

Stainless steel, seagrass, aluminium

h 80cm w 47cm d 50cm

h 31 ½ in w 18 ½ in d 19 ¾ in

Consolidated & Technical, UK

61

Christophe Pillet

Chaise longue, *Agatha Dreams*

Cherrywood

h 73cm w 64cm l 172cm

h 28 ¾ in w 25 ⅛ in l 67 ¾ in

Ceccotti Aviero SpA, Italy

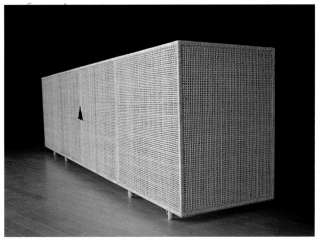

66
Tsutomu Kurokawa and
Masamichi Katayama
Lecturer's Table
Stainless steel, rattan
h 104cm l 400cm d 70cm
h 40 ⁷⁄₈ in l 157 ³⁄₈ in d 27 ¹⁄₂ in
H. Design, Japan

69
Natanel Gluska
Chair
Poplar
h 95cm w 40cm d 40cm
h 37 ³⁄₈ in w 15 ³⁄₄ in d 15 ³⁄₄ in
(Limited batch production)

68
Natanel Gluska
Chair
Elm
h 95cm w 65cm d 60cm
h 37 ³⁄₈ in w 25 ¹⁄₂ in d 23 ⁵⁄₈ in
(Limited batch production)

67
Natanel Gluska
Chair
Elm
h 100cm w 90cm d 143cm
h 39 ³⁄₈ in w 35 ³⁄₈ in d 56 ¹⁄₄ in
(Limited batch production)

70

**Vico Magistretti and
Patricia Urquiola**

Armchair, *Flower*

Rigid polyurethane, chrome-
plated metal

h 80cm w 59cm d 57cm

h 31 ½in w 23 ¼in d 22 ⅜in

e DePadova, Italy

71

Toshiyuki Kita

Chairs, *Aki, Biki, Canta*

Polyurethane foam, polyester
fibre, steel, polyurethane coated
steel, fabric

Aki: h 74cm w 62cm d 68cm

h 29 ⅛in w 24 ⅜in d 26 ¾in

Biki: h 68cm w 72cm d 68cm

h 26 ¾in w 28 ⅜in d 26 ¾in

Canta: h max. 107cm w 73cm
d 71cm

h max. 42 ⅛in w 28 ⅝in d 28in

Adele C, Italy

72
Marco Acerbis
Table, *On*
Opalcore, glass
h 63cm di 54cm
h 24 ¾in di 21 ¼in
Acerbis International SpA, Italy

74
Fernando and Humberto Campana
Screen
Metal, plastic string
h 175cm w 80cm d 25cm
h 68 ⅞in w 31 ½in d 9 ⅞in

73
Fernando and Humberto Campana
Chair
Metal, plastic garden hose
h 110cm w 40cm d 50cm
h 43 ¼in w 15 ¾in d 19 ⅝in

75
Fernando and Humberto Campana
Inflatable table
Aluminium, plastic
h 45cm (deflated) 18cm di 40cm
h 17 ¾in (deflated) 7in di 15 ¾in

76
Peter Christian
Occasional table, *Axle*
Cast aluminium, ash, plastic
h 62cm di 39cm
h 24 ³⁄₈ in di 15 ³⁄₈ in
(Prototype)

77
Stefano Giovannoni
Adjustable stool, *Bombo*
Polypropylene
h 80cm w 46cm
h 31 ½ in w 18 ½ in
Magis srl, Italy

78

Pascal Mourgue

Folding garden chair, *Dune*

Steel, Batyline fabric (PVC-coated

polyester fibre)

h 84cm w 45/51cm d 40cm

h 33 ¼in w 17 ¼/20in d 15 ¼in

Fermob, France

While Starck is against using history to validate design solutions, there are some designers whose work he feels other designers should consider. One such is Alberto Meda, whom Starck praises for his technical rigour. The integration of support, seat and frame in the chaise longue for Alias is clear evidence of this mastery. The keen profile of the headboard also shows a taut balance of forces, while the use of aluminium and net is wholly contemporary.

79

Alberto Meda

Chaise longue, *Longframe*

Aluminium, net

h 90cm w 54cm l 146cm

h 35 ½ in w 21 ¼ in l 57 ½ in

Alias srl, Italy

A simple solution for a singular problem. Edward Geluk's *XES* table is deliberately small in plan. It is intended as a stand for a single drink or plate next to a chair, where it can be placed out of the way. The weighted base in its neat conical form ensures that the table will not tip over easily. This is one of the first products from the new Dutch company, Goods.

Amos Marchant and Lyndon Anderson's *Luna* bar stool uses spare or surplus parts from dishwashers to create the seats and footring. This is wit at work, as much as recycling: the handsome stool is a design statement, not a political one.

82
Amos Marchant and
Lyndon Anderson
Bar stool, *Luna*
Aluminium
h 75cm di 45cm
h 29 ½ in di 17 ¾ in
Allermuir Ltd, UK

80
Edward Geluk
Small table, *Xes*
Nylon, aluminium
h 65cm di 13cm
h 25 ⅜ in di 5 ⅛ in
Goods, The Netherlands

81
Mengazzuto, Villis,
Nascimben Arch. Ass.
Bedside table, *ZAR 11*
Wood, metal
h 60cm w 43cm d 35cm
h 23 ⅝ in w 16 ⅞ in d 13 ¾ in
Frezza srl, Italy

83
Stefan Patte
Bench, *Sunlit*
Steel, solar modules, battery l
h 75cm w 180cm d 80cm
h 29 ½ in w 70 ⅞ in d 31 ½
(Prototype)

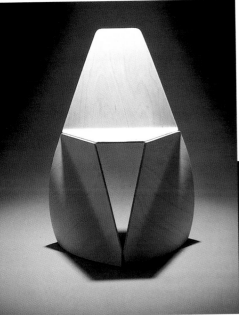

84

Peter Karpf

Stacking chair, *Tri*

Laminated wood

h 80cm w 55cm l 45cm

h 31 ½ in w 21 ⅝ in l 17 ¾ in

Inredningsform AB, Sweden

85

Mitsumasa Sugasawa

Chair for Japanese room,

Origami Zaisu

Curved plywood

h 44cm w 36cm d 50cm

h 17 ⅜ in w 14 ⅛ in d 19 ⅝ in

Tendo Co. Ltd, Japan

86

Nanna Ditzel

Seashell Chair

Wood

h 104.5cm   w 75.5cm   d 68.5cm

h 41 ¼in   w 29 ¾in   d 27in

P.P. Mobler, Denmark

(Prototype)

87
Jan Armgardt
Table, *JAZ28*
Maple
h 70cm w 45cm l 45cm
h 27 ½ in w 17 ¾ in l 17 ¾ in
(Prototype)

88
Lloyd Schwan
Armchair, *Statuette*
Fibreglass, metal
h 98cm w 101cm d 60cm
h 38 ⅝ in w 39 ¾ in d 23 ⅝ in
Cappellini, Italy

Giancarlo Piretti's extensible table for Itachair uses a concertina fold together with fixed and wheeled legs. This allows it to be used in a range of shapes from square to rectangular. While the practical problem of an extending table is neatly solved, the design is hardly novel. What makes this design special is the retention of balanced proportions between top and legs both in the folded and extended state. The self-effacing directness of the design makes it both appropriate and workmanlike.

89
Josep Lluscà
Chair, *Schieratta*
Steel, polypropylene
h 87cm w 49cm d 56cm
h 34 ¼in w 19 ¼in d 22in
Driade SpA, Italy

90
Giancarlo Piretti
Folding table
Steel, wood or laminate
h 71/75cm w 90cm
l 90/220cm
h 27 ⅞/ 29 ½in w 35 ⅛in
l 35 ⅛/ 86 ⅝in
Itachair SpA, Italy

91
Ben Hoek
Table
Metal, wood
h 74cm l 205cm d 95cm
h 29 ⅛in l 80 ¾in d 37 ⅜in
Spectrum, The Netherlands

93
Kuno Prey
Bookshelf, *Libreria*
Stove-enamelled steel
h 16.5cm w 32cm d 16.5cm
h 6 ½ in w 12 ⅝ in d 6 ½ in
Nava Design SpA, Italy

92
Andrea Ponsi
Sawhorses for tables, *On*
Copper, stainless steel
h 72cm w 52cm d 64cm
h 28 ⅜ in w 20 ½ in d 25 ⅛ in
Andrea Ponsi Design, Italy
(Limited batch production)

94
Jan Armgardt
Shelves, *JA 26*
Plywood
h 20cm l 122cm d 20/25/30cm
h 7 ⅞ in l 48in d 7 ⅞ /9 ⅞ /11 ⅞ in

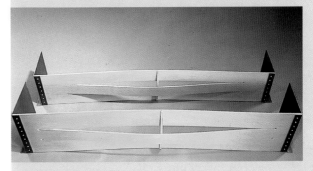

Jan Armgardt's pursuit of recyclable and natural materials in furniture takes a new turn with this plywood bookshelf, where the tension in the wood itself is used to hold the shelf in place, by a wedge passed through a cut section of the lateral plank. This exploration of the properties of natural materials also occurs in his willow and steel stool which uses the natural springiness of willow (a naturally renewable material) to give suppleness and a domical structure to handle the loads.

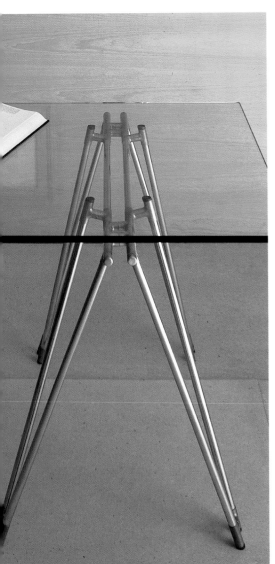

95

Michele de Lucchi and
Mario Rossi Scola

Bookshelf, *Interlife series*

Maple, aluminium

h 200cm w 40cm l 90cm

h 78 ¾in w 15 ¾in l 35 ⅜in

Interlübke: Gebr. Lübke GmbH &
Co. KG, Germany

96

Lucci and Orlandini

Stacking bookshelf, *Filox*

Welded steel, lacquered or
laminated wood, beech

h (between shelves) 36cm

l 108/162/258cm

h (between shelves) 14 ⅛in

l 42 ½/63 ¾/101 ⅝in

d 36in

d 14 ⅛in

Morphos (Divisione della Acerb
International SpA), Italy

97

**Maurizio Giordano and
Roberto Grossi**

Bookshelf, *Libra*

Steel, aluminium, leather

Various sizes

Saporiti Italia, Italy

98

**Lluis Clotet, Enric Miralles
and Oscar Tusquets**

Shelving, *Estanteria Hypostila*

Extruded anodized aluminium

Max. distance between uprights

150cm (59in)

h max. 400cm d max. 25cm

h max. 157 ½ in d max. 9 ⅞ in

Bd Ediciones de Diseño, Spain

100

Angelo Mangiarotti

Bookshelf, *Ipsylon*

Steel sheet

h max. 225cm w 90cm d 60cm

h max. 88 ⅝ in w 35 ⅜ in d 23 ⅝ in

Baleri Italia, Italy

99

Josep Lluscà

Trolley, *Sibilo*

Steel, aluminium, chrome

Top:

h 20cm d 38cm l 66.5cm

h 7 ⅞ in d 15in l 26 ⅛ in

Tall version:

h 111cm d 39cm l 71.5cm

h 43 ¼ in d 15 ⅜ in l 28 ⅛ in

Low version:

h 73.5cm d 39cm l 71.5cm

h 28 ⅞ in d 15 ⅜ in l 28 ⅛ in

Driade SpA, Italy

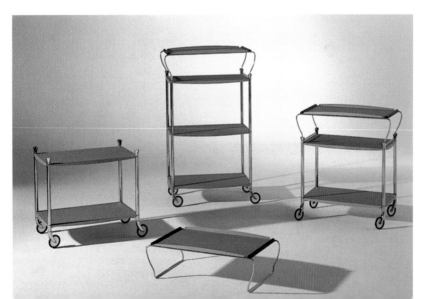

102
Lluis Pau
Bar stool, *Nuta*
Beech, chrome
h 45/60/75cm
h 17 ¾/ 23 ⅝/29 ½in
Mobles 114, Spain

101
David Grimshaw
Chair and stool from the *Janus* range
Beech, epoxy-coated steel
Chair:
h 85cm w 40cm d 52.6cm
h 33 ⅜in w 15 ¾in d 20 ¾in
Stool:
h 107cm w 37.5cm d 52cm
h 42 ⅛in w 14 ⅞in d 20 ½in
Allermuir Ltd, UK

103
Pascal Mourgue
Chair and armchair, *Tempo*
Multiplex and solid beech, lacquered metal
h 80cm l (chair) 44cm
l (armchair) 52cm d 48cm
h 31 ½in l (chair) 17 ⅜in
l (armchair) 20 ½in d 18 ⅞in
Artelano, Italy

104

Frederick Scott

Chair, *Nile*

Tubular steel, moulded

polyurethane

h 83cm   w 57cm   d 48cm

h 32 ⁵⁄₈ in   w 22 ³⁄₈ in   d 18 ⁷⁄₈ in

Allermuir Ltd, UK

105

**Johannes Foersom and
Peter Hiort-Lorenzen**

Chair, *Campus*

Beech or birch

h 76cm w 47/53cm d 49cm

h 29 ⅞in w 18 ½/20 ⅞in d 19 ¼in

Lammhults Möbel AB, Sweden

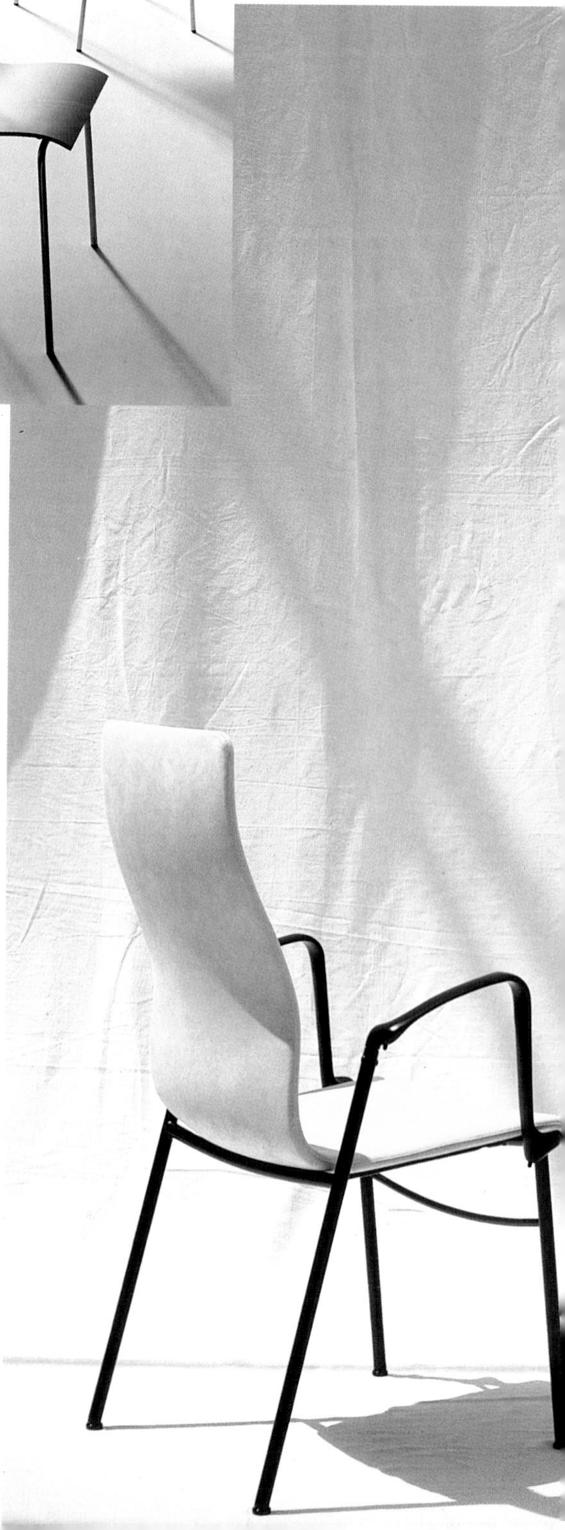

107
**Johannes Foersom and
Peter Hiort-Lorenzen**
Chair, *Qvintus*
Birch, steel
h 77cm w 59cm d 53cm
h 30 ⅛in w 23 ¼in d 20 ⅞in
Lammhults Möbel AB, Sweden

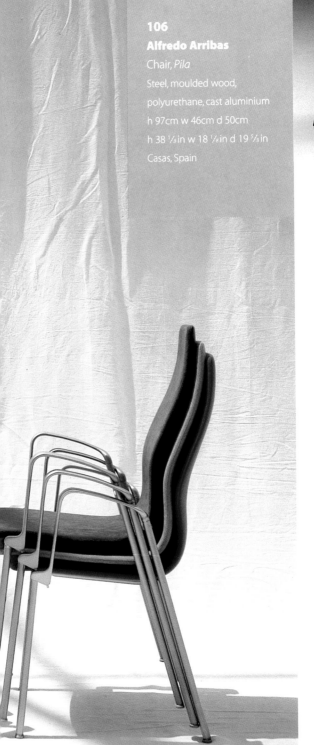

106
Alfredo Arribas
Chair, *Pila*
Steel, moulded wood,
polyurethane, cast aluminium
h 97cm w 46cm d 50cm
h 38 ⅛in w 18 ⅛in d 19 ⅝in
Casas, Spain

108
Hans Jakobsen
Chair, *Aunt Emma*
Elm, steel
h 69cm w 62cm l 44cm
h 27 ⅛in w 24 ⅜in l 17 ⅜in
(Prototype)

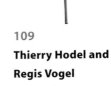

109
**Thierry Hodel and
Regis Vogel**
Chair, *Zébu*
Chromed steel, wood
h 84cm w 35cm d 43cm
h 33in w 13 ¾in d 16 ⅞in
Fou du Roi, France

110
Alfredo Arribas
Stool, *Copa*
Aluminium, steel, polyurethane
h 45/65/80cm di 36cm
h 17 ¾/25 ⅝/31 ½in di 14 ⅛in
Casas, Spain

111
Niels Bendtsen
Sofa and chair, *Long Fellow*
Leather
Sofa:
h 75cm w 158cm d 93cm
h 29 ½in w 62 ¼in d 36 ⅝in
Chair:
h 75cm w 75cm d 93cm
h 29 ½in w 29 ½in d 36 ⅝in
Montis, The Netherlands

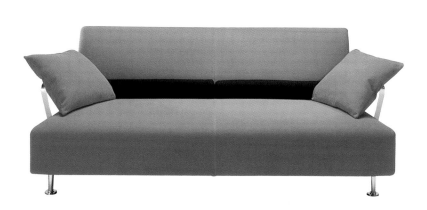

112
Vico Magistretti
Three-seater sofa, *Variantes*
Metal, polyurethane
h 79.5cm l 222cm d 89cm
h 31 ⅛in l 87 ⅜in d 35in
e DePadova, Italy

113
Wulf Schneider
Armchair, *290F*
Beech, aluminium
h 80cm w 55cm d 51cr
h 31 ½ in w 21 ⅝ in d 2
Gebrüder Thonet GmbH
Germany

114

Axel Kufus

System of drawers, *Lader*

Birch plywood

h w & l varied d 51cm d 20in

Moorman Möbel Produktions und

Handels GmbH, Germany

115

**Ann Morsing and
Beban Nord**

Cabinet, *Frost*

Stained birch

h 179cm w 66cm d 42cm

h 70 ½in w 26in d 16 ½in

Box Mobler AB, Sweden

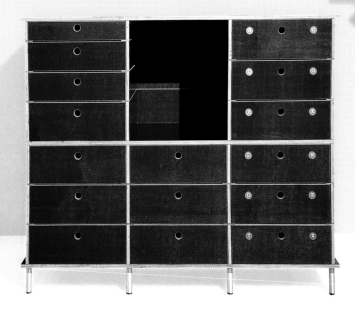

116

Didier Gomez

Stacking chair, *Patio*

Steel, beech plywood, foam,

fabric

h 83cm w 51cm d 54cm

h 32 ⅜in w 20in d 21 ¼in

Roset SA, France

118

Marco Zanuso and Dani
Nava

Armchair, *Litta*

Steel, glass

h 80cm w 54cm l 56cm

h 31 ½in w 21 ¼in l 22in

Arte srl, Italy

117

Design Studio Copenhagen

Swivel chair, *Nevil*

Transparent injected moulded plastic

h 75cm w 55cm d 41cm

h 29 ½in w 21 ⅝in d 16 ⅛in

IKEA, Sweden

120

Herman Wittocx

Chair, *Albert III*

MDF, Triplex

h 79cm w 44cm d 43cm

h 31 ⅛in w 17 ⅜in d 16 ⅞in

Herman Wittocx

Meubelontwerper, Belgium

119

Piero Lissoni

Chair, *Aprile*

Varnished metal

h 77cm w 57cm d 52cm

h 30 ⅓in w 22 ⅜in d 20 ½in

Cappellini, Italy

121

Hans Jakobsen

Chair, *Chairlotte*

Polyurethane textile, aluminium

h 78cm w 57cm d 64cm

h 30 ¾in w 22 ⅜in d 25 ⅛in

(Prototype)

122
Marco Zanuso and Daniele Nava
Table, *Soncino*
Steel, wood
h 74cm w 90cm l 200cm
h 29 ⅛in w 35 ⅜in l 78 ¾in
Arte srl, Italy

123
Piero Lissoni
Chair, *Ariel*
Beech, poplar, fir, cherrywood, ebony,
walnut, polyurethane, polyester fibre
h 80cm w 70cm d 65cm
h 31 ½in w 27 ½in d 26in
Living Divani srl, Italy

125
MDF Design Team
Storage system, *Frame*
Glass, anodized aluminium, wood
h 180/223cm w max. 190cm
h 70 ⅞/87 ¾in w max. 74 ¾in
MDF, Italy

124
Piero Lissoni
Chair, *Frog*
Iron, woven hemp cord
h 80cm w 80cm d 90cm
h 31 ½in w 31 ½in d 35 ⅛in
Living Divani srl, Italy

126

**Jochen Reichenberg
and Volker Weiss**

Garden chairs

Galvanized steel, larchwood

h 82cm w 45/62cm

h 32 ¼in w 17 ¾/24 ⅜in

Reichenberg Weiss, Germany

127

**Jochen Reichenberg
and Volker Weiss**

Garden tables

Galvanized steel, larchwood

h 43/73cm w 215cm

h 16 ⅞/28 ¾in w 84 ⅝in

Reichenberg Weiss, Germany

128

William Sawaya

Chair, *Waterproof*

Plywood, metal

h 78cm w 43cm

h 30 ⅝in w 17in

Sawaya & Moroni, Italy

lighting

Lighting has become mainstream. If furniture design is beginning to emerge, chastened, from recession, lighting design has in the meantime seized the opportunities created by new technologies coming downstream. No longer reserved for engineers, the new potentials of lighting are being more and more widely exploited. Low-voltage systems with compact transformers, optical fibre, miniaturized lamps, sophisticated control systems – all these have become everyday tools for designers who did not necessarily have a lighting background. So Bär and Knell have extended their research into recycled plastic waste for furniture into lamps, and the Japanese designer Masayo Ave's Shibori fabric creations now glow. This process of empowerment has encouraged a new range of designers into lighting, and enabled experienced designers to go even further. Ingo Maurer's work, for example, has moved from independent fittings into what can only be called light environment sculptures.

A key example of the potential of new technology is Artemide's *Metamorphosi* system, for which a number of prototype designs were shown in Milan in April 1996 (Michele de Lucchi's *Telemaco* is shown here). The concept is simple (getting it to work has been the hard part). Three 100-watt halogen bulbs with green, red and blue dichroic filters create a beam of monochromatic light, supplemented by white light from a 150-watt halogen bulb. By varying the intensity of the three colours, an immense range of light atmospheres and colours can be produced. This is done using a remote control fitted with a patented microchip, which has 12 preset and 42 programmable options (the theoretical range of options is over 12 million). If you want a Californian sunrise or a Norwegian dusk, you can have it. This new technology is an important example of invisible design – it reduces the design problem to a solution, not to a form. It leaves the user in control.

1
Bernhard Dessecker
Chandelier, *Rosa Prosa*
Aluminium, felt, metal, plastic
10 x 20w halogen bulbs
h 60cm di max. 60cm
Vase: di 10cm
h 23 ⅝in di max. 23 ⅝in
Vase: di 3 ⅞in
Luzon GmbH & Co., Germany
(Limited batch production)

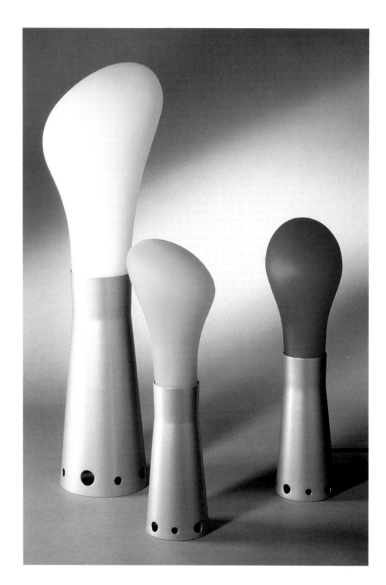

2

**Klok Design (Lydia Kümel
and Koen Ooms)**

Light Box

Plexiglas

T2 Sylvania lamp

h 4.6cm w 10.6cm l 56.6cm

h 1 ⅞in w 4 ⅛in l 22 ¼in

Vezet, Belgium

(Prototype)

3

Frédéric Sofia

Desk light, *Extrait de Naissance*

Aluminium, glass

13w fluorescent bulb

h 35/55cm di 11/16cm

h 13 ¼/21 ⅝in di 4 ⅜/6 ½in

Wombat, France

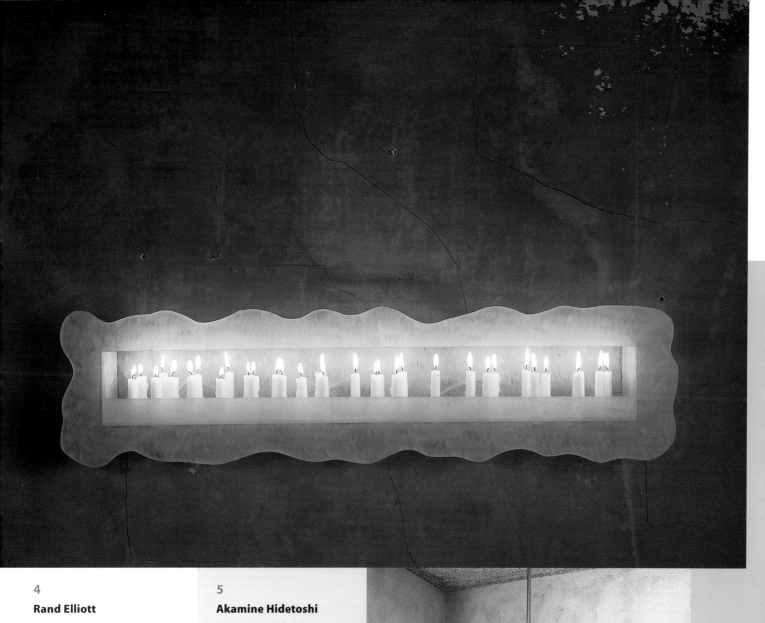

4
Rand Elliott
Candelabra, *Goodnight*
Acrylic
32 candles
h 34.3cm l 137cm d 11.5cm
h 13 ½ in l 54in d 4 ½ in
Custom Plastic, USA

5
Akamine Hidetoshi
Suspension light, *Kaj*
Satin-finished nickel, folded
polycarbonate sheet
50w E27 halogen or
incandescent bulb
l 100–200cm di 50cm
l 39 ⅜–78 ¾ in di 19 ⅝ in
Antonangeli srl, Italy

6
Penny Smith
Standard lamp, *Series Cone 6*
Stoneware, porcelain
Low-energy bulbs
h 150cm di 35cm
h 59in di 13 ¼ in
Design in the Round, Australia
(One-off)

7

Andrea Branzi

Portable lights, *Wireless 01-03*

Metal, wengé wood, rice paper,

rechargeable 6v battery

10w halogen bulb

h 31/54cm di 20/50cm

h 12 ¼/21 ¼in di 7 ⅞/19 ⅝in

Design Gallery Milano, Italy

(Limited batch production)

Andrea Branzi's *Wireless* collection for Design Gallery Milano is a series of domestic enlightenments: simple shapes and even kitchen utensils with integral light sources and shades of rice paper or Dacron. But the intention is serious: *Wireless* is a metaphor for our current coexistence with technology. As Branzi puts it, 'All the advanced technologies have been born without a specific cultural identity, without a space to refer to. In this condition the "ties" of the old knowledge systems are breaking, the "wires" of the old ideologies have disappeared, we have thus all become "wireless" but we don't know what to do with this freedom.'

8

Gijs Bakker
Table lamp, *Ballroom lamp*
Tulle, steel
PLC Philips bulb
di 45cm
di 17 ¼in
Artimeta BV, The Netherlands

9

Riccardo Pellizzato

Table lamp, *Coccode*

Murano glass, lacquered wood

100w E27 bulb

h 33/40cm l 30/43cm

h 13/15 ³⁄₄in l 11 ³⁄₄/17in

Murano Due srl, Italy

10

Giovanni d'Ambrosio

Table lamp/bedside light, *Hebi*

Satined Murano glass, enamelled nickel metal

2 x 100w E27 bulbs (table lamp), 1 x 60w E14 and

1 x 40w E14 bulbs (bedside light)

Table lamp:

h 56cm di 18cm

h 22in di 7in

Bedside light:

h 41cm di 13cm

h 16 ¹⁄₈in di 5 ¹⁄₂in

Murano Due srl, Italy

Big Switch for Segno is – like so much of Giovannoni's work – both direct and witty. The twin 40-watt bulbs are in the translucent white base, and the switch mechanism in the big blue bar on top. The whole design looks like a cartoon image of a light switch, the kind of object Claes Oldenburg would leave to dominate some city square. In the same way Giovannoni's light plays with scale to achieve a surprising – and useful – effect.

11
Stefano Giovannoni
Wall light/table lamp, *Big Switch*
Plastic
2 x 40w bulbs
h 13cm l 21cm d 18cm
h 5 ⅛in l 8 ¼in d 7in
Segno, Italy

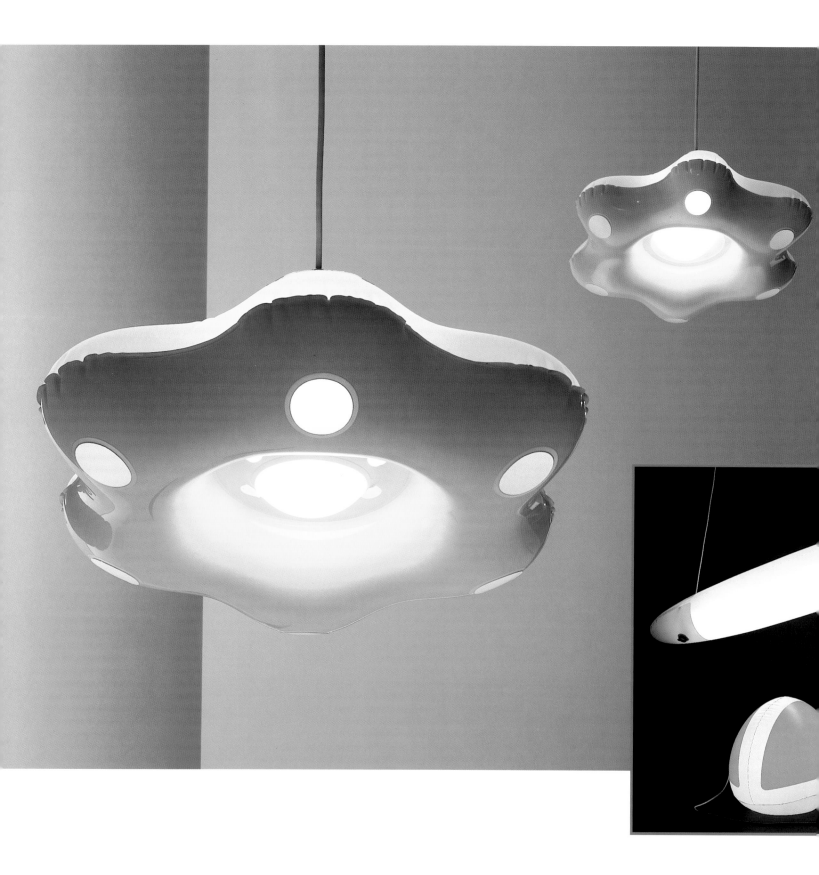

ck Crosbie

eiling light

/C, polypropylene

hilips energy-saving bulb

10cm di 43cm

3 ⁷⁄₈in di 16 ⁷⁄₈in

flate, UK

13

Oval

Unbreakable inflatable lights,

Bumperlights (*Nina* and *Rosie*)

PVC

11w bulb (*Rosie*), 58w bulb (*Nina*)

Nina:

l 190cm di 25cm

l 74 ³⁄₄in di 9 ⁷⁄₈in

Rosie:

h 45cm w 55cm d 45cm

h 17 ³⁄₄in w 21 ⁵⁄₈in d 17 ³⁄₄in

Droog Design label, produced by

Quasar and distributed by DMD BV,

The Netherlands

(Prototype)

14

Rodolfo Dordoni

Table lamp, *Oci*

Hand-blown Murano glass

75w 12v bulb

h 80cm di 18.5cm

h 31 ¹⁄₂in di 7 ¹⁄₄in

Flos Murano, Italy

15
Katsuhiko Ogino
Ceiling light, *K2*
Bronze
h 25/21.5cm di 40cm
h 9 ⅞/8 ½ in di 15 ¾ in
Yamagiwa Corporation, Japan

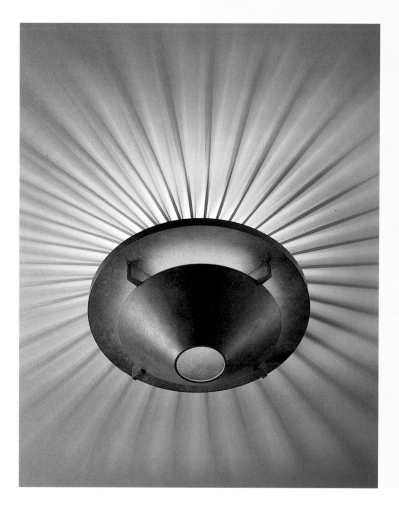

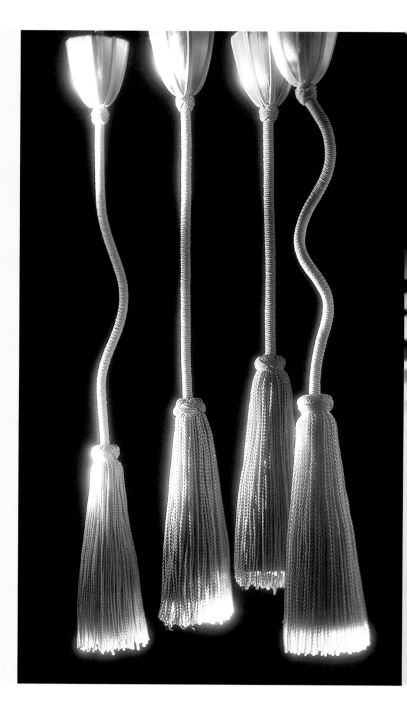

Katsuhiko Ogino's *K2* lamp uses a fluted bronze reflector to project a circle of soft beams of light from the central source. Mounted on a ceiling this gives the shadowed effect of a pleated hanging, but the light can also be floor-mounted, a dark hearth-flame, reflecting an alternative approach to lighting in Japanese culture, as celebrated in Tanizaki's influential 1935 book *In Praise of Shadows*.

16
Christian Ploderer
Suspension light, *Kordel*
Silk rope, metal
50w E27 halogen reflector bulb
l 200cm di 15cm
l 78 ¾ in di 5 ⅞ in
Vest Leuchten GmbH, Austria

17

Ingo Maurer and team
Suspension light, *Pierre ou Paul*
Aluminium, gold plate
h 56cm (adjustable) di 100cm
h 22in di 39 ¼ in
Ingo Maurer GmbH, Germany
(Limited batch production)

19

Hella Jongerius
Knitted light
Glassfibre, PMMA
4 x 25w 22v E27 bulbs
h 40cm w 25cm d 25cm
h 15 ¾in w 9 ⅞in d 9 ⅞in
Droog Design label, produced and
distributed by DMD BV, The Netherlands
(Prototype)

18

**Bernhard Dessecker,
Ingo Maurer and team**

Suspension light, *Lucetto*
Glass, transparent plastic
75w 230/125v E27 bulb
h adjustable di 28cm
h adjustable di 11in
Ingo Maurer GmbH, Germany

20

**Fernando and
Humberto Campana**

Lamp
Metal, rubber
h 67cm w 30cm d 11cm
h 26in w 11 ¾in d 4 ¼in

22
Fabio Crippa and Paolo Sironi
Floor lamp, *Diventuno*
Wood, zinc-plated iron
h 217cm w 48cm d 12cm
h 85 ³/₈ in w 18 ⁷/₈ in d 4 ⁵/₈ in
(Prototype)

23
**Fabio Falanghe and
Giorgio Giorgi**
Table lamp, *Uauá*
Polycarbonate, aluminium, wood
60w incandescent bulb
h 35cm di 17cm
h 13 ³/₄ in di 6 ⁵/₈ in
ONI Design, Brazil

24
Christian Ploderer
System of wall/mirror lights, *Rotkelfer*
Chrome-plated metal, porcelain
25w E27 bulb
h 12cm w 4cm d 10cm
h 4 ³/₄ in w 1 ⁵/₈ in d 4in
Vest Leuchten GmbH, Austria

21
Frédéric Sofia
Wall light, *Nestor*
Metal, plastic, textile
60w E27 bulb
h 160cm w 30cm
h 63in w 11 ³/₄ in
Wombat, France

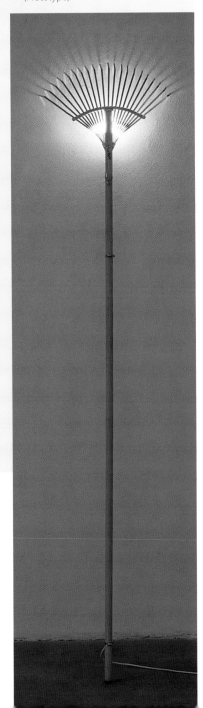

25
Piero Fornasetti
Table lamp from the *Quadra* range
Satined glass, nickel metal or gold
100w E27 or 150w halogen E27 bulb
h 65cm w 40cm d 26cm
h 25 ⁵/₈ in w 15 ³/₄ in d 10 ¹/₄ in
Antonangeli srl, Italy

The names of Masayo Ave's new collection of Shibori textile sculptures with integrated lights come from Tove Jannson's *Moomintroll* books for children. The author's own images of her characters are too well-known to be imitated; rather, according to Ave, her creations – literally – should illuminate the personalities of the characters, gentle, social, intuitive and aware.

26
Masayo Ave
Table lamps, *My* and *Little My*
Metal, wood, Shibori textile (polyester)
25w bulb
h 36.5/47.5cm di 24cm
h 14 ⅜/18 ¾ in di 9 ¼ in
(Limited batch production)

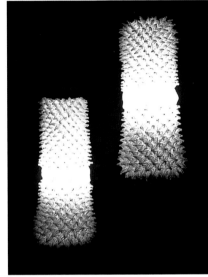

28

Masayo Ave

Table lamp, *Hattifatteners*

Plexiglas, Shibori textile (polyester)

7w bulb

h 25cm di 12cm

h 9 ⅞ in di 4 ⅝ in

29

Masayo Ave

Table lamp, *Ninni*

Metal, wood, Shibori textile

(polyester)

60w bulb

h 36cm di 36cm

h 14 ⅛ in di 14 ⅛ in

7

Marlies von Soden

ght object, *N.T.*

olypropylene

bular compact energy-saving

w fluorescent bulb

63cm di 16cm

24 ¾ in di 6 ¼ in

imited batch production)

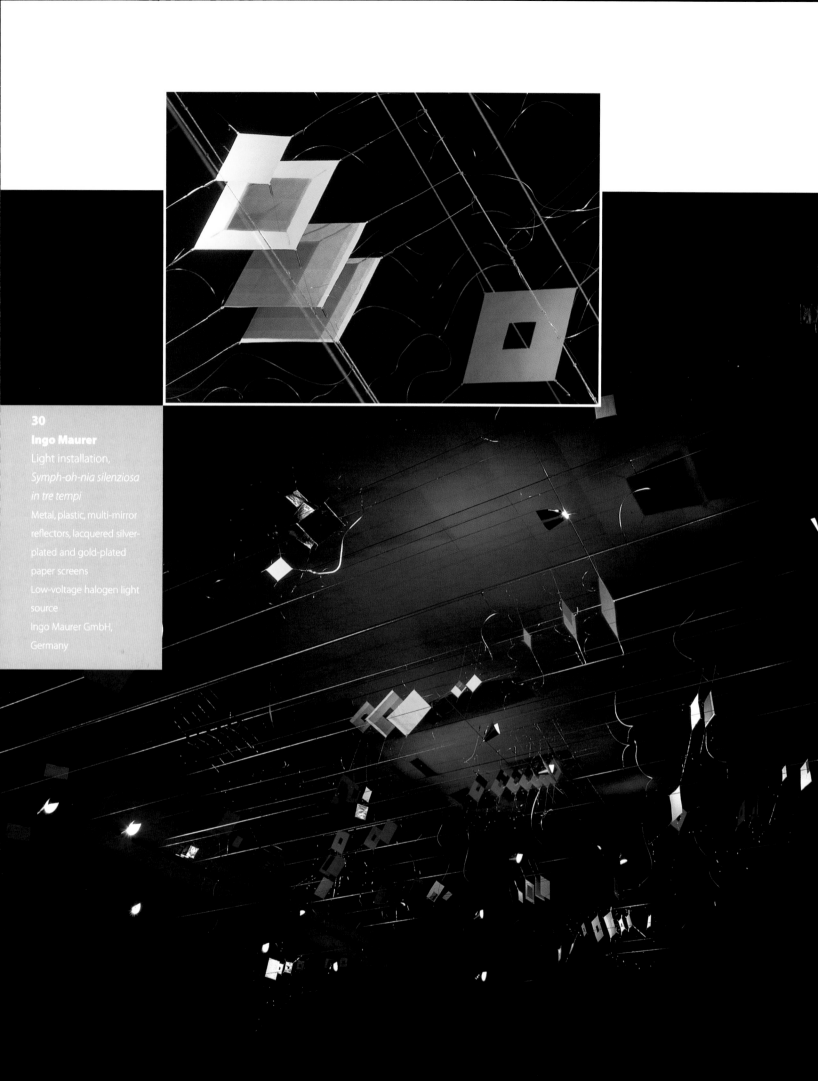

30
Ingo Maurer
Light installation,
*Symph-oh-nia silenziosa
in tre tempi*
Metal, plastic, multi-mirror
reflectors, lacquered silver-
plated and gold-plated
paper screens
Low-voltage halogen light
source
Ingo Maurer GmbH,
Germany

'I am religious without a religion. I like to work in different ways. Sometimes it's more the emotional expression, and at other times the pure, the reduced and technical expression I look for.' Maurer's *Symph-oh-nia* shown at the Spazio Krizia brilliantly embraced both of these approaches. A lattice of fine parallel wires, lit by halogen, was strung with gold paper squares, pierced blue rhomboids and multi-faceted mirrors. It presents a new aspect from every angle, a powerful and poetic statement.

32
Edward van Vliet
Suspension light, *Buba*
Birch plywood, Plexiglas
60w bulb
w 26.5cm l 41cm
w 10 ⅜ in l 16 ⅛ in
Equilibrium, The Netherlands

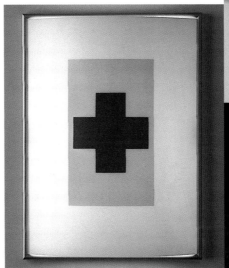

31
Peter Christian
Wall light, *Icon*
Aluminium, printed polycarbonate
Compact fluorescent bulb
h 40cm w 30cm d 8cm
h 15 ¾ in w 11 ⅞ in d 3 ⅛ in
Aktiva, UK
(Limited batch production)

33
Javier Mariscal
Copylight
Plastic, film
h 30cm w 30cm
h 11 ¾ in w 11 ¾ in
Mobles 114, Spain

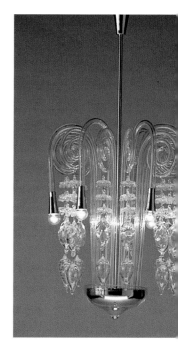

36
Carlo Scarpa
Chandelier
Crystal
6 x 60w bulbs
h 92cm di 52cm
h 36 ¼in di 20 ½in
Flos, Italy

35
Venini
Chandelier
Murano glass
12 x 60w E14 bulbs
h 110cm di 105cm
h 43 ¼in di 41 ½in
Flos Murano, Italy

34
Gio Ponti
Chandelier
Murano glass
12 x 60w E14 bulbs
h 77cm di 88cm
h 31 ½in di 33 ½in
Flos Murano, Italy

Edward van Vliet started Equilibrium, his own brand of lights and furniture, at the end of 1995, and first showed at Cologne and Milan in 1996. He runs it in parallel with his other interior and product design work in Amsterdam. Functionality and integrity are, he feels, the main values he aims for in his designs, which are mainly in plastic, metal and textile. 'They must be products that share the same mentality.' He feels that there is a secure market in The Netherlands for the work of young designers, offering quality products at affordable prices. These cheerful and colourful lights are part of this vision.

37

Edward van Vliet
Bedside light, *Nap*
Coated or nickel-plated
aluminium, Neoprene
40w bulb
h 24cm w 12cm
h 9 ³⁄₈ in w 4 ³⁄₄ in
Equilibrium, The Netherlands

39
Jane Atfield
Wall chandelier
Discarded HDPE bottles,
rubber gromets
Fairy lights
w 26cm l 104cm
w 10 ¼ in l 40 ⅞ in
No Sign of Design, UK
(Limited batch production)

38
Gabriele Allendorf
Suspension light/table
lamp, *Celeste*
Felt, plastic
20w halogen bulb
h 25cm di 16cm
h 9 ⅞ in di 6 ½ in
Luzon GmbH & Co., Germany
(Limited batch production)

40

**Beata Bär,
Gerhard Bär and
Hartmut Knell**

Lighting installation for
the exhibition 'Plastics
2000 - Visions of
Recycled Plastics'

Light column (and
detail, right)
Post-consumer waste
plastics
Fluorescent tube
h 230cm di 30cm
h 90 ½ in di 11 ⅞ in
Bär & Knell Design,
Germany
(Limited batch
production)

'Recycling is not just an option, it is

a necessity. All products should be

planned to be wholly recyclable,

and be created with minimum

expenditure of energy. Our

designs are not alternatives to

mainstream design, but a

statement of how all products

should be conceived.' Bär and

Knell's designs all use carefully

sorted recycled plastics from a

low-energy recycling station. They

have moved from furniture into

lighting, with a tubular floor light

and a range of wall-mounted

flat luminaires. Ironically, their

minimalist approach conveys best

the decorative possibilities of their

chosen material.

Sophie Chandler's *DIY Chandelier* is a simple assembly of eighteen glass bottles held in two rings and suspended by chains from the ceiling. Candles can be fitted into each bottle. It is an example of direct reuse, and a design that can be adapted to whatever materials are to hand. In the prototype version, the blue colour of the glass diffuses the light which also glints off the chains.

41
Sophie Chandler
DIY Chandelier
Blue glass bottles, chain
60w bulb
d 30cm di 61cm
d 11 ¾in di 24in
(Limited batch production)

42
Franco Cervi and Paolo Olivari
Table lamp, *C1P8*
Chromed metal, bicycle lamp
12v bulb
h 17cm w 9cm d 7cm
h 6 ⅝in w 3 ½in d 2 ¾in
(Prototype)

44
Mikala Naur
Table lamp, *Fish-Lamp*
Frosted glass, brass
Max. 40w E27 bulb
h 22cm w 24cm d 24cm
h 8 ⅝in w 9 ⅜in d 9 ⅜in
(Limited batch production)

43
Jorge Beschizza
Table lamp, *Parabólica*
Aluminium
10w 12v halogen bulb
h 29cm di 12cm
h 11 ⅜in di 4 ⅝in

45
Feddow Claassen
Carton light, *Take It*
Plain carton
h 16cm w 7.5cm
h 6 ⅓in w 3in
Droog Design label,
produced by Quasar and
distributed by DMD BV,
The Netherlands

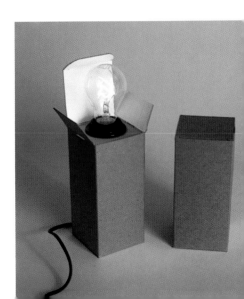

46

Jakob Gebert

Verso

Aluminium, etched glass,
bakelite

100w krypton E27 bulb

h 30cm w 30cm

h 11 ¼in w 11 ¼in

Belux AG, Switzerland

48

Mengotti and Prandina

Ceiling light, *Pacific 3 & 4*

Opaline glass

3 x 60w E14 or 3 x 11w E14
fluorescent bulbs (*Pacific 3*),

4 x 60w E14 or 4 x 11w E14
fluorescent bulbs (*Pacific 4*)

Pacific 3:

h 30cm l 34cm

h 11 ¾in l 13 ¼in

Pacific 4:

h 30cm l 46cm

h 11 ¾in l 18 ⅛in

Prandina srl, Italy

47

**Etienne Ruffieux,
Georges Adatte and
Eric Giroud for
Adatte Design**

Standard lamp, *Spoon*

Aluminium, ash or beech

12w/50w bulb

h 190cm di 30cm

h 74 ¼in di 11 ¼in

Belux AG, Switzerland

50
Miguel Ciganda
Ceiling light, *Veroca*
Metal, fabric
4 x 36w bulbs
l 170cm w 170cm
l 66 ⁷⁄₈ in w 66 ⁷⁄₈ in
Vanlux SA, Spain

49
Marcello Ziliani
Wall light, *Scroeder*
Die-cast aluminium,
blown glass
Arteluce SpA, Italy

51
Júlio Sannazzaro
Standard lamp, *Eletra*
Metal, blue glass bottle
40w incandescent bulb
h 180cm di of base 22cm
h 70 ⁷⁄₈ in di of base 8 ⁵⁄₈ in

52
Nazanin Kamali
Light shade, *Aero Paper Pendant*
Paper, epoxy-coated mild steel
60w bulb
h 32cm di 20cm (conical),
180cm (cylindrical)
h 12 ⁵⁄₈ in di 7 ⁷⁄₈ in (conical),
70 ⁷⁄₈ in (cylindrical)
Aero, UK

Sebastian Bergne's new light fitting for Radius in Germany uses a minimal technical solution to an interesting problem: how to have a light that acts either as a downlighter or an uplighter. The answer is in the steel reflector, which can be switched to fit either above or below the lamp. This gives a partly diffused downlight and strong uplight when in the lower position, or a strong downlight and slight uplight when fixed above.

53
Christian Ploderer
Suspension light, *Ral*
Satinized aluminium
100w E27 bulb
h 45cm di 30cm
h 17 ¾in di 11 ⅞in
Vest Leuchten GmbH, Austria

54
Carlo Nason
Ceiling light, *Actus*
Blown Murano glass,
chromed metal
60w E14 opaline bulb
h 90cm w 86cm
h 35 ⅛in w 33 ⅞in
iTre srl, Italy

55
Sebastian Bergne
Suspension light,
Lampshade
Steel
w 13cm l 36cm
w 5 ⅛in l 14 ⅛in
Radius GmbH, Germany

57

Paolo Piva

Ceiling/wall light, *Spèra*

Blown glass, chromed metal

100w E27 bulb

di 40/50cm

di 15 ¼/19 ⅝ in

AVMazzega Murano srl, Italy

56

Christophe Pillet

Suspension light, *Flap Drop*

Acidized blown glass, metal

100w E27 or 20w fluorescent
bulb

h 25cm di 55cm

h 9 ⅞ in di 21 ⅝ in

AVMazzega Murano srl, Italy

59

Michele de Lucchi

Suspension light, *Caolina*

Porcelain, platinum, painted metal

100w E27 incandescent bulb

h 21cm di 22cm

h 8 ¼ in di 8 ⅝ in

Produzione Privata, Italy

58

Didier Gomez

Standard lamp, *Rif*

Steel, chintz, metal

220v bulb

h 160cm di 35cm

h 63in di 13 ¾ in

Roset SA, France

60

Michele de Lucchi

Suspension light, *Acquatinta*

Murano blown glass, chromed metal

100w E27 incandescent bulb

h 24cm di 22cm

h 9 ⅜ in di 8 ⅝ in

Produzione Privata, Italy

Produzione Privata is Studio de Lucchi's new range of lighting, tableware and furniture designs, intended to provide an alternative outlet to de Lucchi's mainstream design and architectural work for Olivetti and others. These suspension lights, designed by de Lucchi, with simple Murano glass, porcelain or metal shades, show how a carefully defined minimal solution can produce elegant anonymity.

61

Andreas Hagn

Desk light, *TL 122 Fifties-Style*

Metal, chrome plate

25w 220v E27 bulb

h 50cm w 30cm d 40cm

h 19 ⅝ in w 11 ¾ in d 15 ¾ in

di'(sain) Hagn & Kubala OEG, Austria

62

Giampiero Derai

Table lamp, *Giuggiola*

Painted metal, thermoformed glass

100w E27 bulb

h 46cm di 47cm

h 18 ⅛ in di 18 ½ in

F. Fabbian & F.lli SNC, Italy

63

Lievore Asociados

Table lamp, *Esa*

Blown satinized glass, chromed metal

100w E27 incandescent bulb

h 47cm w 44cm d 21cm

h 18 ½ in w 17 ¼ in d 8 ¼ in

Foscarini SpA, Italy

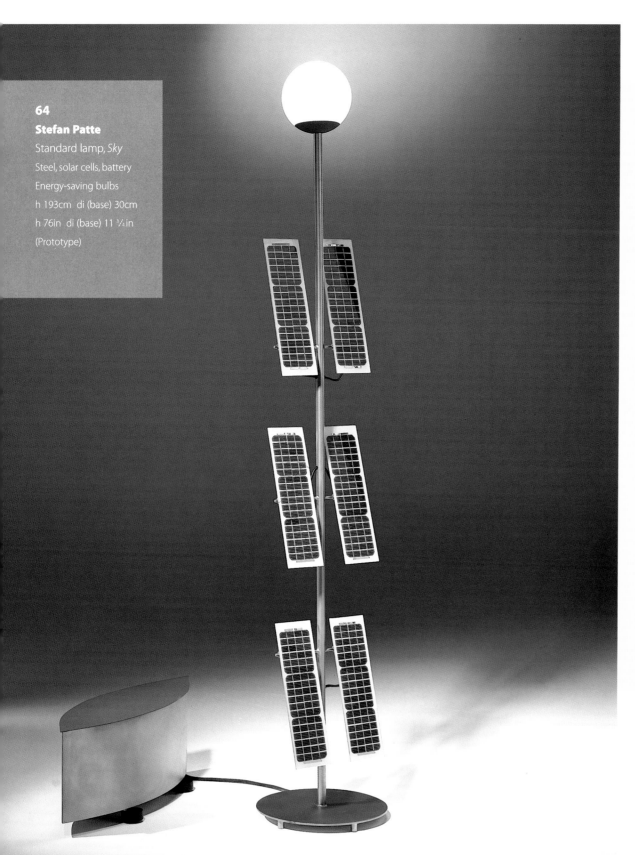

A lamp that works by storing solar energy sounds like a perpetual energy machine: sunlight falls on the six solar panels mounted on the support all day, is stored in the battery and provides light at night. An average day's sunlight stores up to 24 watts of electricity, and the fully charged battery has 70 hours' life. While efforts to save energy are to be encouraged, it is not clear that, as a prototype or one-off only, the total energy equation for this design is finally favourable, when the cost of the steel frame and fabrication and of the solar panels is taken into account. But Patte hopes that further development will lead to more general (and so more economic) production.

65

Ezio Didone

Wall light, *IP555*

Anti-shock technopolymer,

painted steel

18w bulb

d 8cm di 20cm

d 3 ⅛in di 7 ⅞in

Flight div. di Flos, Italy

66

Klok Design (Lydia Kümel and Koen Ooms)

Light object, *Un-Block*

Plexiglas, bath chain, plug

T2 bulb

h 30/50.5cm w of tube 3cm di 14cm

h 11 ⅞/19 ⅞in w of tube 1 ⅛in di 5 ½in

Vezet, Belgium

(Prototype)

67

Tobias Grau and Florian Borkenhagen

George

Plastic, glass, wood

150w bulb

h 30/100cm di 17cm

h 11 ¾/39 ⅜ in di 6 ⅝ in

Tobias Grau KG GmbH & Co.,

Germany

69
**Michele de Lucchi and
Giancarlo Fassina**
Suspension light, *Tolomeo*
Metal, thermoplastic resin, anodized
aluminium
2 x 100w E27 incandescent bulbs
h 74–120cm di max. 150cm
h 29 ⅛–47 ¼in di max. 59in
Artemide, Italy

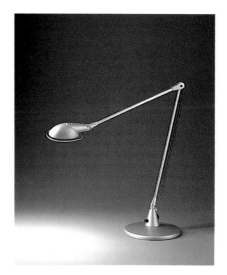

68
Riccardo Blumer
Table lamp, *Mandraki*
Anodized and polished aluminium
100w clear incandescent, 100w
halogen E27 or 15w fluorescent E27
bulb
l 111cm di 26 cm
l 43 ¾in di 10 ¼in
Artemide SpA, Italy

70
Hannes Wettstein
Table lamp, *Spy*
Painted metal
60w E27 incandescent opaline or
75w frosted halogen bulb
h 78cm w 30cm di (base) 21cm
h 30 ¾in w 11 ⅞in di (base) 8 ¼in
Artemide SpA, Italy

71
[Zed]
Table lamp, *Rodope*
Anodized aluminium, steel
50w 12v halogen bulb
h 122cm di (base) 24cm
h 48in di (base) 9 ⅜in
Artemide SpA, Italy

72

Reto Schoepfer

Suspension light, *Updown*

Aluminium

T26 fluorescent tube

l 126–156cm

l 49 ⅝–61⅜ in

Belux AG, Switzerland

74

Michele de Lucchi

Standard lamp, *Telemaco*

Aluminium, painted steel

150w halogen bulb and 3 x

100w halogen bulbs

h 180cm w 47cm d 40cm

h 70 ⅞ in w 18 ½ in d 15 ¾ in

Artemide SpA, Italy

73

Masafumi Katsukawa

Table lamp, *Onda*

Chrome, Pyrex glass,

polycarbonate

20w 12v bulb

h 40cm di 30cm

h 15 ¼ in di 11 ⅞ in

(Prototype)

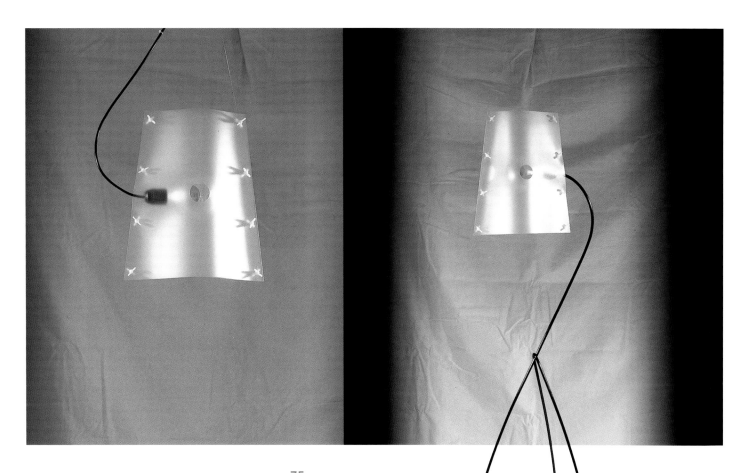

75
Siggi Fischer
Series of lights, *Minima*
Metal, polycarbonate
60w bulb
h 40/170cm w 36cm d 16cm
h 15 ¹/₄/66 ⁷/₈ in w 14 ¹/₈ in d 6 ¹/₄ in
Siggi Fischer Design, Germany
(Prototype)

77

Hannes Wettstein

Lighting system, *CYOS*
(Create Your Own System)

Aluminium

Max. 230v bulb

h 22.5/30.5cm d 13/24cm

h 8 ³/₄/12in d 5 ¹/₈/9 ¹/₂in

Belux, Switzerland

76

Dante Donegani

Ceiling light from *Strip Family*

Aluminium, polycarbonate

18w fluorescent bulb

h 8.5cm w 74cm l 74cm

h 3 ¹/₈in w 29 ¹/₈in l 29 ¹/₈in

Luceplan, Italy

78

Gaspar Glusberg

Lighting fixture, *X257*

Enamelled metal, aluminium

50w 12v dichroic bulb

h 30cm di 6cm

h 11 ⁷/₈in di 2 ³/₈in

Modulor SA, Argentina

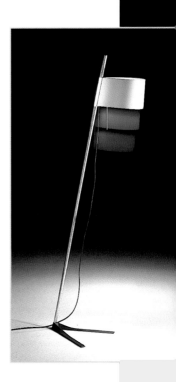

79

**Michele de Lucchi and
Giancarlo Fassina**
Standard lamp, *Tessalo*
Extruded aluminium
3 x 55w fluorescent bulbs
h 185cm w 35cm
h 72 ⅞in w 13 ¾in
Artemide SpA, Italy

81

Yamada
Recessed wall light, *Astra*
Sheet metal, enamelled reflector
Compact fluorescent bulb
iGuzzini, Italy

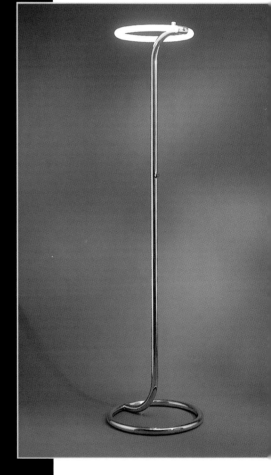

80

Miguel Milá
Standard lamp, *Proxima*
Aluminium, metal
100w E27 bulb
h 170cm w 60cm l 40cm
h 99 ⅞in w 23 ⅝in l 15 ¾in
Antonio Almerich SL, Spain

82

Andrew Martin
Standard lamp, *Halo*
Aluminium
Fluorescent bulb
h 190cm di 45cm
h 74 ¼in di 17 ¾in
(Limited batch production)

83

Fabio Reggiani

Wall/ceiling light, *Morphy*

Die-cast aluminium

200w metal-halide or linear halogen bulbs

h 20.5cm di 18.3cm

h 8in di 7 ¼in

Reggiani SpA, Italy

84

Marcello Ziliani

Outdoor installation, *Allumette*

Painted extruded aluminium, opal technopolymer

Compact fluorescent TC-E 2G11 bulb

h max. 210cm w 9.8cm d 6.6cm

h max. 82 ⅝in w 3 ⅞in d 2 ⅝in

Flight div. di Flos, Italy

85

Megalit

Bollard light, *Planar Bollard*

Injection-moulded aluminium

Low-voltage halogen or compact fluorescent bulb

h 70cm di 15cm

h 27 ½in di 5 ⅞in

Artemide, Italy

87

Shozo Toyohisa

Lighting system, *Mylight*

Silica glass-core optical fibre

150w metal-halide bulb

h 26.8cm w 17cm d 29cm

h 10 ½in w 6 ⅝in d 11 ¼in

Asahi Glass Co. Ltd, Japan

86

Perry A. King and Santiago Miranda

Bollard, *Borealis*

Aluminium

100w incandescent, 50w HME and 26w TCD bulbs

h 115cm di 30cm

h 45 ¼in di 11 ⅞in

Louis Poulsen & Co. A/S, Denmark

88

Mario Cucinella

Exterior floodlights, *Woody* and *Miniwoody*

Die-cast aluminium

50/100w halogen bulbs

Woody: h 23cm d 16.5cm di 14cm

h 9in d 6 ½in di 5 ½in

Miniwoody: h 20.5cm d 10cm di 8.5cm

h 8 ⅛in d 3 ⅞in di 3 ¼in

iGuzzini, Italy

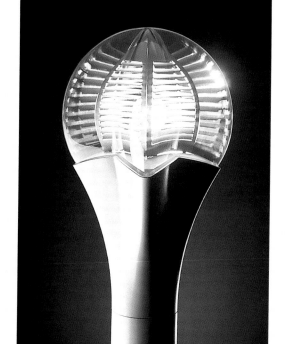

tableware

'Beauty is now an obsolete
concept', wrote Starck recently. 'Beauty is only of
use or interest in a period of luxury. That is not
the case now: beauty has become dangerous.' So
the indulgent, all-consuming, self-regarding
design of a few years ago is no longer relevant at
all. Rather, society is approaching a crisis –
politically, socially and environmentally. Not,
however, just the crisis of need, which others, from
a narrow economic framework, have been
predicting, but the crisis of information and
communication in which, he argues, the arrival of
truly global access to information will oblige
mankind to look at itself, in its imperial clothes,
anew.
The link between such global
projections and the domestic rituals of the table
seems at first sight thin. But the coming change is
so profound that it will run deepest into the most
embedded of social rituals. In such a context, beauty
is an irrelevant and histrionic distraction. Sensibility,
intelligence, awareness and wit are what is
needed. Qualities neatly summed up in Nick
Crosbie's perky inflatable eggcup, a polite bow
to the Domestic Landscapes of the past and
also a machine-washable contribution to the
future. Or Jane Atfield's simple, unpretentious
bowl in recycled plastic.

(page 122)

1

Ettore Sottsass

Chinese vase, *Omega*

Lacquered chestnut, anodized
aluminium, blown glass
h 73cm w 59cm d 28cm
h 28 ¾in w 23 ¼in d 11in
Design Gallery Milano, Italy
(Limited batch production)

2

Ettore Sottsass

Chinese vase, *D*

'Ambuina' briarwood, anodized
aluminium, gold-plated brass
h 86cm w 69cm d 37cm
h 33 ⅜in w 27 ⅛in d 14 ⅛in
Design Gallery Milano, Italy
(Limited batch production)

3

Ettore Sottsass

Chinese vase, *W*

'Zebrano' veneer, blown glass
h 60cm w 50cm d 40cm
h 23 ⅝in w 19 ⅝in d 15 ¾in
Design Gallery Milano, Italy
(Limited batch production)

4

Michael Rowe

Vase No. 1

Brass, tin

h 51cm w 18.5cm d 22cm

h 20in w 7 ¼in d 8 ⅝in

Michael Rowe, UK

(One-off)

6

Michael Rowe

Vase No. 5

Brass, tin

h 58cm w 19cm d 20cm

h 22 ⅞in w 7 ½in d 7 ⅞in

Michael Rowe, UK

(Limited batch production)

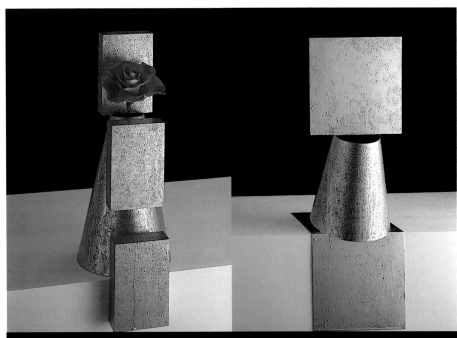

5

Michael Rowe

Vase No. 4

Brass, gold leaf

h 30cm w 26cm d 40cm

h 11 ⅞in w 10 ¼in d 15 ¾in

Michael Rowe, UK

(One-off)

7

Michael Rowe

Vase No. 2

Brass, tin

h 16cm w 54cm d 35cm

h 6 ¼in w 21 ¼in d 13 ¼in

Michael Rowe, UK

(Limited batch production)

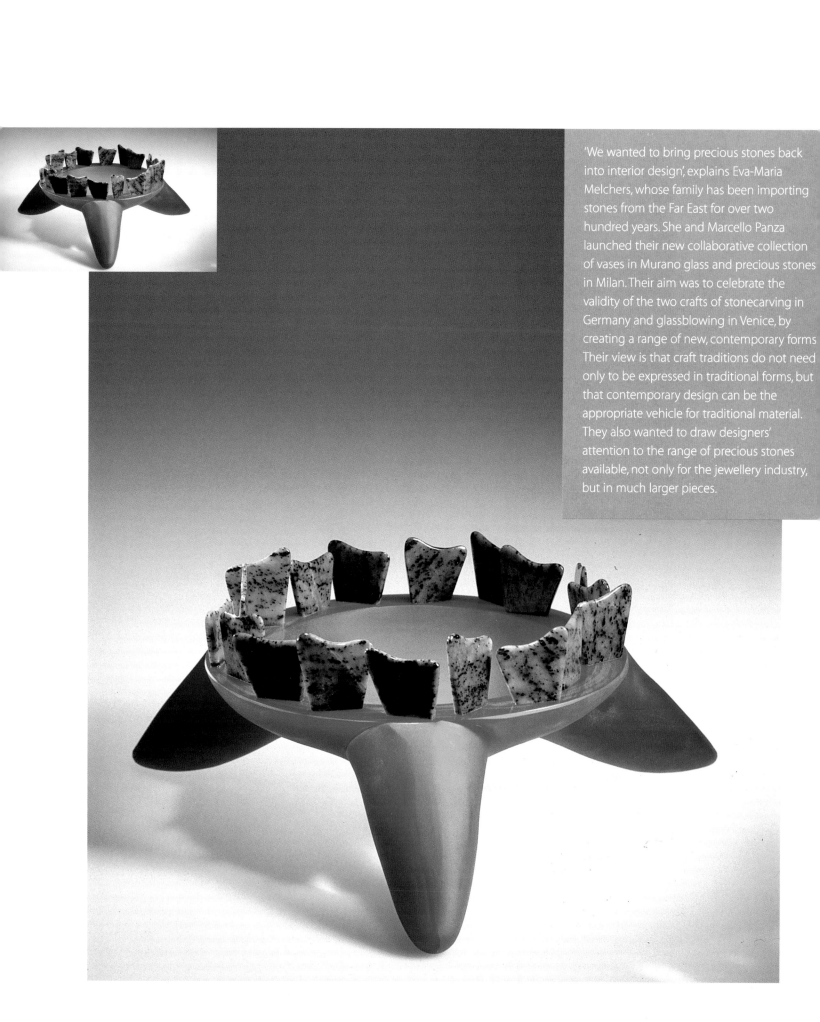

'We wanted to bring precious stones back into interior design', explains Eva-Maria Melchers, whose family has been importing stones from the Far East for over two hundred years. She and Marcello Panza launched their new collaborative collection of vases in Murano glass and precious stones in Milan. Their aim was to celebrate the validity of the two crafts of stonecarving in Germany and glassblowing in Venice, by creating a range of new, contemporary forms. Their view is that craft traditions do not need only to be expressed in traditional forms, but that contemporary design can be the appropriate vehicle for traditional material. They also wanted to draw designers' attention to the range of precious stones available, not only for the jewellery industry, but in much larger pieces.

8

Marcello Panza

Bowl, *Zoe*

Murano glass,

precious stones

h 11cm di 32cm

h 4 ³/₈ in di 12 ⁵/₈ in

Eva-Maria Melchers,

Germany

(Prototype)

9

Penny Smith

Stoneware vases

h 20/30cm di 10/14cm

h 11 ⁷/₈/7 ¹/₈ in di 3 ⁷/₈/5 ¹/₂ in

Penny Smith, Australia

10

Hannes Rohringer

Coffee-pot or teapot,

Isadora D

Porcelain

h 22cm w 10cm l 29cm

h 8 ⁵/₈ in w 3 ⁷/₈ in l 11 ³/₈ in

(Prototype)

11
Luk van der Hallen
Vase, *Pento*
Aluminium
h 28cm di 12cm
h 11in di 4 ¾in
Art & Design, Belgium
(Limited batch production)

12
Luk van der Hallen
Vase, *Flox*
Aluminium
h 23cm di 10cm
h 9in di 3 ⅞in
Art & Design, Belgium
(Limited batch production)

13
Luk van der Hallen
Vase, *Papilio I*
Aluminium, steel
h 20cm w 22cm d 10cm
h 9in w 8 ⅝in d 3 ⅞in
Art & Design, Belgium
(Limited batch production)

14
Sergio Asti
Boxes, *Bon Bon, Bonbis, Bontris*
Silver
h 14cm di 9/12/18cm
h 5 ½in di 3 ½/4 ¾/7in
Gabriele de Vecchi, Italy
(Limited batch production)

15
Antonio Cagianelli
Ashtray, *Pipa*
Resin
h 18cm | 28cm
h 7in | 11in
Edizioni Galleria Colombari,
Italy

16
Borek Sípek
Candlestick
Sterling silver, Bohemian crystal
h 40cm w 12cm
h 15 ¾in w 4 ¾in
Steltman Collection,
The Netherlands

17
Borek Sípek
Egg-cup, *S 176*
Gilded Dutch sterling silver
h 10cm di 5cm
h 3 ⅞in di 12in
Steltman Collection,
The Netherlands
(Prototype)

18
Borek Sípek
Bowl, *Apollo*
Crystal, metal
h 8cm di 19cm
h 3 ⅛in di 7 ½in
D. Swarovski & Co., Austria

19

Borek Sípek

Vase, *Celine I - II*

Porcelain, crystal

h 70cm di 20/24cm

h 27 ½in di 7 ⅞ / 9 ½in

Driade SpA, Italy

20

Borek Sípek

Vase, *Herbert*

Crystal

h 52cm w 32cm d 15cm

h 20 ½in w 12 ⅝in d 5 ⅞in

Driade SpA, Italy

21

Borek Sípek

Vase, lemon squeezer, oil/vinegar set,

Herold, Melusina, Eulalie

Herold: Crystal

h 35cm di 10.5cm

h 13 ¾in di 4 ⅛in

Melusina: Porcelain

h 21cm di 9.5cm

h 8 ¼in di 3 ¾in

Eulalie: Crystal

h 20cm w 16cm d 10cm

h 7 ⅞in w 6 ¼in d 3 ⅞in

Driade SpA, Italy

22

Borek Sípek

Stand, *Verdun*

Porcelain, glass

h 26cm w 22cm d 14.5cm

h 10 ½in w 8 ⅝in d 5 ¾in

Driade SpA, Italy

23

Borek Sípek

Dinner set, *Albert*

Porcelain

Plate:

h 2.5cm l 34.5cm d 13/27cm

h 1in l 13 ½in d 5 ⅛/10 ⅝in

Egg cup:

h 4.5cm di 11cm

h 1 ¾in di 4 ¼in

Cup:

h 10.2cm w 15cm d 10.5cm

h 3 ⅞in w 5 ⅞in d 4in

Driade SpA, Italy

24
Borek Sípek
Dessert cutlery, *S172*
Sterling silver
l 20cm
l 7 ⅞in
Steltman Collection,
The Netherlands
(Prototype)

25
Denis Santachiara
Glass, *Kognac*
h 14.5cm di 11.5cm
h 5 ¼in di 4 ½in
Goto, Massimo Lunardon
Glass Collection, Italy
(Limited batch production)

26
Camille Jacobs
Bowl, *Wagga-Wagga*
Float glass, bamboo
h 7cm l 55cm d 29cm
h 2 ¾in l 21 ⅝in d 11 ⅜in
(Limited batch production)

27
Alfred Kainz
Plate
Crystal, Botticcino marble
h 3cm w 30cm
h 1 ⅛in w 11 ⅞in
Wohnobjekte und Design
Alfred Kainz, Germany
(One-off)

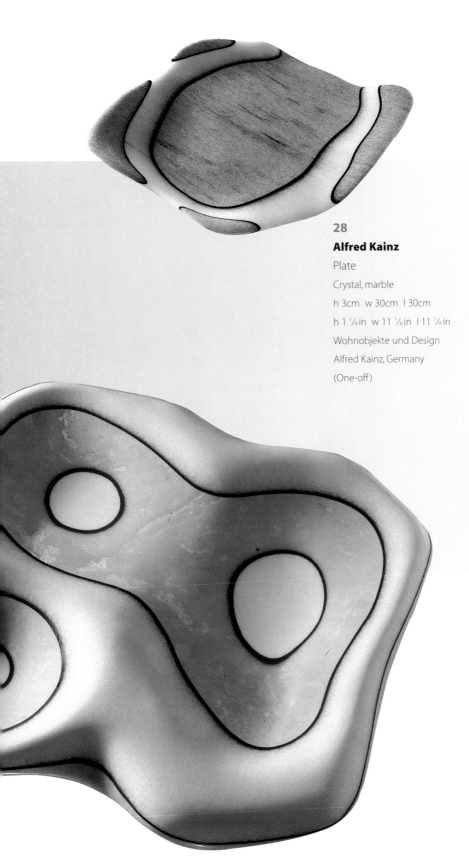

28
Alfred Kainz
Plate
Crystal, marble
h 3cm w 30cm l 30cm
h 1 ⅛ in w 11 ⅞ in l 11 ⅞ in
Wohnobjekte und Design
Alfred Kainz, Germany
(One-off)

29
Reinhard Paulus
Honey server
Porcelain, pearwood, aluminium
h 17cm di 2.8cm
h 6 ⅝ in di 1 ⅛ in
Radius GmbH, Germany

30

Mikala Naur

Vase

Rubber, frosted glass

h 25cm di 14cm

h 9 ¾in di 5 ½in

(Limited batch production)

'We wanted to make a range of products for the breakfast table that would be affordable and exciting – something to make it worth getting up in the mornings.' Having worked together on inflatables at design school, Nick Crosbie and Michael Sodeau launched Inflate in 1995. The response to their inflatable products – lights, bowls and egg-cups – has been good. While they intend to keep away from large-scale pieces (such as furniture), they see a continuing market for their cheerful, inviting designs (see also pages 90, 208 and 221).

31
Michael Sodeau
Egg-cup, *Farm Fresh*
PVC
h 3cm di 12cm
h 1 ⅛in di 4 ¼in
Inflate, UK

32
Guido Niest
Cutlery, *Caribe*
Silver-plated brass alloy
Spoon:
h 21.5cm h 8 ½ in
Fork:
h 20.3cm h 8in
Spoon:
h 20.5cm h 8in
Guido Niest A.T.E.L.I.E.R.,
Italy
(Prototype)

These prototypes for childre
cutlery are based, the
designers say, 'on the sword
the spade and the dungfork
a collection of iconic image
which suggests a design
process rethought – literally
from the ground up.

33

Metz.Schlett.Kindler
Children's cutlery, *Knopf and Friends*
Cromargan (metal)
h 1.3cm w 3.5cm l 13cm
h ½ in w 1 ⅜ in l 5 ⅛ in
WMF, Germany
(Limited batch production)

34
Metz.Schlett.Kindler
Kitchen knives, *Plugs*
Wood, refined steel
Various sizes
Robert Herder KG, Germany
(Prototype)

35
Anna Castelli Ferrieri
Cutlery, *Segnale*
Stainless steel
Spoon:
w 4.7cm l 20.4cm d 2.3cm
w 1 ⅞in l 8in d ⅞in
Fork:
w 2.1cm l 20.4cm d 2.3cm
w ⅞in l 8in d ⅞in
Knife:
w 1.6cm l 23.2cm d 0.5cm
w ⅝in l 9 ⅛in d ¼in
Sambonet SpA, Italy

36
Takeshi Kimura
Glasses from the *Kikatsu* series
Glass
h (average) 17.5cm w 4.2cm
h (average) 6 ⅞ in w 1 ⅝ in
Kimura Glass Co. Ltd, Japan
(Limited batch production)

37
Michele de Lucchi
Glass vases,
Vaso Bottiglia
Aluminium, glass
h 25cm w 15cm
l 10cm di 12cm
h 9 ⅞ in w 5 ⅞ in
l 3 ⅞ in di 4 ¾ in
Produzione Privata, Italy

The *Bottiglia* range of vases are simple in concept: take a used
bottle, cut it below the neck, seal the lid and mount a circular
aluminium ring there. Turn it neck downwards and you have a
vase on a base. De Lucchi describes the aim of Produzione
Privata, his new collection, as 'opening a dialogue with the
market, verifying ideas and so proposing a small variety of
objects whose identity goes beyond the aesthetic result'.

40

Karim Rashid

Multi-use servers, *Jimmy*

Polished mixed metal alloy

h 10cm di 7cm

h 3 ⅞in di 2 ¾in

Nambe Mills Inc., USA

39

Nigel Coates

Vases

Hand-blown glass, lead crystal

h 32–56cm di 24–28cm

h 12⅝–22in di 9 ⅜–11in

Handmade for Simon Moore

(Prototype)

38

Sergio Asti

Coffee-pot from the *Nuvola* set

Porcelain

h 25cm di 12cm

h 9 ⅞in di 4 ¾in

Richard-Ginori 1735 srl, Italy

41

Lodovico Acerbis

Vase, *Dorik*

Opal

h 32cm di 20cm

h 12 ⅝ in di 8 ⅞ in

Acerbis International SpA, Italy

42

Philip Baldwin and

Monica Guggisberg

Vase, *Yellow Zebravase*

Blown glass

h 32cm di 20cm

h 12 ⅝ in di 7 ⅞ in

Verrerie de Nonfoux,

Switzerland

43
Anna Gili
Vase, *Rigato*
Blown glass
h 31cm di 11cm
h 12 ¹⁄₄in di 4 ³⁄₈in
Salviati srl, Italy

44
Lodovico Acerbis
Vase, *Sung Sung*
Opal
h 33cm di 22cm
h 13in di 8 ⁵⁄₈in
Acerbis International SpA, Italy

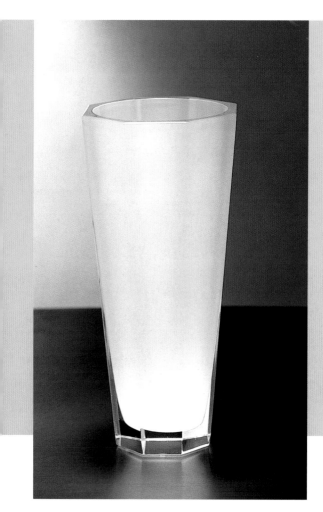

45
Lena Bergström
Vase
Crystal
h 32cm di 15.5cm
h 12 ⅝in di 6 ⅛in
Orrefors-Kosta Boda AB, Sweden
(Limited batch production)

46
Lena Bergström
Vase
Crystal
h 32cm di 15.5cm
h 12 ⅝in di 6 ⅛in
Orrefors-Kosta Boda AB, Sweden
(Limited batch production)

47
David Huycke
Set of seven bowls
Black patinated silver
h max. 8cm di 30.5cm
h max. 3 ⅛in di 12in
(One-off)

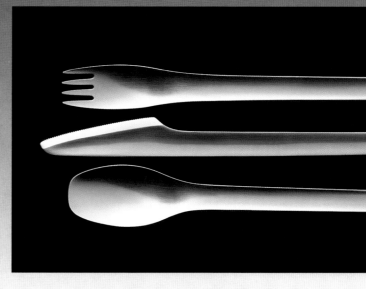

48

Masayuki Kurokawa

Cutlery, *CU-A.Accent Series*

Stainless steel

Spoon:

h 19cm w 3.5cm

h 7 ½ in w 1 ⅜ in

Fork:

h 19cm w 2.4cm

h 7 ½ in w ⅞ in

Knife:

h 21.5cm w 2.4cm

h 8 ½ in w ⅞ in

Takenaka Works Co. Ltd,

Japan

50

Carsten Jorgensen

Bread basket, *Arkade*

Plastic

h 7.7cm w 18.8cm l 2.8cm

h 3in w 7 ⅛ in l 1 ⅛ in

Bodum, Switzerland

49

Erik Magnussen

Cutlery

Satin-finished stainless steel

Spoon:

h 20.5cm

h 8 ⅛ in

Fork:

h 20.5cm

h 8 ⅛ in

Knife:

h 22in

h 8 ⅝ in

A/S Stelton, Denmark

51

Josep Lluscà

Cutlery, *Sevruga*

Stainless steel

Spoon:

h 27cm w 4.3cm

h 10 ⅝ in w 1 ⅝ in

Fork:

h 19.6cm w 2.4cm

h 7 ¾ in w ⅞ in

Knife:

h 23.4cm

h 9 ¼ in

W.M.F. AG, Germany

52

Richard Sapper

Cutlery, *RS01*

Stainless steel

Fork: l 20cm l 7 ⅞ in

Knife: l 20cm l 7 ⅞ in

Spoon: l 19.2cm l 7 ½ in

Alessi SpA, Italy

54

Eleanor Kearney

Lidded pot

Cast pewter

h 7.5cm w 5cm

h 3in w 2in

(Limited batch production)

56

Jürgen Lehl

Vase

Copper

h 30cm di 21cm

h 11 7/8in di 8 1/4in

Jürgen Lehl Co. Ltd, Japan

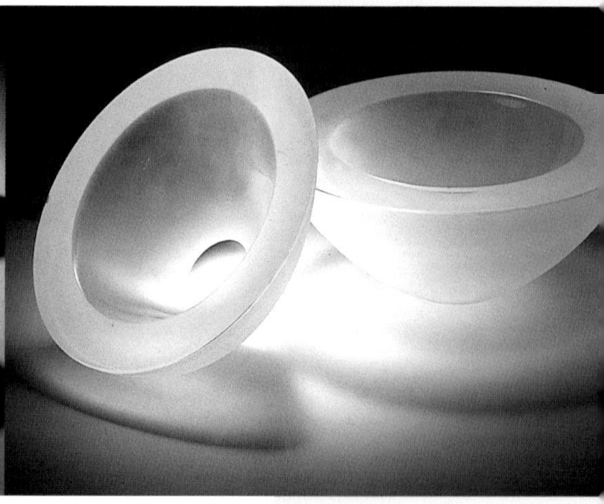

53

Hans Maier-Aichen

Tumbler and bowls, *Cup*

Recyclable polypropylene

Tumbler: h 8.5cm di 9cm

h 3 3/8in di 3 1/2in

Bowl 1: h 9cm di 13.5cm

h 3 1/2in di 5 3/8in

Bowl 2: h 6cm di 20.5cm

h 2 3/8in di 8in

Authentics, Germany

55

Vincent de Rijk

Bowl, *Kom BV*

Resin, ceramic

h 12.5cm di 25cm

h 4 7/8in di 9 7/8in

Goods, The Netherlands

57

Anne Nilsson

Bowls, *Lothar*

Crystal

h 6.1/6.5/10cm w 15.7/20/29.5cm

h 2 3/4 /2 1/2/3 7/8in w 6 1/8 /7 7/8 /11

Orrefors-Kosta Boda AB, Sweden

58
Hans Maier-Aichen
Fruit bowl, *Buco*
Recyclable polypropylene
h 21cm d 26cm
h 8 ½in d 10 ¼in
Authentics, Germany

59
Jennifer Lee
Ceramic, *Pale pot*
Stoneware, T. material, clay, oxides
h 20.5cm di 12cm
h 8in di 4 ¾in
(One-off)

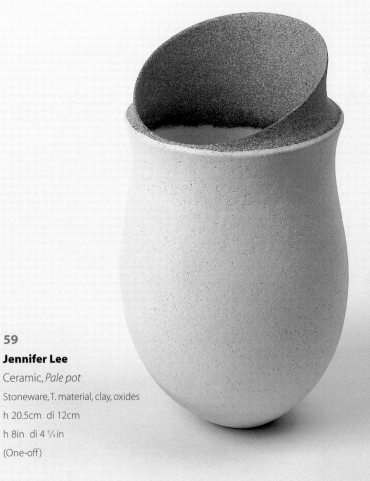

60

Osiris Hertman

Soup plate

Glazed stoneware

h 4cm di 25cm

h 1 ⅝ in di 9 ⅞ in

T-Sign Royal Tichelaar

Makkum,

The Netherlands

61

Jane Atfield

Fruit bowl

Post-consumer recycled plastic

h 10cm di 34cm

h 3 ⅞ in di 13 ⅜ in

No Sign of Design, UK

62

Massimo Iosa Ghini

Vacuum flask, *Thunderbird*

SAN

h 91cm

h 35 ¾ in

21, Germany

64
Nick Allen
(with graphic design by
Birgit Eggers)
Drinking vessel, *Radar Glass*
Lead crystal
Glass: h 5.8cm di 8cm
h 2 ¼in di 3 ⅛in
Base: h 4.7cm di 4.8cm
h 1 ⅞in di 1 ⅞in
Nick Allen, UK

65
Zaha Hadid
Coffee and tea service
Sterling silver
Coffee pot: h 24.6cm w 9.2cm
d 10cm
h 9 ¾in w 3 ½in d 3 ⅞in
Teapot: h 25.8cm w 15cm
d 7.6cm
h 10in w 5 ⅞in d 3in
Milk jug and sugar bowl:
h 27.6cm w 13cm d 10.4cm
h 11in w 5 ⅛in d 4in
Sawaya & Moroni, Italy

63
Michele de Lucchi and
Kubo Masahiko
Salt- and pepper-shakers,
Ginger and Fred
Porcelain, stainless steel
h 14cm di 4cm
h 5 ½in di 1 ⅝in
Rosenthal AG, Germany

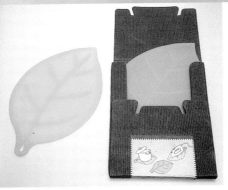

66
Santina Bonini and
Ernesto Spicciolato
Table mat, *Trivet*
HTV silicon rubber
h 0.6cm w 19.5cm l 31cm
h ¼in w 7 ⅝in l 12 ¼in
Viceversa, Italy

textiles

Starck's
most recent foray into textile
design is the Saba smart jacket,
which acts as a whole body amplifier
for a sound or radio system built into the
material. His selection for the Yearbook has
both a mineralogical edge – as with Ulf
Moritz's fabrics woven with copper and brass –
and a technological one, with Philippa Brock's
computer-aided designs and Clodagh's random
micropatterns in which the design subtly and slightly
varies from metre to metre.
Overall, however, as in previous Yearbooks,
the Japanese contribution is dominant. The Japanese
designers' ability to extract endless variations of
innovation and quality in fabric design poses two
conflicting questions. Is the existence of a long tradition
of exquisite and exacting design enough to explain the
continuing vitality of Japanese work? Or is their ability to
respond to a series of technical innovations (both in
materials and processes) with ever more subtle and
intelligent designs simply the result of contemporary
awareness? Part of the answer might lie in the
absence of status for the artist in traditional Japanese
society, so bypassing the absurd European myth of
the artist as sole creator endowed with individual
genius, in favour of positioning the maker –
artist or designer – firmly in and as part of
society.

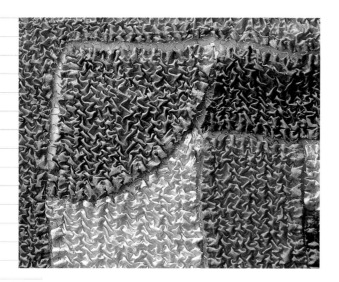

2

Yoshiki Hishinuma

6SHW4–27

100% polyester

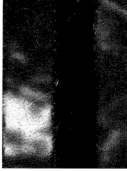

4

Yoshiki Hishinuma

6WSL3–01

70% nylon, 30% polyurethane

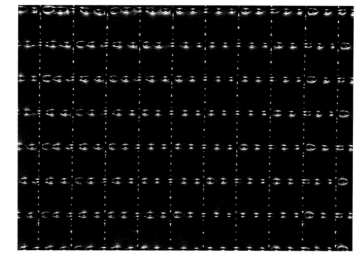

5

Yoshiki Hishinuma

6S3D6–13

50% polyester, 50% polyurethane

(page 152)

1

Yoshiki Hishinuma

6SRE6–11

100% polyester

7
Yoshiki Hishinuma
6WIM4–21
60% polyester, 40% rayon

6
Yoshiki Hishinuma
6WM04–01
60% polyester, 40%
rayon

9
Yoshiki Hishinuma
6S3D4–31
50% polyester, 50%
polyurethane

10
Yoshiki Hishinuma
6WCC1–28
80% rayon, 20% polyester

8
Yoshiki Hishinuma
6SBO2–22
100% polyester

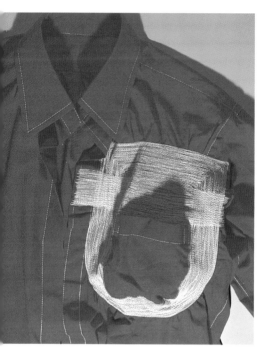

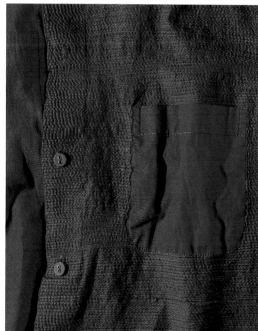

12

Koji Hamai

Textile, *14 ½ – 4, – VI*

Cotton

w 60cm l 90cm

w 23 ⅝ in l 45 ½ in

Hamai Factory Inc., Japan

11

Koji Hamai

Textile, *14 ½ – 4, – I*

Cotton

w 60cm l 90cm

w 23 ⅝ in l 45 ½ in

Hamai Factory Inc., Japan

13

Philippa Brock

Woven Jacquard, *Formed 2*

Cotton warp; linen and lycra

weft

h 5cm w 5cm

h 2in w 2in

CAD Woven Textiles, UK

(Prototype)

14
Philippa Brock
Woven Jacquard,
Formed 1
Wool crêpe and lurex
warp; lurex and lycra weft
h 5cm w 5cm
h 2in w 2in
CAD Woven Textiles, UK
(Prototype)

15
Reiko Sudo
Fabric, *Coal*
Polyester
w 109cm
w 42 ⅞ in
Nuno Corporation, Japan

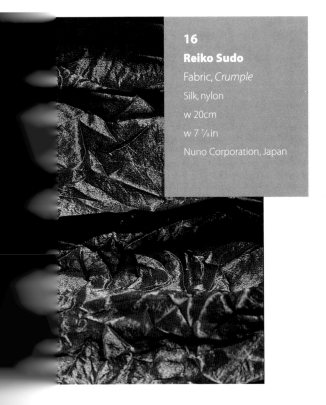

16
Reiko Sudo
Fabric, *Crumple*
Silk, nylon
w 20cm
w 7 ⅞ in
Nuno Corporation, Japan

17
Reiko Sudo
Fabric, *Mica*
Polyester
w 65cm
w 25 ⅝ in
Nuno Corporation, Japan

The technical mastery of Japanese designers is well shown in Reiko Sudo's new collection for the Nuno Corporation: *Cellophane* uses silk yarn and polyester to imitate the visual and textural qualities of cellophane, solving the technical problem of getting polyester to lie flat in the process. *Coal* employs polyester monofilament, normally used for fishing line. *Mica* uses polyester, which holds pleats well: here the fabric is pleated by heat moulding (a little-used process) by hand and by machine to create a glittering, multi-layered fabric.

18
Reiko Sudo
Fabric, *Cellophane*
Silk, polyester
w 110cm
w 43 ¼ in
Nuno Corporation, Japan

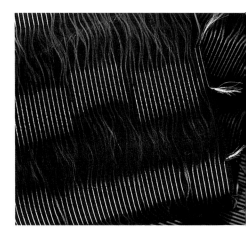

19
Reiko Sudo
Fabric, *Pack Ice*
Silk, rayon
w 115cm
w 45 ¼ in
Nuno Corporation, Japan

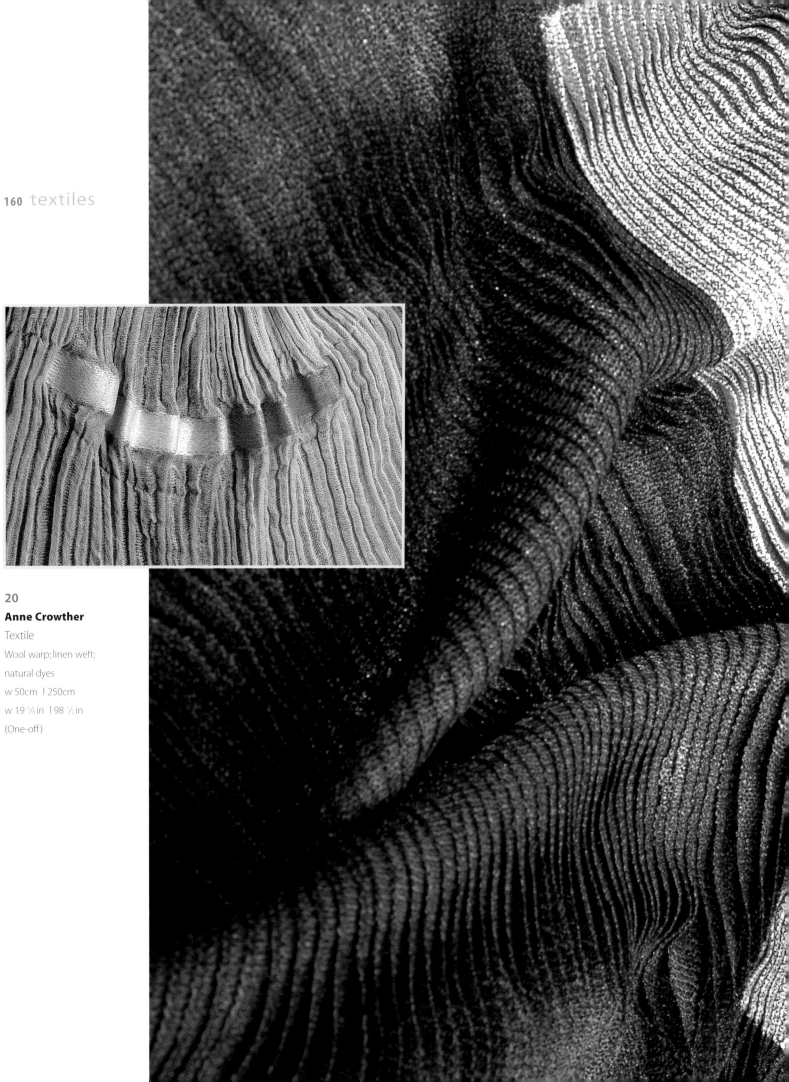

20

Anne Crowther

Textile

Wool warp; linen weft;
natural dyes
w 50cm l 250cm
w 19 ⅛ in l 98 ½ in
(One-off)

22
Gary Rooney
Textile throw, *Pleat 2*
Lurex
w 90cm I 150cm
w 35 ½ in I 59in
Shima Seiki Machine Builders,
UK
(Limited batch production)

21
Gary Rooney
Textile throw, *Pleat 4*
Lurex
w 90cm I 150cm
w 35 ½ in I 59in
Shima Seiki Machine Builders,
UK
(Limited batch production)

24
Ann Richards
Woven textile,
Crepon Blocks
Spun silk, crêpe silk
w 25cm I 150cm
w 9 ⅞in I 59in
(Prototype)

23
Ann Richards
Woven textile, *Crepon Spot*
Spun silk, crêpe silk
w 25cm I 150cm
w 9 ⅞in I 59in
(Prototype)

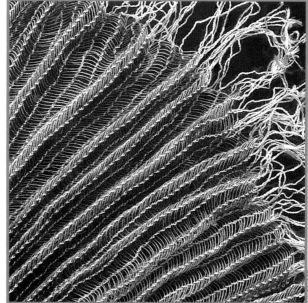

25
Ann Richards
Woven textile, *Gauze Pleat*
Mohair, tussah silk
w 25cm l 145cm
w 9 ⅞in l 57in
(Limited batch production)

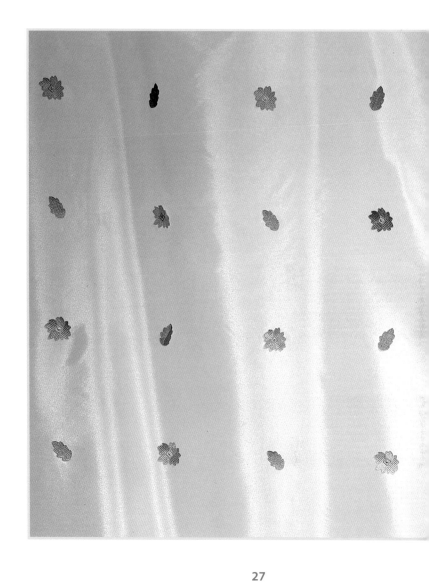

27

Heinz Röntgen

Embroidery on organdy,

Adora

Viscose, polyester

w 180cm

w 70 ⅞ in

Nya Nordiska, Germany

26

Susie Freeman

Scarf/drape, *Rich Mix*

Nylon monofilament

w 20cm l 30cm

w 7 ⅞ in l 11 ⅞ in

(Limited batch production)

28
Heinz Röntgen
Curtain fabric, *Plissee*
Polyester, polyamide
w 280cm
w 110 ¼ in
Nya Nordiska, Germany

29
Heinz Röntgen
Decorating fabric, *Stratos*
Polyester, pes-metal
w 155cm
w 61in
Nya Nordiska, Germany

30
Vibeke Rohland
Pillow, *Queenie Standstills*
Silkscreen, pigment print
h 90cm w 90cm d 25cm
h 35 ½ in w 35 ½ in d 9 ⅞ in
(Limited batch production)

A rug marks out space in a room.

This one, from the Belgian

designers Weyers and Borms,

marks out an intellectual space as

well. Never shy of promoting their

own quirky and original work, the

design on the rug is their own

logo, a piratical skull and

crossbones centred in a flaming

grenade: design by visual

subversion.

31
Weyers and Borms
Rug, *Nonx*
Wool
w 200cm l 400cm
w 78 ¼ in l 157 ½ in
Vera Vermeersch-Gilson, Belgium
(Limited batch production)

32
Ulf Moritz
Curtain fabric, *Lyrica*
Viscose, silk
w 142cm
w 55 ⁷⁄₈ in
S. A. Hesslein & Co.,
Germany

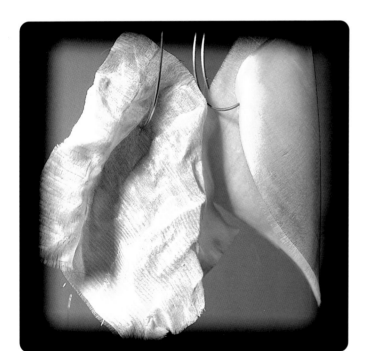

33
Ulf Moritz
Curtain fabric, *Lyrica Gold*
Metal, cotton, polyester
w 158cm
w 62 ¹⁄₄ in
S. A. Hesslein & Co., Germany

Ulf Moritz's new work for the Sahco Hesslein collection makes use of metal inserts to add points and lines of contrast and colour to the fabric base. These give a high reflectivity to the surface, enabling the final fabrics to be used both in fashion and furnishing design.

34
Ulf Moritz
Curtain fabric, *Colombine*
Silk, acetate, polyester
w 150cm
w 59in
S. A. Hesslein & Co., Germany

Ulf Moritz

Upholstery fabric, *Pharao*

Cotton, copper, copper yarn

w 150cm

w 59in

S. A. Hesslein & Co., Germany

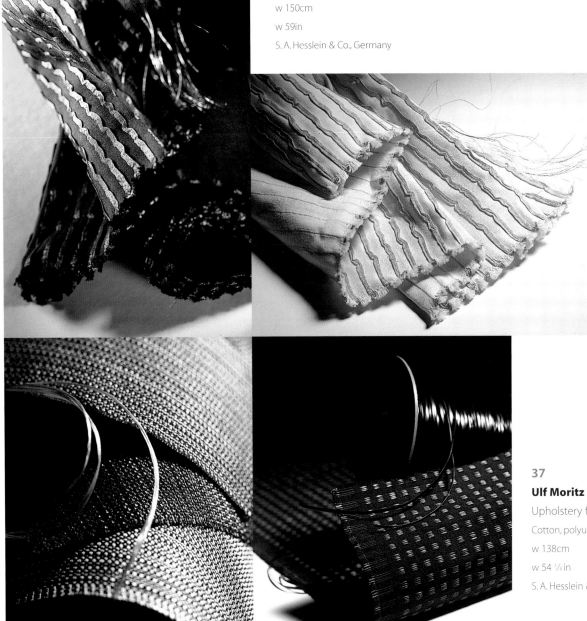

36

Ulf Moritz

Upholstery fabric,

Titanin

Cotton, polypropylene,

polyamide, nylon

w 130cm

w 51 ¼in

S. A. Hesslein & Co.,

Germany

37

Ulf Moritz

Upholstery fabric, *Epoca*

Cotton, polyurethane, viscose

w 138cm

w 54 ⅜in

S. A. Hesslein & Co., Germany

39
Louise Sass
Handprinted textile
Cotton, printed with chemical
resist and discharge
w 143cm
w 56 ¼ in
(One-off)

38
Jhane Barnes
Upholstery fabric,
Honeycomb
Polyester, rayon, nylon
w 137cm
w 54in
Knoll Textiles, USA

40
Renata Bonfanti
Rug/tapestry, *Algeria 24*
Wool, flax
w 195cm l 235cm
w 76 ¾ in l 92 ½ in
Renata Bonfanti Snc, Italy

41
Maddalena de Padova
Rug, *Fès 1*
Wool, natural fibre
w 90–250cm l 200–350cm
w 35 ½–98 ½ in l 78 ¾–
137 ¾ in
e. DePadova, Italy

Clodagh is one of the few designers to provide an email address: the accompanying design is equally contemporary. This metallic fabric contains a watermark of random shape and frequency which surfaces and disappears in the manner of a hologram. The deliberate choice of a random process echoes the happenstance of searching the World Wide Web.

42
Clodagh
Textile, *Tara*
Cotton, rayon
w 137cm
w 54in
Designtex, USA

products

Domestic product design, from
door handles to hi-fi, and from sinks to Web servers,
has long been a semiological battleground. Does the
product have to be mute (like hardware), dependent on the
user's knowledge or intuition, and appealing to taste rather than
practice, or must it be 'user friendly' (like software, supposedly). Can
a product declare itself through its appearance and still conform to
norms of expectation? This year's selection suggests a victory for
what might be termed the positive interface. That is to say, a
semantic content to the product which does not merely invite the
user but actively explains purpose and function without reference to
a hierarchy. Starck's own work for Thomson is a good example of this.
The *Moa Moa* radio, with its Brancusi form, positively asks to be
picked up and carried.

        The traditional definition of a good interface was its
transparency and neutrality – like classic typography never
interfering with the reader's understanding of the words. Now that
the new typography has reminded us that text is never independent
of context, we can expect other interfaces not to be passive, but to
support and instruct. Products are never, in fact, inert. In a highly
mediatized world they are themselves communications, and must be
designed as such.'I am a computer' is no longer enough:'I am the
computer that will get you on to the Web/travel with you on the
train/help your children learn' is now the necessary statement.

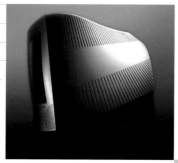

(page 172)
1
Thomas Meyerhoffer,
Gary Schultz,
Naoto Fukasawa and
Tim Brown for IDEO
Product Development
CRT monitor,
NEC Multisync M500
Plastic, ABS
h 40.6cm w 37.2cm l 40.5cm
h 16in w 14 ⅝in l 15 ⅞in
NEC Corporation, Japan

2
Hartmut Engel
TV set, *Loewe Planus*
Plastics
h 60.2cm w 81.6cm d 49cm
h 23 ¾in w 32 ⅛in d 19 ¼in
Loewe Opta GmbH, Germany

3

Mitsuru Takami

Liquid crystal display for car
dashboard, *TR-7LC4*

ABS

h 12.8cm w 18.8cm d 3.5cm

h 5in w 7 ⅜in d 1 ⅜in

Matsushita Electric Industrial Co. Ltd
(Television Sector), Japan

5

Sony

LCD television, *KL-37 HW1*

Plastics

h 82.5cm w 92cm d 39cm

h 32 ½in w 36 ⅛in d 15 ⅓in

4

Philips Corporate Design

Television, *FL5 Range*

Mono-materials, waterbased
suede paints

h 50.6cm w 64.8cm l 49.3cm

h 19 ⅞in w 25 ½in l 19 ⅜in

Philips Corporate Design,
The Netherlands

6

**Scott Stropkay, David Privitera,
Mark Nichols, Alan Vale and
Otto DeRuntz for IDEO Product
Development**

TV-top receiver and universal
remote control, *VideoGuide*

Recyclable plastic

Base unit:

h 10.7cm w 20.3cm d 12cm

h 4 ¼in w 8in d 4 ¾in

Remote:

h 16.5cm w 6.3cm d 3.2cm

h 6 ½in w 2 ½in d 1 ¼in

VideoGuide Inc., USA

7

**Toshiba Corporation
Design Centre**

Personal handyphone system
terminal, *DL-S22PL Carrots*
ABS, plastics
h 13.5cm w 4.3cm d 2.4cm
h 5 ³/₈in w 1 ⁵/₈in d 1in
Toshiba Corporation, Japan

9

**Christian Schwamkrug and
Simon Fraser for Porsche
Design GmbH**

Cord and cordless telephone
Plastic
h 12/13cm w 14/24cm d 15/18cm
h 4 ³/₄ /5 ¹/₈in w 5 ¹/₂ /9 ³/₈in d 5 ⁷/₈/7in
Samsung Electronics Co., Korea

8

**Design Centre
Communication and
Audio Systems Group**

Telephone, *JD-P2, PHS
Compatible Digital Cordless
Phone*
h 11.2cm w 4.3cm l 2.7cm
h 4 ³/₈in w 1 ⁵/₈in l 1in
Sharp Corporation, Japan

10

Steve McGugan

Telecommunications
headset for *Vois* (MPA) and
Vois plus (Telephone)
ABS plastic
h 3.5cm l 14cm d 9cm
h 1 ³/₈in l 5 ¹/₂in d 3 ¹/₂in
GN Netcom A/S, Denmark

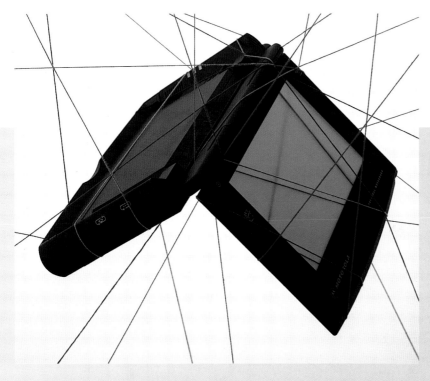

11
**frogdesign global
creative network**
Personal wireless
communicator,
Motorola 'Envoy'
ABS
h 2.8cm w 4.8cm l 8.2cm
h 1 ½in w 1 ⅞in l 3 ¼in
Motorola, USA
(Limited batch production)

12
Sony
Personal MD File PDF-5
h 25.5cm w 30.8cm d 5.6cm
h 10in w 12⅛in d 2 ⅛in

13
**Cheryl Felix and
Larry Kuba for Herbst
LaZar Bell Inc.**
Space heater, *Holmes Heater*
ABS, plastic
h 24cm w 31.7cm d 15.8cm
h 9 ½ in w 12 ½ in d 6 ¼ in
Holmes Product Corporation,
USA

14
**Steve McGugan, Thomas
Dickson, Sally Beardsley,
Brüel & Kjaer**
Sound-level measuring
instruments, *SLM 2260* and
SLM 2236
ABS plastic
h 4/6cm w 9.5/13cm
l 25/40cm
h 1 ⅝/2 ⅜ in w 3 ¾/5 ⅛ in
l 9 ⅞/15 ¾ in
Brüel & Kjaer A/S, Denmark

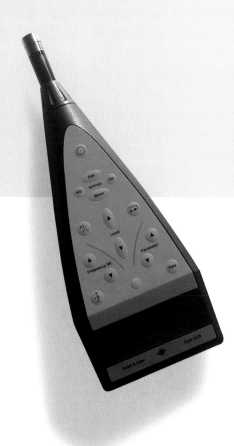

15

**Marcello Cutino and
Stefano Como**

Remote control

ABS

h 17cm w 9cm l 8cm

h 6 ¾ in w 3 ½ in l 3 ⅛ in

Compania Roca Radiadores SA,
Spain

Developing three-dimensional models in computer-aided design is normally done in one of two ways. Either the model is created as a series of two-dimensional planar images and assembled on screen in three dimensions, or a physical model is scanned three dimensionally to create the computer model. Both approaches have their advantages and disadvantages, and neither takes maximum benefit from the capabilities of modern computer hardware and software. The main problem is devising an input tool which has the flexibility of physical modelling but is also accurate. Gianni Orsini, an Italian designer working in Holland, has devised a new system, *TIME*, to meet this need. With a drawing tablet as a basis, *TIME*'s key element is the 'watch', a hand-held device that allows the designer to create 3D models and navigate three dimensionally through the design while using a stylus with the other hand (as opposed to the one-handed approach normally used on screen). A number of Dutch designers, including Droog Design, Ninaber/Peters/Krouwel and Philips Corporate Design, contributed to the research on the project, which is expected to go into production soon.

16

Gianni Orsini

Computer for modelling
3D objects, *TIME* (3D Input,
Modification and Evaluation)

Recyclable thermoplastic blend of
PC and ABS

h 8cm l 53cm d 40cm

h 3 ⅛ in l 20 ⅞ in d 15 ¾ in

(Prototype)

Lunar Design's long association with the computer hardware industry means that the Californian company has played a major role in creating the product semantics of the IT revolution. What should a modem look like, for example (it is a plastic box containing chips and wires, and its function, purely electronic, has no bearing on its form)? Should a hand controller for computer games still be a joystick, in the age of the Stealth bomber you can now fly across the screen? Lunar Design's solutions to these two problems show both attention to ergonomic detail and a keen understanding of the man/machine interface in its widest, most imaginative sense.

17

David Laituri, Gil Wong and Jeff Hoefer for Lunar Design; Ray Riley, Rick Jackson and Cal Seid for Apple Computer

Game machine/Internet appliance, *Pippin/Atmark*
ABS, sheet metal
Box:
h 9cm w 26cm l 27cm
h 3 ½ in w 10 ¼ in l 10 ⅝ in
Container:
h 4.5cm w 16cm l 10cm
h 1 ¼ in w 6 ⅓ in l 3 ⅞ in
Apple Computer for
Bandai Co. Ltd of Japan, USA

18

Max Yoshimoto, Jeff Salazar, Larry Kerila and Alex Ross for Lunar Design; Michael Trupiano and Louis Ornelas for Farallon Computing

Modem, *Netopia*
ABS, polycarbonate, sheet metal
h 6cm w 27cm l 24cm
h 2 ⅜ in w 10 ⅞ in l 9 ⅜ in
Farallon Computing Inc., USA

19
John Edson, Max
Yoshimoto, Gil Wong and
Alex Ross for Lunar
Design;
Amy Bayersdorfer, John
Cary, Andy Stavros and
Jim Nealon for Global
Village Communication
Fax/modem connector,
Power Port Platinum Pro
Connector
PVC, polycarbonate
h 2.3cm w 4cm l 4.3cm
h ⅞in w 1 ½in l 1 ⅝in
Global Village
Communication, USA

20

**Kyushu Matsushita
Electric Co. Ltd**

Laser printer, *KX-P6100*

Plastic

h 28.7cm w 13.2cm l 37.8cm

h 11 ¼in w 5 ⅛in l 14 ⅞in

Kyushu Matsushita Electric

Co. Ltd, Japan

21

King-Miranda Associati

Air-conditioner and

remote control, *Climapiu*

Plastics, metals

h 35cm w 88cm d 16.5cm

h 13 ¾in w 34 ⅝in d 6 ½in

Olimpia Splendid SpA, Italy

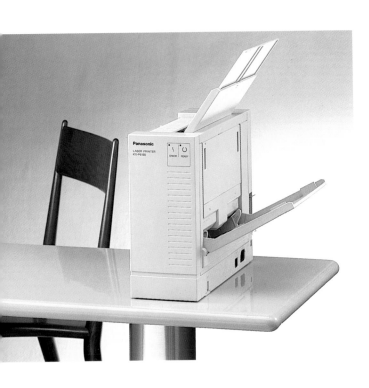

22
Yves Béhar
Portable electronic assistants,
Dyna Book and *GPS Receiver*
Rubberized translucent
thermoplastic, lycra polypropylene
h 3cm w 22.5cm l 28cm
di of *GPS* 1/3cm
h 1 ½in w 8 ⅞in l 11cm
di of *GPS* ⅜/1 ½in
Lunar Design, USA
(Prototype)

24
**Michele de Lucchi and
Alessandro Chiarato**
Personal computer,
Minitower M6 6200
Plastic, sheet metal
h 22cm w 34cm l 43cm
h 8 ⅝in w 13 ¾in l 17in
Olivetti SpA, Italy

23
Michele de Lucchi
Portable computer,
Echos 20
Plastic
h 26.5cm w 34cm
h 10 ½in w 13 ¾in
Olivetti SpA, Italy

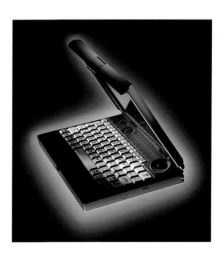

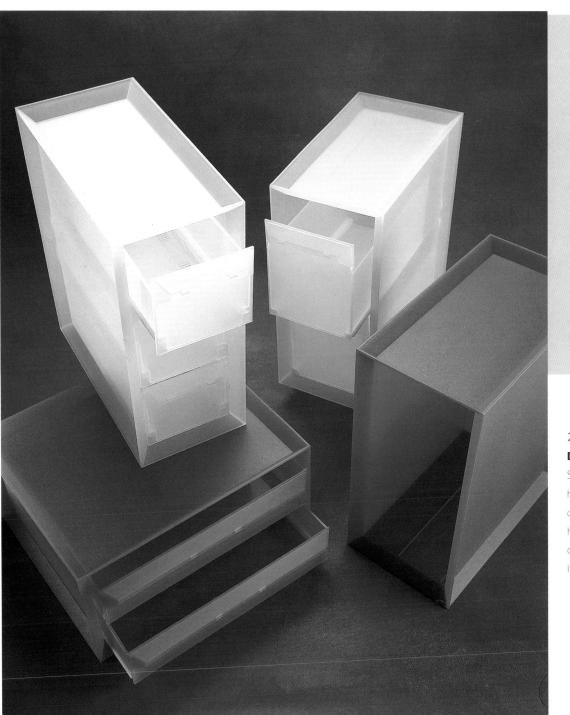

25

Design Studio Copenhagen

Storage containers, *Box*

h 17/35cm w 15.7/17/35cm

d 30cm

h 6 ⅝/13 ¾ in w 6 ⅛ /6 ⅝ /13 ¾ in

d 11 ⅞ in

IKEA, Sweden

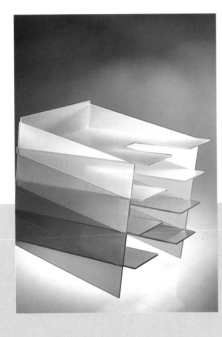

27

Sebastian Bergne

Letter tray, *DIN A4*

Polystyrene

h 7.5cm w 25cm l 35cm

h 3in w 9 ⅞in l 13 ¾in

Authentics, Germany

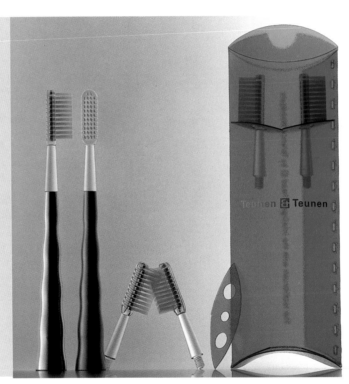

26

Theo Williams

Disk containers

PVC, nylon

Various sizes

Nava Design SpA, Italy

28

Terence Woodgate

Toothbrush

Steel, nylon

l 17.5cm

l 6 ⅞in

Teunen & Teunen, Germany

30

Mario Ruiz Rubio for Costa Design

Rucksack, *Integral*

Cord, aluminium

h 50cm w 27cm l 38cm

h 19 5/8in w 10 5/8in l 15in

Casa Artiach SA, Spain

29

Kazuyo Komoda

Photograph holder, *Photogenia*

PVC, polycarbonate

Small:

h 15/16cm l 15/16cm d 10cm

h 5 7/8/6 1/4in l 5 7/8/6 1/4in d 3 7/8in

Large:

h 20/22cm l 20/22cm d 13cm

h 7 7/8/8 5/8in l 7 7/8/8 5/8in d 5 1/8in

Oggetti Latini srl, Italy

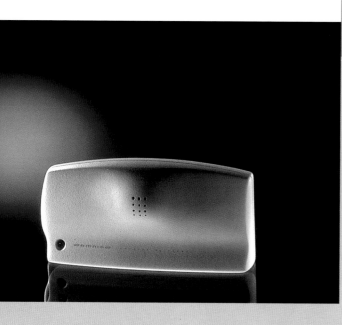

32
Setsu Ito and Bruno Gregori
Humidifier, *Machine*
Porcelain
h 19.2cm l 12cm d 5cm
h 7 ½in l 4 ⅝in d 2in
Ceramica Il Coccio, Italy

31
Mario Ruiz Rubio for Costa Design
Sleep inducer, *Somnios*
ABS
h 6.5cm w 2.5cm l 13.5cm
h 2 ½in w 1in l 5 ¼in
Somnios SL, Spain

33
Mario Ruiz Rubio for Costa Design
Insect exterminator, *Extertronic*
ABS
h 32cm di 28cm
h 12 ⅝in di 11in
Electronica Escuder SL, Spain

34
Mario Ruiz Rubio for Costa Design
Electronic rele, *Gare*
Lexan
h 9cm w 17cm l 10cm
h 3 ½in w 6 ¾in l 3 ⅞in
Disibeint Electronics SL, Spain

IDEO's new cable storage system for American Power Conversion deals with one of the problems of the modern office – the spaghetti of cables needed to keep modern computers and communication systems going. Each half-moon can take five plugs, with the wires coming in and out through a channel. Two half-moons can be linked to make a circle of ten sockets. The device includes a current surge protector to safeguard the end equipment.

35
**Scott Stropkay, Mark
Nichols, David Weissburg
and Bob McCaffrey
for IDEO Product
Development**
Emergency communications
control system, *Lifeline
CarePartner Communicator*
Plastic
h 8.9cm w 17.8cm d 8.9cm
h 3 ½ in w 7in d 3 ½ in
Lifeline Systems Inc., USA

36
**Mark Nichols, Scott
Stropkay, Hayden Taylor,
Harald Quintus-Bosz,
David Privitera, Tim
Proulx and Bob McCaffrey
for IDEO Product
Development**
Surge-protected power strip,
APC Surge Arrest E10
Plastic
h 5.8cm w 12.7cm l 30.5cm
h 2 ¼ in w 5in l 12in
American Power Conversion, USA

37

Yoshitaka Sumimoto

Saw for high branches,
Silky Hayauchi
Steel, aluminium
w 12cm l 63cm d 3cm
w 4 ¾in l 24 ¾in d 1 ½in
UM:Kogyo Inc., Japan

38

Yoshitaka Sumimoto

Saw, *Silky Gomtaro-Pro*
Steel, plastic
h 7cm w 36cm l 24cm d 2.2cm
h 2 ¾in w 14 ⅛in l 9 ⅜in d ⅞in
UM:Kogyo Inc., Japan

39

Mitsushige Sumimoto

Saw, *Silky Super Accel-21*
Steel, aluminium, plastic
h 4cm w 23cm l 21cm d 2.2cm
h 1 ⅝in w 9in l 8 ¼in d ⅞in
UM:Kogyo Inc., Japan

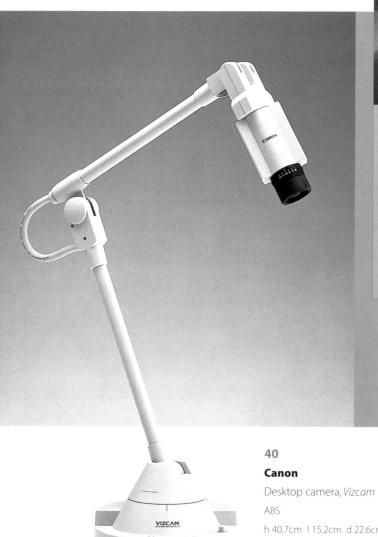

41
Jonathan Marshall
Camera, *126 Desk Camera*
Aluminium, cherry wood
h 8.5cm l 11cm d 4cm
h 3 ⅜in l 4 ⅜in d 1 ½in
(Prototype)

40
Canon
Desktop camera, *Vizcam*
ABS
h 40.7cm l 15.2cm d 22.6cm
h 16in l 6in d 8 ⅞in
Canon, Japan

42
Canon
Camera, *Prima Sol*
Polycarbonate, resin
h 6.7cm l 12.4cm d 4.5cm
h 2 ⅝in l 4 ⅞in d 1 ¾in
Canon, Japan

43
JVC
Digital video camera,
GR-DV1
Aluminium, plastics
h 14.8cm w 4.3cm d 8.8cm
h 5 ⅞in w 1 ¾in d 3 ⅞in

44

Edda Design

Knife sharpener, *Carrot*

Plastics

h 5cm w 5cm l 25cm

h 2in w 2in l 9 ⅞ in

Fiskars, Finland

(Prototype)

46

Edda Design

Knife sharpener, *Motion*

Plastics

h 5cm w 5cm l 25cm

h 2in w 2in l 9 ⅞ in

Fiskars, Finland

(Prototype)

45

Philips Corporate Design

Portable multimedia LCD
projector, *ProScreen 1200*

ABS, acrylic, silicon rubber,
steel plate

h 20.7cm w 28cm l 9.7cm

h 8 ⅛ in w 11in l 3 ⅞ in

Philips Corporate Design,
The Netherlands

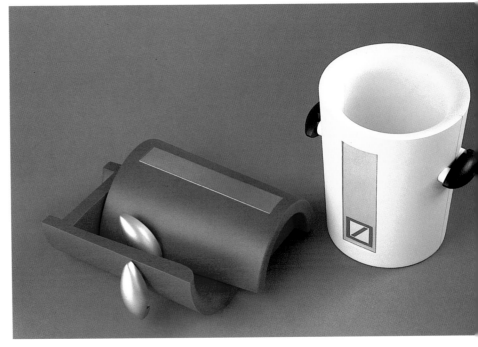

47

Jochen Henkels

Sparkling-wine cooler,
B.Fridge

Plastics, alloy

h 20cm di 16cm

h 7 ⅞ in di 6 ¼ in

(Prototype)

The *Soft Fan* is a simple statement about centrifugal force: three pieces of fabric hang from the spinner of a fan, making a soft sculpture when not in use and a shimmering disc of colour when in motion, as the fabric stretches and fills with air. Unlike a metal or plastic blade fan, the moving parts present no danger, and so no protective guard is needed. By working with the Aeronautics Department at Imperial College in London, Paul Priestman refined the fabric assembly to a performance comparable with a conventional fan, one distributing a gentle breeze over a wide area (like a ceiling fan) rather than the forced draught of a desk fan. 'I see it as a passive, safe and tactile modern product with a tinge of green thinking', the designer says, 'and I'm thinking about large-scale soft fans as architectural features on walls and ceilings. In beautiful fabrics these could be wonderful, like the sails of ships.'

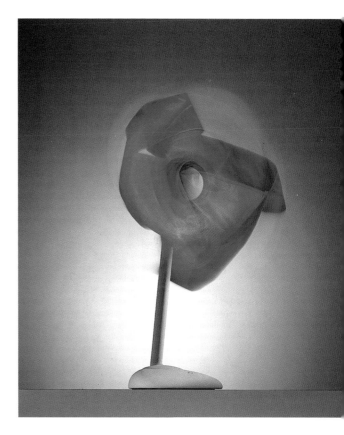

48
Paul Priestman
Desk fan, *Soft Fan*
Fabric, plastics
h 34cm w 20cm l 24cm
h 13 ³/₈ in w 7 ⅞ in l 9 ³/₈ in
(Prototype)

49

Jasper Startup

Desk fan, *Basket Fan*

Willow

h 48cm w 35cm d 30cm

h 19 ⅞in w 13 ¾in d 11 ¾in

John Frietas, UK

(Prototype)

51

Carsten Jorgensen

Coffee-grinder, *EL*

ABS, SAN

h 27cm w 16cm l 21cm di 14.5cm

h 10 ⅝in w 6 ¼in l 8 ¼in di 5 ¾in

Bodum, Switzerland

50

Richard Sapper

Automatic teapot, *Bandung*

Stainless steel, wicker

h 20.8cm w 12.3cm l 21.5cm

h 8 ⅛in w 4 ⅞in l 8 ½in

Alessi SpA, Italy

52
Josep Lluscà
Electronic keyring
ABS, elastomer
h 6cm w 4cm d 1.5cm
h 2 ¼in w 1 ½ in d ½in
Ingenieria de Control SA,
Spain

53
**Mark Dziersk, Jim Hand,
Phil Anthony, Carl Price
and Dave Pacchini for
Herbst LaZar Bell Inc.**
Carpet cleaner, *Marathon*
Polyethylene, aluminium,
PVC rubber
h 91.4cm w 49.6cm l 109.2cm
h 36in w 16in l 43in
Breuer/Tornado Corporation,
USA

54

Sony

CD player and hi-fi system,

CMT-M1 56

Aluminium

CD player:

h 12.5cm w 14.2cm d 25.2cm

h 4 ⅞ in w 5 ⅝ in d 9 ⅞ in

Speakers:

h 20cm w 12.5cm d 21.5cm

h 7 ⅞ in w 4 ⅞ in d 8 ½ in

55

**Erwin Driessens and
Maria Verstappen**

Massager, *Tickle Machine*
Aluminium, silicone or
urethane rubber caterpillar
tracks
h 2.4cm w 7.8cm l 8cm
h ⁷⁄₈in w 3in l 3 ¹⁄₈in

56

**Ninaber/Peters/Krouwel
Industrial Design**

Cycle-track with Excel computer
Steel, ABS
Cycle-track:
h 40cm w 59cm d 58cm
h 15 ³⁄₄in w 23 ¹⁄₄in d 22in
Computer:
h 4cm w 12.5cm d 10cm
h 1 ⁵⁄₈in w 4 ⁷⁄₈in d 3 ⁷⁄₈in
Technische Industrie Tacx,
The Netherlands

This robot tickling machine comes with a selection
of different tracks, to generate different effects on
the skin. Battery driven, the motion sensors within
it ensure that when it reaches an edge it turns or
retreats, and so remains on the body. But whether
Tickle is therapy or toy is not to the point. Not Not
Design is a Dutch group, based in Amsterdam. A visit
to their Web site explains their interest in random
behaviour, for there they also show a series of three-
dimensional virtual constructions (both interior and
exterior) generated by applying evolutionary rules
to an initially random assembly of fixed units. They
also offer software with random generation systems
for language. *Tickle*, with its self-programming
movement, carries this research over into the real
world.

58

Christof Schwarz

Child's toy, *Beachball*

Alucubond, polycarbonate

l 33cm di 22.5cm

l 13in di 8 ⁷⁄₈in

Hafenatelier, Germany

(Limited batch production)

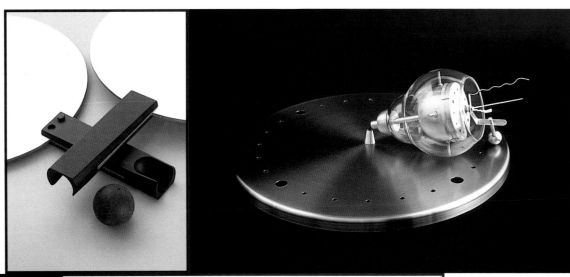

59

Masafumi Katsukawa

Clock, *Holos-On*

Prototype

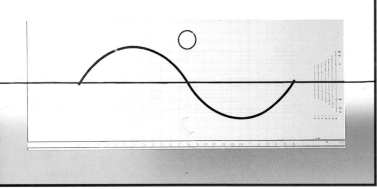

60

Andrea Ponsi

Wall solar clock, *Cielo*

Metal, Plexiglas

h 28cm w 4cm l 70cm

h 11in w 1 ½in l 27 ½in

Andrea Ponsi Design, Italy

(Limited batch production)

57

Industrial Bohner & Lippert

Sports spectacles,

Uvex Bulletproof Codex

Metal, pearled nylon, rubber,

bulletproof lenses

Uvex Sports GmbH & Co. KG, Germany

61

Sergio Calatroni

Container, *Mama*

Plastic

h 25cm w 12cm l 30cm d 13cm

h 9 ⅞in w 4 ¾in l 11 ⅞in d 5 ⅛in

Afro City, Italy

(Limited batch production)

62

Lois Walpole

Laundry basket,

Juice Cartons

Juice cartons

h 85cm w 65cm d 52cm

h 33 ⅜in w 25 ½in d 20 ½in

(One-off)

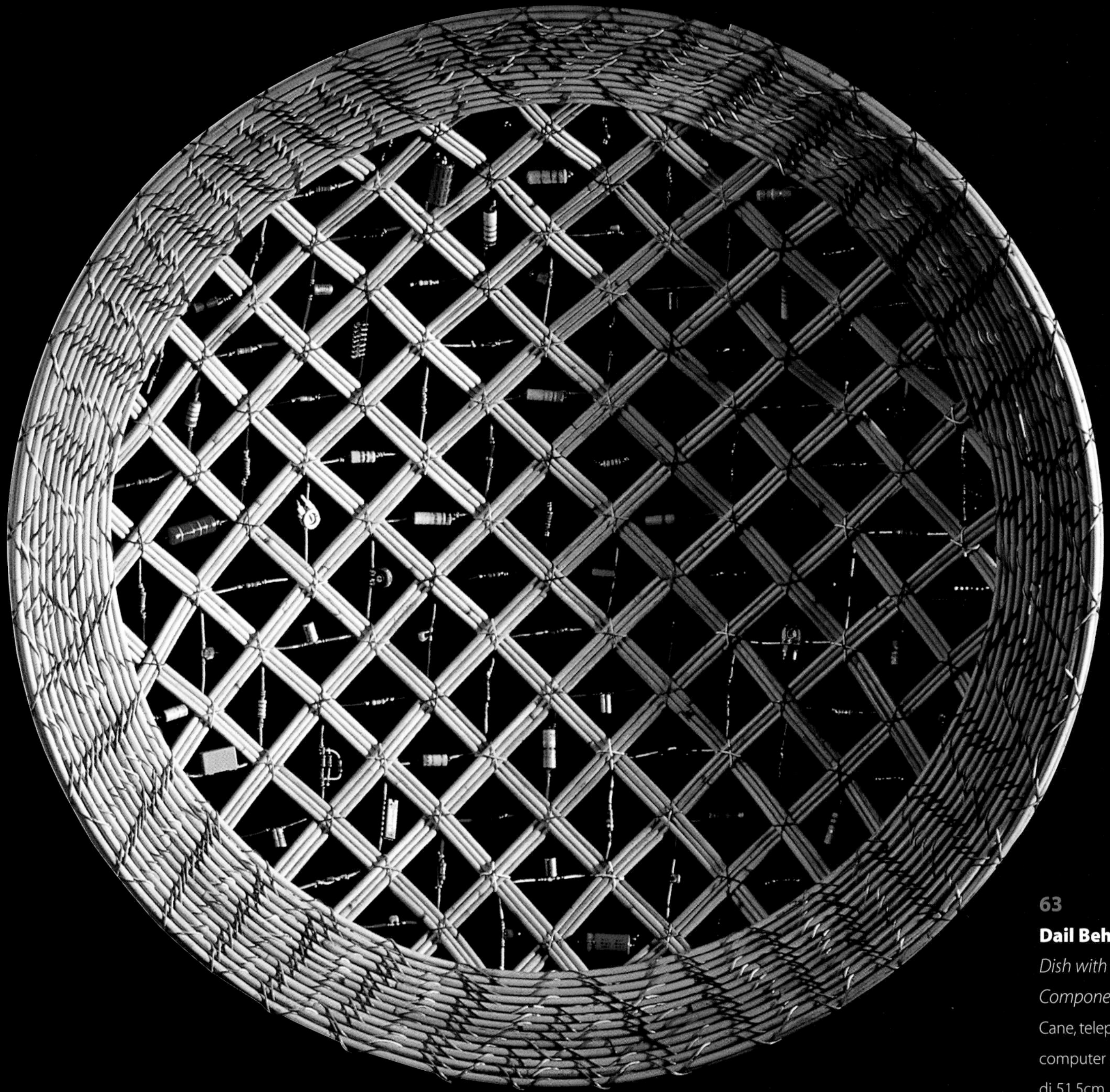

63
Dail Behennah
Dish with Computer Chip
Components
Cane, telephone wire,
computer components
di 51.5cm
di 20 ¼ in
(One-off)

64

Thomas Krause

Cocktail radio

Ready-made Alessi cocktail
shaker, plastic, wood, brass
h 35cm di 10cm
h 13 ¾ in di 3 ⅞ in
(One-off – Alessi project at
the Royal College of Art,
London)

66

Michael Marriott

*Sardine Tin Collector's
Cabinet*

Sardine tins, MDF, fuel line,
wing nuts
h 25.5cm l 5cm d 10cm
h 10in l 2in d 3 ⅞ in
(Limited batch production)

65

Jos van der Meulen

Wastepaper basket,
Paperbag
Unused billboard posters
h 20–90cm di 12–70cm
h 7 ⅞–35 ⅛ in di 4¾–27½ in
Goods, The Netherlands

Every time billboard posters are printed, there are a number of surplus copies: some
are the result of the printing machine running on, some spares to replace damaged
posters on site. Normally they would be scrapped after the campaign, but Jos van
der Meulen has come up with the idea of reusing the unwanted sheets, folding and
sewing them to turn them into wastepaper baskets.

Eva-Maria Melchers' *Nature* wash-stand is

a simple metaphor: the traditional bowl

placed on a table becomes an iconic

object in oak, glass and bronze. The

combination of simple, mnemonic forms

and 'noble' materials creates an object

rich in significance and celebration.

67
Eva-Maria Melchers
Wash-stand, *Nature*
Oak, glass, bronze
h 96cm w 42cm l 60cm
h 37 ¾in w 16 ½in l 23 ⅝in
Eva-Maria Melchers, Germany

Konstantin Grcic's new wastepaper

baskets for Authentics validate Starck's

judgement of him as one of the key

minimalists. The shape is simple,

self-evident and inviting, the handles

rounded to provide an even grip,

proof of what the designer calls the

'minimal design language' of the

product. This design approach also fits

in with Authentics' declared approach

of providing basic household

products in a range of simple colours

which exploit the translucence of

recyclable polypropylene.

68
Konstantin Grcic
Basket, *2 Hands*
Recyclable polypropylene
h 24.5cm d 54.5cm
h 9 ⅝ in d 21 ½ in
Authentics, Germany

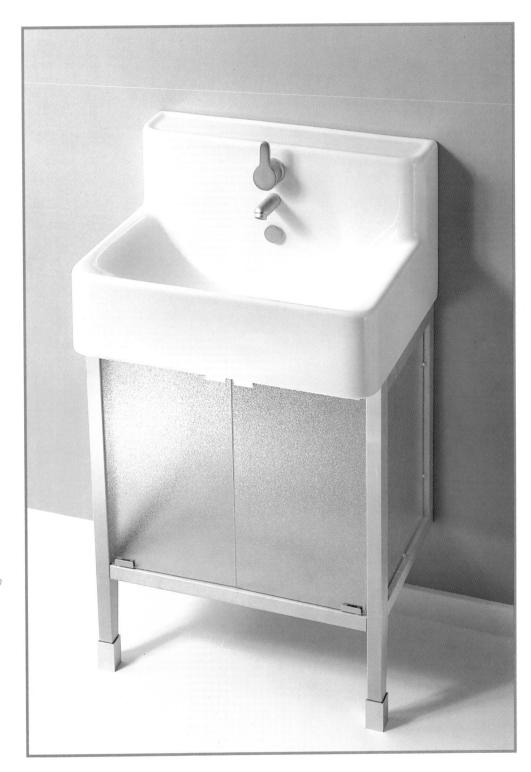

69
**Design Studio
Copenhagen**
Wash-basin with cabinet, *Ann*
Porcelain, glass, wood
h 100cm w 60cm d 45cm
h 39 ⅛ in w 23 ⅝ in d 17 ¾ in
IKEA, Sweden

70

**Josep Massana and
Josep Tremoleda**

Bathroom accessories, *Siria*

Stainless steel

Various sizes

Mobles 114, Spain

71

Claus Lippe

Bottle, *Pineo*

Glass

h 31cm w 8.8cm l 31cm di 8.8cm

h 12 ¼in w 3 ½in l 12 ¼in di 3 ½in

Naturquell SA, Germany

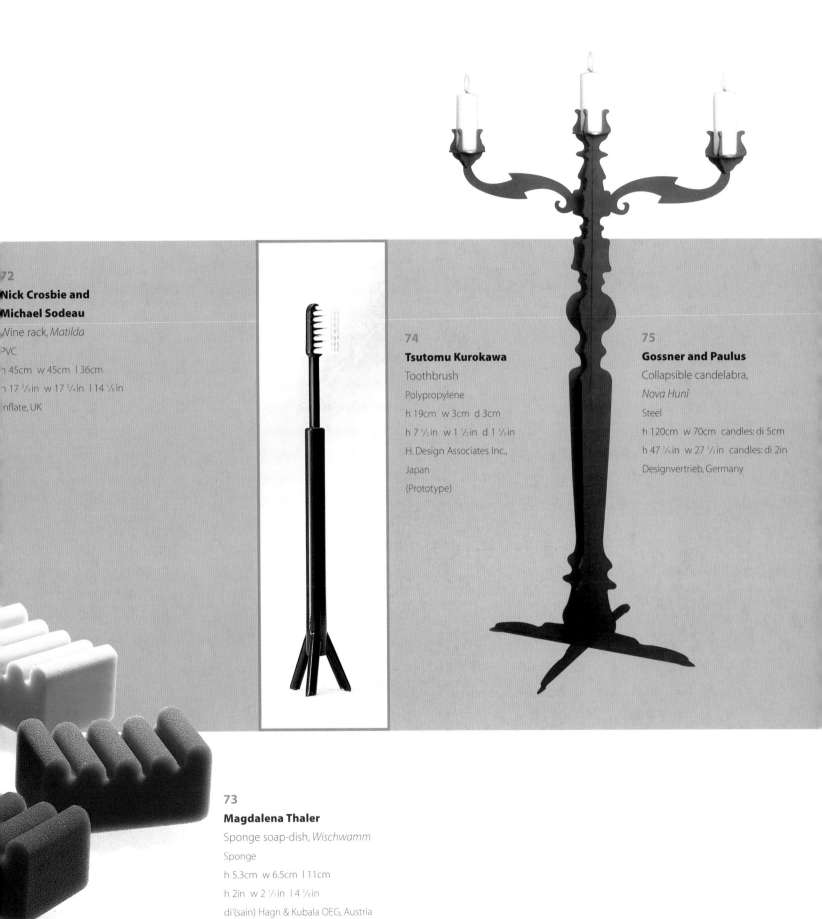

72

**Nick Crosbie and
Michael Sodeau**

Wine rack, *Matilda*

PVC

h 45cm w 45cm l 36cm

h 17 ¾ in w 17 ¾ in l 14 ⅛ in

Inflate, UK

74

Tsutomu Kurokawa

Toothbrush

Polypropylene

h 19cm w 3cm d 3cm

h 7 ½ in w 1 ½ in d 1 ½ in

H. Design Associates Inc.,

Japan

(Prototype)

75

Gossner and Paulus

Collapsible candelabra,

Nova Huni

Steel

h 120cm w 70cm candles: di 5cm

h 47 ¼ in w 27 ½ in candles: di 2in

Designvertrieb, Germany

73

Magdalena Thaler

Sponge soap-dish, *Wischwamm*

Sponge

h 5.3cm w 6.5cm l 11cm

h 2in w 2 ½ in l 4 ⅜ in

di'(sain) Hagn & Kubala OEG, Austria

76
Feldmann & Schultcher
Christmas tree, *Spiralbaum*
Lasercut plywood and steel
h 0.5–160cm w 110cm l 110•
h ¼–63in w 43 ¼in l 43 ¼ir
Werth Forsttechnik, Germany
(Prototype for mass productio

This minimalist Christmas tree

neatly solves the problem of what

to do with the tree for the other

351 days of the year. Feldmann

and Schultchen's design, for Werth

Forsttechnik, is a circle of plywood

cut with a helical pattern leading

to the centre. Pull the centre up,

hang it, and you have a swirling

tree shape with slots for candles.

It then packs flat after use.

77
Pietro Silva
Coat hook, *Signor T*
Brushed steel
h 10.4cm w 23.7cm
h 4 ⅛ in w 9 ⅜ in
Tevere SpA, Italy

78
Enrico Quell and Diego Lemme
Clothes drier, *Lo Stendino*
Wood, metal
h 64cm l 78cm d 11cm
h 25 ⅛ in l 30 ¾ in d 4 ⅜ in
(Limited batch production)

79
Mark Rogers
Magazine rack
Birch ply, aluminium
h 32cm w 22cm l 36cm
h 12 ⅝ in w 8 ⅝ in l 14 ⅛ in
BUT, UK
(Limited batch production)

80
Kuno Prey
Libreria/CD
Varnished metal sheet
h 22cm w 11.5cm
h 8 ⅝ in w 4 ½ in
Nava Design SpA, Italy

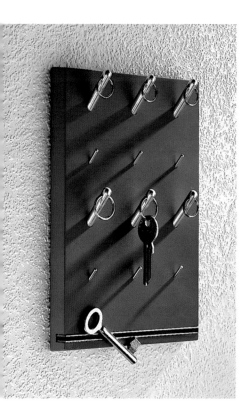

81
Winfried Scheuer
Key storage, *Pin*
Aluminium, MDF
h 25cm w 18cm l 1.5cm
h 9 ⅞in w 7in l ⅝in
Emform, Germany

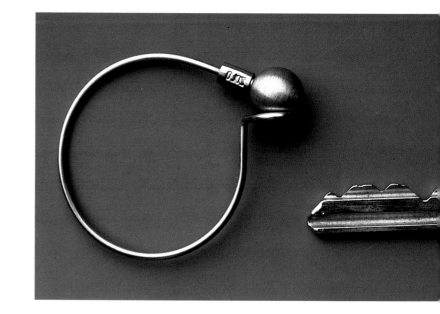

82
Sven Heestermann
Keyholder, *Keypr*
Steelwire, brass
di 3.7cm
di 1 ½in
Radius GmbH, Germany

A traditional board for storing keys safely

required hooks. Winfried Scheuer's new

keyholder offers a direct alternative: rather

than hanging on a hook, the key slides into

an angled slot.

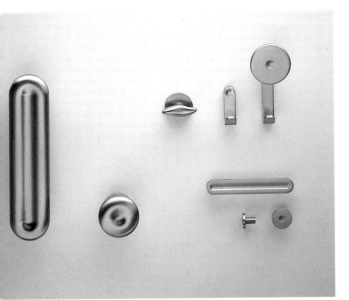

84

Sir Norman Foster

Door handle and accessories,

NF Novantacinque

Brass, wood, rubber

h 6.9cm w 4.4cm l 14.7cm

h 2 ¾ in w 1 ¾ in l 5 ¾ in

Fusital srl, Italy

83

**Industrial Bohner &
Lippert**

Watch and weather station

Metal

h 10cm w 10cm l 3.5cm

h 3 ⅞ in w 3 ⅞ in l 1 ⅜ in

Barigo, Germany

85

**Constantin Boym and
Laurene Leon**

Door handle, *Egg*

Brass, porcelain

d 10cm di 10cm

d 4in di 4in

Boym Design Studio, USA

(Prototype)

86
**Frogdesign Global
Creative Network**

Network computer,
Oracle 'NC'
Plastics
h 26.3cm l 23.7cm d 23.7cm
h 10 ⅜in l 9 ⅜in d 9 ⅜in
Oracle, USA
(Prototype)

88
**Frogdesign Global
Creative Network**

Computer trackball,
Logitech 'Palmball'
Polycarbonate
h 10.4cm w 15.8cm d 4.9cm
trackball: di 4.5cm
h 4in w 6 ¼in d 1 ⅞in
trackball: di 1 ¾in
Logitech, USA

87
**Frogdesign Global
Creative Network**

Multimedia computer,
*Packard Bell 'Corner
Computer'*
ABS
h 14cm w 42cm d 42cm
h 5 ½in w 16 ½in d 16 ½in
Packard Bell, USA

The *Oracle* computer is the first major
challenge to the dual hegemony of the IBM
PC and the Apple Mac in a decade. Called
the *NC* (for Network Computer), it is designed
to offer a low-cost alternative for home,
leisure and business computing by using
the Internet. Rather than buying an
expensive machine with dedicated screen
and hard disk, *Oracle* proposes a low-cost
communication system that will link to the
Internet, so using downloaded programs
from the Net rather than storing your own
software, and which will output to a standard
television, though the laptop version will
have an integral screen. The system offers
customers the pleasures of direct access to
the Internet and World Wide Web.
Frogdesign's design for the main unit also
adopts a visionary stance in line with the
challenge of the product. The different tower
units (such as loudspeakers) plug into a base
unit. The whole has an uncanny echo of
Norman Bel Geddes's 1939 *Futurama* designs
for a modern city linked by motorways, an
exact simile for the invisible information
highways of cyberspace.

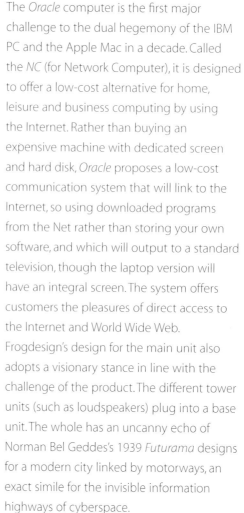

89
Shinichi Sumikawa
Pillcase, *Pecon*
Plastic, rubber
w 5cm l 9cm d 1.3cm
w 2in l 3 ½in d ½in
Sumikawa Design Studio,
Japan
(Prototype)

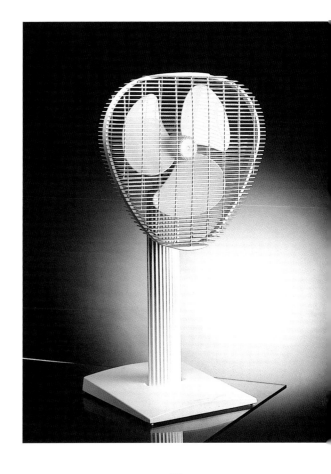

91
Ramon Graells
Fan, *Europa 16°C*
h 156cm w 50.7cm d 42cm
h 61 ¼in w 29in d 16 ½in
Taurus, Spain

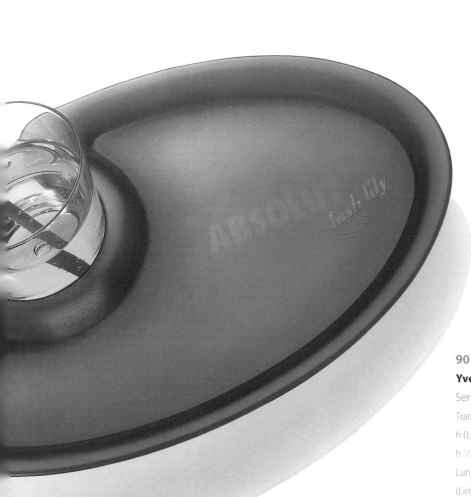

90
Yves Béhar and David Malina
Serving trays, *Lush Lily Tray System*
Translucent polypropylene
h 0.5cm w 4cm l 4.6cm
h ¼in w 1 ¼in l 1 ¾in
Lunar Design, USA
(Limited batch production)

92

Marco Gorini

Storage system, *Pareti*

Aluminium, maple, stainless steel, glass

Panel:

h 290cm w 108/116cm d 2.5cm

h 114 ⅛in w 42 ½/45 ⅝in d 1in

Strato srl, Italy

93

Miki Astori

Kitchen, *High-Tech Room*

Aluminium, stainless steel

Worktop:

h 85cm

h 33 ⅛in

Utensil bar:

l 120cm

l 47 ⅛in

Aluminium shelf:

l 200cm d 15cm

l 78 ⅝in d 5 ⅞in

Driade Chef SpA, Italy

94
Kristiina Lassus
Trivet, *Tundra*
Stainless steel
h 1.7cm di 17.8cm
h ⅝in di 7in
Alessi SpA, Italy

96
Metz.Schlett.Kindler
Coffee-maker, *Pull It!*
Glass, ABS, metal
h 20cm w 16cm l 10cm
h 7 ⅞in w 6 ⅓in l 3 ⅞in
WMF, Germany

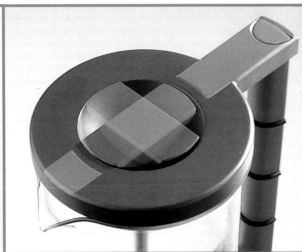

97
Metz.Schlett.Kindler
Rolling pin, *Mr Bull*
Wood
w 7cm l 45cm
w 2 ¾in l 17 ¾in
Alessi SpA, Italy
(Prototype)

98
Jochen Henkels
Wet shaving unit, *Best Boy*
Aluminium, ABS
l 13cm di 6cm
l 5 ⅛in di 2 ⅜in
(Prototype)

95
Marco Ferreri
Tisane instiller, *Tisaniera*
Porcelain, copper, silver,
malachite
h 21.7cm d 8.5cm
h 8 ½in d 3 ⅜in
Faraone, Italy

100
Metz.Schlett.Kindler
Ladle, *Miss Top*
Cromargan (metal)
h 6cm w 9.5cm l 35cm
h 2 ¼ in w 3 ¾ in l 13 ¾ in
WMF, Germany

99
Rainer Lehn
Bottle opener, *Froschkönig*
PS, gold-plated metal
h 12.5cm w 6.5cm
h 4 ⅞ in w 2 ½ in
Koziol, Germany

101
Stefano Giovannoni
Watch, *Rollerball*
Plastic, metal, liquid silicone rubber
w 3.7cm l 18cm d 3.9cm
w 1 ⅜ in l 7in d 1 ½ in
Seiko, Italy
(Prototype)

102
Stefano Bocchini
Dustpan, *Veronica*
Plastic
h 90cm w 34cm d 20cm
h 35 ⅜ in w 13 ⅜ in d 7 ⅞ in
(Prototype)

103
Constantin Boym
Souvenirs,
Missing Monuments
Bronze (wood prototypes)
h 12.7cm l 5–12.7cm
h 5in l 2–5in
Boym Design Studio, USA
(Prototype)

Souvenirs are tactile 'nostalgia for world culture' in Osip Mandlestam's phrase. But what souvenirs are there of a building that is long gone or never existed – be it Paxton's Crystal Palace, Loos' Chicago Tribune Tower, Tatlin's Monument to the Third International, or the Trylon and Perisphere for the New York World's Fair of 1939? Made in bronze, Boym's collection is a serious attempt to reassert the importance of the souvenir. 'Such small objects,' says the designer, 'become indispensable things, the only material manifestation left of a memory or of an idea.'

104
Lawrence Laske
Ashtray, *Vesuvius*
Aluminium
h 23.5cm w 10cm
h 9 ¼in w 3 ⅞in

105
Michal Fronek and Jan Nemecek
Comb, *Serpentine*
Silver
w 6cm I 16cm
w 2 ⅜in I 6 ¼in
Olgoj Chorchoj, Czech
Republic

107
Winfried Scheuer
Wall-hook, *Take Five*
Polypropylene
h 18cm w 15cm I 3cm
h 7in w 5 ⅞in I 1 ⅛in
Authentics, Germany

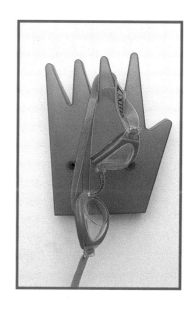

106
Ulf Moritz
Magnetic objects for
pleating curtains, *Scarabae*
Acrylic, copper, iron, brass
h 3.5cm w 5cm I 10.5/14cm
h 1 ⅜in w 2in I 4 ¼/5 ½ in
h 3.5cm di 5.5cm
h 1 ⅜in di 2 ⅛in
Art-line Wohndecor GmbH,
Germany

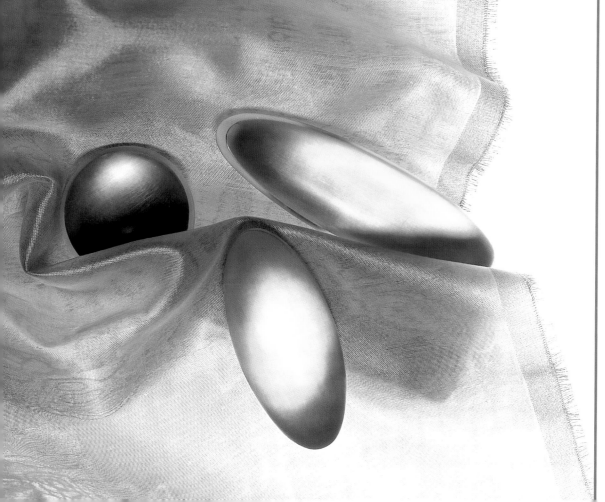

109
Nick Crosbie
Ashtray
PVC, aluminium
h 12cm w 26cm
h 4 ¾ in w 10 ¼ in
Inflate, UK

110
Nick Crosbie
Picture frame, *Cheese*
PVC
h 28cm w 20cm d 4cm
h 11in w 7 ⅞ in d 1 ⅝ in
Inflate, UK

108
**Mark Sodeau,
Nick Crosbie and
Michael Sodeau**
Mirror
PVC, mirror glass
h 28cm w 4cm l 20cm
h 11in w 1 ½ in l 7 ⅞ in
Inflate, UK

biographies

Lodovico Acerbis is president of the family-owned furniture design company Acerbis International, which was founded in 1870. Born in Albino, Bergamo, in 1939, he graduated in economics and business studies from Milan University. He not only takes an industrialist's interest in Acerbis International but, along with Giotto Stoppino, has created some of the company's most important designs. Some of his works have won major international design awards such as the Compasso d'Oro, and a number can be seen in the permanent collections of the Victoria and Albert Museum, the Neue Sammlung Staatliches Museum für Angewandte Kunst, Munich, the Museum of Contemporary Art, Chicago and in the City Hall of Shanghai. 3.41, 44

Marco Acerbis was born in Bergamo. He is currently in the fourth year of the architectural course at the University of Milan. He has also attended English courses and Anglo-American culture courses at the American School of London. In 1996 Acerbis International produced two of his designs. 1.72

Adatte Design SA, a Swiss company based in Le Mont sur Lausanne, was set up by Georges Adatte in 1990. The design team consists of Georges Adatte, Etienne Ruffieux and Eric Giroud. The company is active in Swiss watch design, shop and furniture design, consumer products and packaging. 2.47

Werner Aisslinger was born in 1964 and studied design under Professor Nick Rierícht at the Hochschule der Künste in Berlin. He worked as assistant to Jasper Morrison, London, and in the de Lucchi studio, Milan, before forming his own practice. Current clients include the Lufthansa Design Centre, Porro and Cappellini. He has been awarded various design prizes for his work including the Compasso d'Oro. 1.52

Nick Allen is a Fine Arts graduate from Epsom College of Art, Surrey, UK. He designs furniture using fine woods with intricate veneers, inlay and marquetry as well as metal patinations. He is also developing a range of glassware items. He has exhibited in Europe, the USA and Hong Kong and his pieces can be found in the permanent collection of the Victoria and Albert Museum, London. 3.64

Gabriele Allendorf was born in Munich in 1956. He attended the Academy of Fine Arts in Nuremberg, where he studied interior design whilst at the same time designing workwear, children's toys, packaging, exhibition stands and advertising materials and brochures. Since 1988 he has been involved in the design, production and marketing of numerous lamps and light fittings, as well as lighting schemes such as that for the Kandinsky Exhibition in the Lenbachhaus, Munich (1996). 2.38

Bruno Anderle worked in construction for four years and since 1994 has worked on the design of special one-off furniture pieces. 1.45

Phil Anthony is project manager and senior mechanical engineer for Herbst, LaZar and Bell. He holds a BSME from Lehigh University, Bethlehem, Pennsylvania, and a MSME from Northwestern University, Evanston, Illinois. He is experienced in a range of mechanical engineering subjects, including electro-mechanical products, plastic components, power tools, water filtration and automated mechanisms. 5.53

Ron Arad was born in Tel Aviv in 1951 and studied at the Jerusalem Academy of Art and the Architectural Association, London (from 1974 to 1979). In 1981 he founded One Off Ltd with Dennis Groves and Caroline Thorman, and in 1983 designed One Off's first showroom in Neal Street, Covent Garden. He started to exhibit both nationally and internationally, and hosted shows for other designers, notably Danny Lane, Tom Dixon and Jon Mills in 1986. In 1988 he won the Tel Aviv Opera Foyer Interior Competition with C. Norton and S. McAdam, and the next year formed Ron Arad Associates in order to realize the project, moving the firm's premises to Chalk Farm, London. As well as the design and construction of the new One Off Design Studio, furniture gallery and workshop in 1990, recent projects have included furniture design for Poltronova, Vitra, Moroso and Driade, and the design of interior installations and domestic architectural projects. Exhibitions include 'Breeding in Captivity', a one-man show at the Edward Totah Gallery, London; joint shows with Ingo Maurer at the Galleria Internos and the Galleria Facsimile, Milan; and 'Gaz Naturel, L'Energie Créative' at the Grand Palais, Paris. 1.3, 11, 13

Jan Armgardt was born in 1947. He trained initially as a cabinet-maker and later in interior design. After gaining practical experience in a firm involved in furniture design, he opened his own furniture studio in Bensheim, Germany, in 1974. He collaborates with companies such as de Padova, de Sede, Knoll and Wittman, and also designs kitchen and table accessories, office equipment and lamps. He has been the recipient of numerous awards and prizes. 1.87, 94

Alfredo Arribas was born in Barcelona in 1954 and studied architecture at the Superior Technical School of Architecture of Barcelona, where from 1978 to 1980 he was Professor of Projects. From 1982 to 1985 he was President of INFAD (the Association of Interior Designers) and in 1990 received a FAD Gold Medal in recognition of his career. Arribas founded his own company in 1986, and recent projects have included the Spanish Contemporary Art Museum, Marugame, Japan (1991 to 1993); Acuarinto Children's Hall, Nagasaki, Japan (1992 to 1993); the opening/closing ceremonies at the Olympic Games in Barcelona (1992); the Gran Velvet bar in Badalona (1992 to 1993); and a café/pavilion annexe at the Schim Kunsthalle, Frankfurt (1993). 1.106, 110

Sergio Asti set up his own studio in 1953. He was one of the founding members of the ADI (Associazione per Il Disegno Industriale) and is still an honorary member. He designs furniture, lighting, glassware, wooden products, ceramics, electrical appliances, interiors, stores and exhibitions and works with some of the most important manufacturing companies. He has received numerous awards, including the gold medal at the XI Milan Triennale and a Compasso d'Oro (1962). 3.14, 38

Miki Astori graduated in 1991 with a design for the shipbuilding industry. He designed prefabricated building components and worked with Antonia Astori, mainly on architectural projects, before joining the Philippe Starck practice in Paris (1992 to 1993). In 1994 he opened his own practice in Milan, specializing in furniture and interior design. He designed Driade's new offices at Fessadello di Coarso (Piacenze) and now works for Atlantide, Driade and O-Luce. 1.57; 5.93

Jane Atfield trained in architecture before completing a master's degree in furniture design at the Royal College of Art, London, in 1992. Since graduating she has worked as a freelance furniture designer for companies such as Formica, Habitat and Katharine Hamnett Ltd. Some commissions involving collaborations with architects are the University of Westminster Student Bar and designs for L!ve TV. Recent exhibitions include the Contemporary Arts Society 'Every Angle' at the ITN Building, London (1994); ECO Design in Brussels (1994); and 'Not so Simple' in Barcelona (1995). Jane Atfield recently set up Made of Waste, a new agency for recycled materials. 2.39; 3.61

Masayo Ave was born in Tokyo in 1962 and graduated from the architectural department at Hosei University. After working in the architectural office of Ichiro Ebihara, she moved to Milan and completed a master's degree in industrial design at the Domus Academy, establishing her own design studio, Ave Design Co., in 1992. Since then she has received international acclaim in the fields of industrial, furniture and textile design, theatre sets and architecture. She is interested in the potential of the Shibori textile, and in the fusion of traditional Japanese tie-dyeing techniques with modern technology. 2.26, 28, 29

Gijs Bakker was born in Amersfoort, The Netherlands, in 1942. He studied at the College of Arts and Crafts (now the Rietveld Academy), Amsterdam, in the Department of Jewellery Design, and later at the Konstfackskolan, Department of Industrial Design in Stockholm. From 1962 to 1963 he worked as a designer at Van Kempen & Begeer in Zeist, then until 1986 was a freelance designer for companies such as Bussum and Artifort Maastricht. From 1987 to 1989 he was a partner in the design studio BRS Premsela Vonk in Amsterdam. Today he is head of the 'Man and Living' Department of the Eindhoven Academy of Industrial Design, and design advisor for Keramische Industrie Cor Unum. In 1993 Bakker established Keizersgracht 518 in Amsterdam. His work can be seen in design collections at the Stedelijk Museum, Amsterdam; the Power House Museum, Sydney; the Denver Museum of Art, Colorado; the Cooper-Hewitt Museum, New York; and the Victoria and Albert Museum, London. 2.8

Michela Baldessari has a Diploma in Industrial Design from the European Institute of Design, Milan. Before founding Baldessari and Baldessari in Rovereto (Trento) she collaborated with Studio Aroldi, and with Isao Hosoe in Milan. She currently runs her own practice with Giulio and Paolo Baldessari and concentrates on research and industrial, visual and interior design, working for such companies as Alias, Artemide, Bernini and Progetti Horm. She manages exhibition displays in Italy and other countries and is consultant for the city displays advertising the International Rovereto Festival of Theatre–Dance. 1.2

Philip Baldwin and **Monica Guggisberg** trained in Sweden at the Orrefors Glass School and later with the studio of Ann Wolff and Wilke Adolfsson. In 1982 they established their own design and hot glass studio near Lausanne in Switzerland. They divide their time between their hand-blown collection, produced in Nonfoux, one-off sculptural pieces and design for the glass industry, working for companies such as Rosenthal, Steuben and Bernini. Their work is represented in museums in Europe and the USA. 3.42

Jhane Barnes started her career by designing clothing and won her first COTY for menswear in 1980. She has her own practice and distributes garments and contract textiles throughout North America, South America, Japan and Europe. 4.38

Bär and Knell Design is the design studio of Hartmut Knell and Beata and Gerhard Bär. Hartmut Knell trained as a carpenter and co-founded Bär and Knell in 1992. Beata and Gerhard Bär studied interior design and architecture and worked together from 1987. The studio, which specializes in designs using post-consumer plastic packaging materials, has clients such as Thonet, Steelcase and Artifort. Two of its chairs have been purchased by the Vitra Design Museum, Weil am Rhein. Since 1995 the studio has been responsible, along with the Deutsche Gesellschaft für Kunststoffrecycling, for the touring exhibition 'Plastics 2000 – Visions of Recycled Plastics', and has also taken part in 'Design and Identity, Aspects of European Design' at the Louisiana Museum of Modern Art, Denmark. 1.34, 35; 2.40

Carlo Bartoli was born in Milan where he graduated with a degree in architecture from the Polytechnic. Today his interests lie in the design of domestic furnishings and objects. He teaches the Advanced Course of Industrial Design in Florence and Rome and has exhibited his work extensively. The *Gaia* armchair is part of the permanent collection at the Museum of Modern Art, New York, and the *Sophia* chair is in the collection of the Architectural Museum in Ljubljana. 1.50

Sally Beardsley is an American graphic designer living in Copenhagen. She graduated from the Rhode Island School of Design, and before moving to Denmark worked in design studios in Italy and England. Her book *Conversations at the Interface: Product-People Communication* is published by the Danish Design Centre. She is currently a UN guest lecturer at the Central Academy of Arts and Design in Beijing, China. 5.14

Yves Béhar, born in Switzerland in 1967, is a senior industrial designer at Lunar Design. He graduated in industrial design from the Art Center College of Design, Pasadena, and worked for Steelcase before moving to San Francisco. He practised exhibit and furniture design with Bruce Burdick and now leads the Lunar Design team that creates designs for Hewlett Packard's home products division. He recently joined Frogdesign as Design Project Leader. 5.22, 90

Dail Behennah was born in 1953 and attended the London College of Furniture, studying for a City and Guilds Diploma in basketry. She set up her own workshop in 1990 and has exhibited her work throughout the UK and USA. Her work can be found in several public collections, including that of the Crafts Council, London. 5.63

Niels Bendtsen was born in Denmark in 1943. He was educated in both Denmark and Canada and since 1973 has worked as a freelance furniture designer for a number of manufacturers throughout Scandinavia. He is currently based in Vancouver, Canada, where he has his own design practice, Bendtsen Associates. 1.111

Sebastian Bergne formed his own practice in 1990 designing mass-manufactured products in a wide range of areas. His clients include Driade, Cassina, Vitra, O-Luce and Aero Wholesale Ltd. He is a visiting tutor at Central Saint Martin's College of Art and Design and the London Institute, and was a jury member for the *DesignWeek* Awards in 1991. He has taken part in numerous joint shows in London, New York, Hamburg, Tokyo and Brussels. 2.55; 5.27

Lena Bergström was educated at the National College of Art, Crafts and Design, Stockholm. She worked in the workshop of Ann Sutton and in 1989 studied the industrial production of woven textiles under a British Council Scholarship. In 1991 she travelled to Japan where she studied carpet design. She has exhibited in Sweden, Germany, the UK and Spain and was awarded the Excellent Swedish Design Prize in 1992 and 1993. She began her collaboration with Orrefors in 1993. 3.45, 46

Jorge Fernando de Lima Beschizza was born in São Paulo, Brazil, in 1964. He completed his studies at the Zootecnia University and today is working in computer graphics. He began designing lamps in 1989 and presented his designs for the first time in Milan at the 'Brasil Faz Design' exhibition in 1996. 2.43

Francesco Binfare was born in Milan in 1939 and founded Cassina in 1969, Braccio di Ferro in 1962 with Gaetano Pesce and Alessandro Mendini, and the Centre of Design and Communication in 1980. He has participated at the Venice and Helsinki Biennales and several times at the Triennale in Milan, most recently in 1992. He lectures at the Domus Academy in Milan, and has also given seminars at the Institute of Contemporary Arts, London, and at the School of Architecture in Strasbourg. 1.28

Riccardo Blumer received an art diploma before studying architecture at Milan Polytechnic. From 1984 he worked for Mario Botta, responsible for the graphic and photographic archives and for various exhibitions and related publications. He worked on the Banco Gottardo in Lugano, as well as producing lights such as the *Helios* wall lamp for Lumina Italia. In 1989 he set up his own studio in Morosolo, Varese, and designed two administrative buildings, followed by the new headquarters of Lamberti SpA, a chemical factory for Sasschim di Fiorano in Modena, and the restoration and extension of the Villa Ballerio. He continues to produce lighting designs for companies such as Artemide. 2.68

Stefano Bocchini was born in Cesena, Italy, in 1968. He studied science and later architecture at the University of Florence, graduating with honours and with special mention for his plan for a new train station in Rimini. He is now an architect in Cesena collaborating with the Ottagono Associate Studio. 5.102

Matthias Bohner and **Stefan Lippert** (born in 1966 and 1964, respectively) have worked together since 1990, as students at the Kunstakademie in Stuttgart and later in their own company, Industrial Bohner and Lippert. Clients include Adidas, Fraunhofer Gesellschaft, GSM Software, Union Marwi and Raichle Boots. Bohner was awarded the Braun Prize for Technical Design in 1995, and Lippert the Mia Seeger Stipendium from Baden Württemberg in 1994. 5.57, 83

Renata Bonfanti was educated at the Istituto Statale d'Arte in Venice and at the Kvinnelige Industriskole in Oslo in the early 1950s. She produces handwoven rugs and tapestries as well as machine-woven material. She has taken part in various exhibitions and competitions, including the Milan Triennale (1954, '57, '60, '64), the Venice Biennale (1956 to 1960), the Biennale de la Tapisserie of Lausanne (1975 to 1977) and the 'Design since 1945' exhibition at the Philadelphia Museum of Art (1983). In 1962 she received the Compasso d'Oro. 4.40

Santina Bonini and **Ernesto Spicciolato** founded their product design office in Milan in 1990. They are also involved in interior design projects for commercial spaces, booths for trade shows and small-scale architectural schemes. Until 1991 Santina Bonini worked with Andrea Branzi on the new Contemporary Art Museum in Arezzo. She studied architecture in Florence and was a founder member of DIN, Industrial Design Consultants (1992). Ernesto Spicciolato also studied architecture in Florence. He founded Elettra in 1982, Bolidismo in 1985 and co-founded DIN. From 1987 to 1990 he worked with Makio Hasuike before starting his collaboration with Bonini. They have exhibited work internationally, most recently in the New York Museum of Modern Art's show entitled 'Mutant Materials in Contemporary Design' (1995). Clients include Alessi, Cappellini, Colombo Design, Domus Design Agency and Unitalia. 3.66

Tiziano Bono was born in Vercelli, Italy, in 1962. He worked in the design studio of the Carpano Brothers and later with George Ranalli in New York before studying architecture at the Polytechnic in Turin. Since 1991 he has taken part in projects organized by OPOS in Milan, where in 1995 he started his own business. The subject of his degree thesis on the reuse of a factory building in Biella has recently been made into an exhibition at the Valentino Castle in Turin. 1.31

Florian Borkenhagen was born in Frankfurt in 1959 and studied at the Academy of Fine and Applied Arts. He specializes in interior, set and exhibition design, as well as furniture and object design, and in 1990 set up his own studio in Como. 2.67

Fabio Bortolani and **Walter Becchelli** have worked together since 1991, having studied at the University of Florence and the Bologna Academy of Arts, respectively. Their clients include Alessi/Twergi and Ravanni & Castoldi, and their work has been published in design periodicals such as *Abitare* and *Gap Casa*. 1.29, 40, 48

Constantin Boym was born in Moscow in 1955. He graduated from the Moscow Architectural Institute in 1978 and from 1984 to 1985 studied for a master's degree in design at the Domus Academy in Milan. He became a registered architect in the USA in 1988 and today has his own design consultancy in New York. He has designed award-winning products for many international companies, including Morphos, Néotù and the Formica Corporation. Since 1986 he has taught at the Parsons School of Design, New York. Awards include the ID Annual Design Award (1988 and 1990). His work is included in the permanent collection of the Cooper-Hewitt Museum, New York, and in the Musée des Arts Décoratifs in Montreal. 5.85, 103

Andrea Branzi was born in 1938 in Florence, where he studied architecture. Together with Gilberto Corretti, Paolo Deganello and Massimo Morozzi, he founded the avant-garde group Archizoom Associates in 1966. From 1974 to 1976 he was involved with Global Tools, and in the late

1970s set up CDM, a Milan-based group of design consultants. He worked with Studio Alchimia and Memphis from the outset, designing furniture and objects and preparing shows and publications. He has contributed to leading architectural and design reviews. He also teaches, holding conferences at universities in Italy and abroad. He founded the Domus Academy in 1983 and has been its cultural director and vice-president. He has had many one-man shows at the Milan Triennale and at galleries and museums around the world. All his projects were acquired in 1982 by the Communications Study Centre and Archives at the University of Parma. In 1987 he won the Compasso d'Oro/ADI prize in recognition of his entire career. 2.7

Philippa Brock is a research fellow working on computer-aided design and woven Jacquard design at the Winchester School of Art. She designs her own textiles, which she sells internationally. She is also a consultant designer to yarn companies, producing research samples of new yarn developments. 4.13, 14

Tim Brown is Director of IDEO, Europe. Clients include Microsoft, NEC, Sony, Apple and Hewlett Packard. After studying at the Royal College of Art, he joined IDEO in 1987 and subsequently headed IDEO, San Francisco, before returning to London in 1995. 5.1

Brüel and Kjaer is an industrial design and engineering firm formed over fifty years ago. It specializes in the design of precision instruments for measuring sound, vibration, gases and thermal comfort. 5.14

Antonio Cagianelli was born in Pisa in 1964. After studying architecture at the University of Florence he moved to Paris, where he now lives. In 1991 he took part in an international exhibition at the Galleria Clara Scremini in Paris, and in 1993 worked in the same gallery to produce his collection entitled 'Object of Design, Objects of Desire'. He produces works in coloured transparent resin for Edizioni Galleria Colombari. In 1996 Cagianelli took part in the collective exhibition of young designers at the Ubersee Museum, Bremen, and was selected for the Biennale dell'Architetture in Venice. 1.18; 3.15

Sergio Calatroni was born in San Guiletta, Italy, in 1951 and studied at the Accademia di Belle Arti in Milan. He is presently involved in architecture, design and interior design, sculpture and journalism. He is the founder of the design group Zeus and of the Gallery Zeus Arte Milano in New York, as well as the publishing company Editions Marrakech, which specializes in books on design, architecture and art theory. His principal projects include offices in Osaka and Shizuoka, the Kashiyama boutique in Paris, the Fujitaka restaurant in Milan, the Seiren showroom, also in Milan, and the Copy Centre in Shizuoka. He has taught interior design at the European Institute of Design in Milan and product design at the Futurarium in Ravenna. Calatroni is consultant editor on the design magazine *Interni*. 5.61

Fernando and **Humberto Campana** have been working together since 1984. Humberto trained as a lawyer and his brother, Fernando, graduated as an architect. Their work involves the research and combination of different materials. They have held many individual shows in Brazil and have taken part in collective exhibitions in Brazil, Italy and the USA. 1.73–75; 2.20

Anna Castelli Ferrieri studied architecture at the University of Milan. She taught industrial design at the Milan University School of Architecture from 1984 to 1986 and at the Domus Academy Postgraduate Design School from 1987. Projects include the Kartell corporate buildings at Binasco, and the restoration and interior redesign of ancient buildings such as the Bramante cloister in Milan. From 1976 to 1987 she was Art Director for Kartell. Her industrial design projects have achieved international recognition through major design awards such as the Compasso d'Oro, which she has received twice, and the ID Annual Design Award, USA (1983). Her work is included in the permanent collections of the New York Museum of Modern Art; the Design Museum, London; the Stadtmuseum, Munich; the Israel Museum, Jerusalem; the Copenhagen Museum of Decorative Art; and the São Paulo Design Museum. 3.35

Achille Castiglioni, born in Milan in 1918, began his career immediately after the Second World War with his brothers Livio and Pier Giacomo. He is well known for his innovative designs in interiors, furniture and lighting, and his clients include Flos, Phonola, Bernini, Cassina, de Padova, Fontana Arte, Interflex, Kartell, Marcatré, Olivetti, Up & Up and Zanotta. Castiglioni has been honoured nine times with the Compasso d'Oro. His work is in the collections of the Victoria and Albert Museum, London; the Museum of Modern Art, New York; the Israel Museum, Jerusalem; and in museums in Prague, Zurich, Munich, Düsseldorf, Cologne, Hamburg and Helsinki. He is Professor of Industrial Design and Decoration at the University of Milan. 1.22, 23

Franco Cervi and **Paolo Olivari** (born in 1968 and 1969, respectively) founded the Chipster Group in 1993. They are active in the fields of industrial design, advanced 2D/3D computer graphics and in desktop publishing. They work with the Architecture Faculty of Milan Polytechnic, Sottsass Associati, BDDP/Hyphen and *Modo* design magazine. 2.42

Sophie Chandler was born in 1972. She studied design at Staffordshire University, England, specializing in glass. She has worked for SKK Design Consultancy and teaches at both the Crafts Council and Sheffield Hallam University. Her work has been published in numerous leading UK journals and in France and Italy. 2.41

Patrick Seow Leng Chia was born in 1969 and graduated from the industrial design course at the Royal Melbourne Institute of Technology in 1993. He is currently involved in product, graphic, interior and exhibition design. 1.14

Alessandro Chiarato graduated with a degree in architecture from Rome University, then worked for Autonautica Sport and International Boat Italia. In 1983 he studied for a master's degree in design at the Domus Academy under Mario Bellini. He then worked with Olivetti SpA in its consumer products division. Today he is a consultant for Studio de Lucchi. 5.24

Peter Christian was born in 1958. After graduating from the Royal College of Art, London in 1984 he established the furniture design company Flux and manufactured the *Rib Chair*, which is on show in the Victoria and Albert Museum's 20th-Century Furniture Collection. Between 1991 and 1995 Christian ran the lighting studio Aktiva. He is now working independently on a number of new products with various manufacturers and teaches at the Ravensbourne College of Design and the Royal College of Art. 1.76; 2.31

Miguel Ciganda was born in Pamplona in 1945. He founded his interior decoration and design office in 1969 and has collaborated on various schemes such as the Central Building of the Bank Caja de Ahorros, Pamplona, the Hotel Tres Reyes de Pamplona, the Warehouse Unzu Grandes Almacenes, the Museum Santo Domingo in Estella and the VIP floor of the C.A.I. bank in Zaragoza. In 1991 he won first prize in the competition to design the furniture for the Spanish pavilion for Expo '92 and also created its decoration. 2.50

Antonio Citterio was born in Meda, Italy, in 1950. He studied at Milan Polytechnic, and has been involved in industrial and furniture design since 1967. In 1973 he opened a studio with Paolo Nava, and the two have worked jointly and individually for B & B Italia and Flexform, among other clients. In 1979 they were awarded the Compasso d'Oro. In 1987 Terry Dwan became a partner in Studio Citterio Dwan, and the company has undertaken many interior design projects, including a range of schemes for Esprit and offices and showrooms for Vitra. Among the work realized in Japan, in partnership with Toshiyuki Kita, is the headquarters in Kobe for World Company, the Corrente Building in Tokyo and, in 1992, the Daigo headquarters in Tokyo. Citterio has participated in many exhibitions, including independent shows in Hanover, Rome, Amsterdam, Paris and Weil. In 1993 he designed the layout of the exhibition 'Antonio Citterio and Terry Dwan' promoted by Arc en Rêve in Bordeaux, which travelled to both Osaka and Tokyo in 1994. 1.53

Feddow Claassen trained as a photographer and worked in New York, where he also designed accessories and textiles. He opened his own product design studio in The Hague in 1995. 2.45

Clodagh is an interior designer who lives and works in New York. She set up her own fashion design company in Ireland when she was 17 and later, following a move to Spain, founded an architectural design company. Her work ranged from designing the interiors of private homes and restaurants to consultancy on hotel and spa complexes and landscaping. In 1983 she moved to New York and opened Clodagh Design International. She was selected for the 1996 *Architectural Digest* 'AD 100' listing of the world's top interior designers and architects. Projects include the New York department store Felissimo, the New York headquarters of Time Warner's Elektra Records and a new brand launch for Kose Cosmetics in Japan. 4.42

Lluis Clotet, born in Barcelona in 1941, graduated in 1965 from the Escuela Técnica de Arquitectura in Barcelona. In 1964 he founded Studio PER with the architects Pep Bonet, Christian Cirici and Oscar Tusquets and has collaborated on numerous projects with them. He is a founder member of Bd Ediciones de Diseño, for which he still designs furniture and objects. He received the FAD award for the best interior in Barcelona in 1965 and 1972. He has also received the Delta de Oro on three occasions for his industrial design. 1.98

Nigel Coates was born in 1949 in Malvern, England. He studied at the University of Nottingham and at the Architectural Association, where he has lectured since his graduation in 1974. In 1985 he co-founded Branson Coates with Douglas Branson. His projects include work for Jasper Conran and Katharine Hamnett. He has also designed restaurants in Japan, including the Nishi Acabu Wall in Tokyo, and the Sea Hotel restaurant in Otaru. Recent projects include two restaurants at Schiphol Airport, Amsterdam. 3.39

Stefano Como was born in Verona and graduated from the European Institute of Design in Milan. He has worked in collaboration with BDF Studio since 1988. 5.15

Fabio Crippa received a diploma in furniture design from the Institute I.P.S.I.A in Meroni di Lissone and later studied architecture at Milan Polytechnic. In 1995 he received an honourable mention in the Young Design show for his award-winning design for a cupola for the Monza MIA. He has worked in various interior design and architecture studios, including those of G. Vigano and Paolo Sironi, and has carried out product design for clients such as Steel, Swan, Colombo Plus and Bellato. 2.22

Nick Crosbie was born in 1971. He has a degree in industrial design from Central Saint Martin's College of Art and Design, London, and a master's degree from the Royal College of Art. He set up Inflate in 1995 with Michael Sodeau. 2.12; 5.72, 108–110

Anne Crowther studied textile design at Central Saint Martin's College of Art and Design, London graduating with a specialization in woven textiles. With the aid of the Yorkshire and Humberside Art Grants she set up in business and continues to create new work at her studio in Bradford. She has frequently exhibited her work in the UK. 4.20

Mario Cucinella was born in 1960 and studied architecture in Genoa and Lisbon. He has been director of MCA, Mario Cucinella Architects, since 1992. He has designed a Paris showroom, two office buildings, a conference centre and light application centre for i Guzzini, as well as developing the *Woody* and *MiniWoody* lighting system in 1996. Other commissions include an award-winning car park on an archaeological site in Geneva, a sports stadium in Oita, Japan, renovation of five buildings in France for Fiat, and several designs for the European Commission Joint Research Centre in Ispra, Italy. 2.88

Marcello Cuneo studied in Milan, where he is currently based. He worked with Lino Saltini from 1959 until 1962 and later with Gio Ponti until 1970, during which time he developed major architectural projects, including office buildings, department stores, museums and churches. Since 1971 he has worked on a freelance basis, active in all areas of product design. Cuneo has created lamps for Gabbianelli, pre-fabricated bathroom units for F.E.A.L., furniture for La Linea, upholstered pieces for Arflex, Comforto and Cassina, textiles for Jsa of Busto Arsizio and lighting for Valenti and Stilnovo. He has also worked in exhibition design and on architectural lighting projects. He received an honourable mention at the XI Compasso d'Oro in 1979 for the *Cross* chair. 1.20

Marcello Cutino graduated from the Institute of Applied Arts in Verona in 1976 and from Milan Polytechnic in 1978. He is Director of the Industrial Design Section of BDF Studio. 5.15

Giovanni d'Ambrosio was born in Rome in 1959. He studied architecture and advertising graphics, and before setting up his own studio worked for architectural companies such as L. Pellegrin and S. Sartogo Association. As an industrial designer he has worked with clients such as Arteluce, I Tre, Murano Due and Bernini. He is currently working on private building projects. He also has schemes in progress in Asia, including a restaurant/bar in Kuta, Bali, and a boutique in Nusa Dua, Bali. 1.58; 2.10

Christopher Deam holds a master's degree in Urban Design from the University of Notre Dame and a Bachelor of Architecture from California Polytechnic State University. He worked for Antonio Citterio and Matteo Thun in Italy, and upon his return to the USA collaborated with Frank Gehry. He currently lives in San Francisco, where he has his own architecture and furniture design studio. 1.43

Michele de Lucchi was born in Ferrara, Italy, in 1951 and graduated from Florence University in 1975. During his student years he founded the "Gruppo Cavat", a group concerned with avantgarde and conceptual architecture. He worked and designed for Alchimia until the establishment of Memphis in 1981. Today he produces exclusive art-orientated handmade products, industrial consumer items and furniture. His architectural activities range from shop design to large-scale office buildings and private apartment blocks. De Lucchi's work has received many awards and he has exhibited widely. He has taught at design schools and universities such as the Domus Academy, Milan, and the University of Detroit. 1.95; 2.59, 60, 69, 74, 79; 3.37, 63; 5.23, 24

Maddalena de Padova and her husband created the furniture manufacturing company ICF in 1958. The company produced under licence Hermann Miller's furniture by designers such as Eames and Girard. After her husband's death, Maddalena de Padova continued to work at ICF and in 1985 set up Edizioni De Padova, collaborating with designers such as Achille Castiglioni, Dieter Rams and Vico Magistretti. 4.41

Giampiero Derai was born in Venice in 1941 and attended the Academy of Arts, graduating in 1962 with a degree in sculpture and plastic materials. Between 1963 and 1964 he taught Applied Arts at the State Institute for Industry and Handicrafts at Darfo, Brescia whilst at the same time attending a course in industrial design and technology in Venice. He has been working for Fabbian Lighting since 1971. 2.62

Vincent de Rijk studied at the Eindhoven Academy of Industrial Design. He works mainly with ceramics and also makes scale models for OMA, the company of architect Rem Koolhaas. His *Kommetjes* bowls can be seen in the permanent collection of the Museum of Modern Art, New York, and the *Kom BV* in the collection of the Cooper-Hewitt Museum, New York. 3.55

Otto DeRuntz works as a mechanical engineer for IDEO (Boston). Previously he has been employed by companies such as Pioneer Design, Atari Games and Adcotech Corporation. He has a degree in tool design from deAnza College. 5.6

Design Studio Copenhagen was founded in 1988 by Niels Gammelgaard (born in 1944), founder of Pelikan Design, and Lars Engman (born in 1945) from IKEA. The design team has since expanded to include Ehlén Johansson, Tina Christensen, Mia Lagerman and Anna von Schewen. The aim of the design team is to develop products for IKEA in Sweden. 1.117; 5.25, 69

Bernhard Dessecker was born in 1961 in Munich. He studied interior architecture, then from 1983 to 1984 worked at Studio Morsa, New York. From 1984 he was a freelance designer, collaborating with the design team of Ingo Maurer, before creating his own company with his wife Susanne Dessecker. In 1995 he founded Luzon GmbH & Co. KG, a company to develop, produce and distribute light fixtures, furniture and other objects. 2.1, 18

Franco di Bartolomei was born in 1954 in Udine and trained at the Architectural University in Venice. He has received international recognition as an artist, and has exhibited at the Venice Biennale. He has executed many commissions in the fields of architecture and design, and has collaborated with major Italian furniture and lighting manufacturers. 1.21

Thomas Dickson is a Danish designer and architect, born in Los Angeles in 1958. He studied at the Art Center College of Design, Pasadena, and holds a master's degree from the Royal Danish Academy in Copenhagen. He worked as a freelance for Ashcraft Design and Seve Mogugan Industrial Design, and now runs his own studio, Tomcat Design. He lectures at the Royal Danish Academy. 5.14

Ezio Didone was born in 1939 in Milan, where he studied architecture, specializing in industrial design. In 1963, together with Studio G14 and the architect Alberto Colombi, he founded Designers Associati Milano, which he has since left. He collaborates with Valenti, Gruppo Industrial Busnelli and Arteluce. 2.65

Nanna Ditzel was born in 1923 in Copenhagen and graduated from the Kunsthåndvaerkerskolen in 1946. She established an industrial design studio in Copenhagen with Jorgen Ditzel and since then has founded several practices in London and Copenhagen. She is active in furniture, textile, jewellery and tableware design. She has received international acclaim for her work, winning the Gold Medal (with Jorgen Ditzel) at the Milan Triennale in 1960 and the Gold Medal at the International Furniture Design Competition, Asahikawa, Japan in 1990. Her work can be seen in the permanent collections of the Louisiana Museum of Modern Art, Humlebaek, Denmark; the Museum of Decorative Art, Copenhagen; the Museum of Applied Art, Trondheim, Norway; and Goldsmiths' Hall, London. 1.86

Tom Dixon was born in Sfax, Tunisia, in 1959 and moved to the UK when he was four. He formed Creative Salvage with Nick Jones and Mark Brazier-Jones in 1985. His studio, SPACE, is where his prototypes and commissioned works – stage sets, furniture, sculpture, illuminated sculpture, architectural installations, chandeliers and other objects – are made. His clients include Cappellini, Comme des Garçons, Nigel Coates, Ralph Lauren, Vivienne Westwood and Terence Conran. Dixon has exhibited work internationally, most recently in 'A New Century in Design' at the National Museum of Modern Arts, Tokyo. His designs are in the permanent collections of the Victoria and Albert Museum, London; the Musée des Arts Décoratifs and the Centre Georges Pompidou, Paris; the Vitra Chair Museum, Basle; the Crafts Council and the Design Museum,

London; and the Brooklyn Museum, New York. In 1994 Dixon opened the SPACE shop. 1.32

Dante Donegani, born in 1957, graduated in architecture in Florence in 1983. He set up his practice in 1991 and has worked with Andrea Branzi on several architecture competitions. He is also a consultant for Olivetti Corporate Identity and is actively involved in exhibition design, working on such shows as 'Michelangelo. Architetto' at Casa Buonarroti, and 'Mondrian e De Stijl' at the Fondazioni Cini in Venice, and on display systems for Fissler Kitchens and Sant Pauls International Bookstore. Product design clients include Memphis, Stildomus and Luceplan. Donegani is Director of the Industrial Design master's course at the Domus Academy. 1.56; 2.76

Rodolfo Dordoni was born in Milan in 1954 and graduated from the Polytechnic in 1979. After working in the offices of several architects in Milan, he became interested in industrial design and at present works as consultant and designer to companies such as Artemide, Arteluce, Cappellini, De Sede, Driade, Fontana Arte and Foscarini. Dordoni is also involved in pavilion, shop and stand design, and architecture. 2.14

Mark Dziersk is Vice-President of Herbst, LaZar and Bell. He received a BFA in Industrial Design from the University of Michigan, and is a member of the Industrial Designers Society of America. He works as a senior consultant and design manager for several design firms, and has also been a Corporate Designer for the GenRad Corporation. Recognition for his work has included the Industrial Design Excellence Award, Instrumentation. He holds 26 product design and engineering patents in the USA. 5.53

Edda Design (Estudio de Diseño Avanzado) was founded by Jordi Mila in 1995 and is involved in multi-disciplinary and integral design for products, transportation and communication. 5.44, 46

John Edson is a senior product designer for Lunar Design. His work has been featured in several design magazines, including *Design Report* and *ID* magazine. He received his master's degree in mechanical engineering from Stanford University in 1993. 5.19

Rand Elliott & Associates Architects provides services that include master planning; architectural, landscape and interior design; retail space design; image development; civil, structural, mechanical and electrical engineering; graphic design and signage; and product and lighting design. It works on a range of project types from retail, office, restaurant and residential through to municipal, city, state and federal government schemes, museum and historic restorations. It has been awarded over 80 major national and international awards. 2.4

Hartmut Engel was born in Stuttgart in 1939. He studied electrical engineering in Stuttgart and Darmstadt, then industrial design in Pfirzheim. After qualifying as an industrial designer in 1968, he set up his own studio in Ludwigsburg. He has received numerous awards in Germany, including the Industry Forum Design, Hanover 'Top Ten of the Year' Gold Award. 5.2

Fabio Falanghe and **Giorgio Giorgi** are partners in the studio Oni Design, which they founded in 1986. They have been manufacturing their own lamps since 1994 and have exhibited their work in Brazil and also at the 'Brasil Faz Design' exhibition in Milan in 1996; the Design Europeo Anteprima show at the Sottosullo Gallery in Milan in 1993, and at the Internos Gallery, also in 1993. 2.23

Giancarlo Fassina was born in Milan in 1935 and trained at the Superior Engineering Institute in Fribourg and Milan Polytechnic, where he graduated in architecture. In 1970 he joined Artemide, working closely with Enzo Mari. Recently he has collaborated with Marco Zanuso on the lighting of the new Fossati Theatre in Milan and with Mario Bellini for the lighting of the Milan Triennale. 2.69, 79

André Feldmann and **Arne Jacob Schultchen**, born in 1964 and 1965, respectively, have worked as a team since they met at the Hochschule für Bildende Künste, Hamburg, from which they graduated in industrial design in 1992/93. In 1994 they established a studio in Hamburg. Their work ranges from product design, furniture, lighting and interiors to graphics, packaging, exhibition design and experimental works. 1.1; 5.76

Cheryl Felix works for Herbst, LaZar and Bell, where she develops consumer electronic products for leading manufacturers. Prior to joining HLB she worked at Philips Corporate Design, The Netherlands. She is a member of the Industrial Designers Society of America. 5.13

Marco Ferreri was born in 1958 and graduated in architecture from Milan Polytechnic in 1981. He has had his own design studio in Milan since 1984 and is active in architecture, and graphic and showroom design. He has worked for clients such as Adele C. Agape, Danese, Fontana Arte and Robots. His work can be found in the Israel Museum, Jerusalem and the Museum of Modern Art, New York. His furniture designs *Libroletto* and *Bruno Munari* were selected for the 40th Compasso d'Oro. 5.95

Diana Firth studied industrial design at the Wellington Polytechnic School of Design and fine art at the Elam School of Fine Arts, Auckland, New Zealand. She has been working with printing methods in the fashion industry for over ten years, and has exhibited her work nationally. 1.4

Siggi Fischer was born in Cologne in 1954 and studied industrial design in Wuppertal. Since 1990 he has worked independently for clients including Thomas Schulte Designmanufaktur, Vericom GmbH and Best Friends Collection. He has exhibited in Germany, Italy and Japan. 2.75

Uwe Fischer see Ginbande

Johannes Foersom and **Peter Hiort-Lorenzen** are furniture designers, currently working for Lammhults Möbel Design in Sweden. 1.105, 107

Piero Fornasetti is a contemporary artist, painter and sculptor. He also creates stage sets and costumes, and organizes exhibitions and promotions at an international level. He has been awarded the Neiman Marcus Award and his works are displayed in several Italian collections; the Victoria and Albert Museum, London; the Mitchell Wolfson Museum, Miami; and the Bischofberger Collection, Zurich. In 1992 the V&A held a major retrospective of Fornasetti, which then travelled throughout Italy. 2.25

Sir Norman Foster was born in Manchester, England, in 1935 and studied architecture and city planning at the University of Manchester and at Yale University. He established Team 4 in 1963 – with his late wife, Wendy, and Su and Richard Rogers – and founded Foster Associates in 1967. Today he is internationally famous for his high-tech designs, many of which have resulted directly from competitions, such as the Hong Kong and Shanghai Bank (1979 to 1985), and Stansted Airport (1981 to 1989). Recent projects include the Sackler Galleries at the Royal Academy of Arts, London, which was named the RIBA building of the year in 1993; the Centre d'Art, Nîmes; the Reichstag remodelling, Berlin; headquarters for Commerzbank in Frankfurt; and an airport at Chek Lap Kok, Hong Kong. Master plans include the King's Cross development, London. Foster received a knighthood in the Queen's Birthday Honours in 1991, and his work has won over 60 awards and citations. Although primarily concerned with large-scale architectural projects, Sir Norman Foster is also active in furniture and product design. 5.84

Simon Fraser was born in Hamilton, New Zealand. He studied in the School of Fine Arts of the University of Auckland and joined Porsche Design in 1979. 5.9

Susie Freeman was born in 1956 in London. She trained in Manchester and at the Royal College of Art, receiving both a Bachelor of Arts degree in Textiles/Fashion and a Master of Arts in Textiles. She has taken part in exhibitions in the USA, London, Korea and Japan and in 1994 held a one-person show, 'Mobilia', in Massachusetts, USA. Her work can be seen in the collections of the Victoria and Albert Museum, the Geffrye Museum, the Crafts Council and the British Council, London, and the Whitworth Art Gallery, Manchester. 4.26

Frogdesign Global Creative Network was created in Germany in 1968 and today has offices in California, Texas and Germany. It offers industrial design, graphic design, software interface and interactive design, and mechanical engineering services, and works for clients such as Alessi, Apple, AT&T, Logitech, Motorola, Packard Bell and Swatch. Its work is in the permanent collections of the Museums of Modern Art in New York, Philadelphia, Milwaukee and Munich, the Boilerhouse, London, and the Cooper-Hewitt National Design Museum, New York. Frogdesign has twice won the *Time Magazine* and *Business Week* 'Design of the Year' award. 5.11, 86–88

Michal Fronek and **Jan Nemecek** were born in 1966 and 1963, respectively. Both studied at the Academy of Applied Arts in Prague under Borek Sípek. They began their first collaboration as the design group Olgoj Chorchoj, and since then have completed numerous interior design projects in Prague. Artel II was founded in 1993 and exhibited at the Milan Furniture Fair; at the International Conference of Arts and Crafts, London; at the International Design Exhibition, Turin; and at the Gallery Genia Loci, Prague. Currently Fronek and Nemecek teach alongside Sípek at the Academy of Applied Arts in Prague and are designing the interior fittings in Vaclav Havel's Prague house. 5.105

Naoto Fukasawa joined IDEO in 1989. Previously he was chief designer of the R & D design group at Seiko Epson Corporation in Japan. He returned to Japan in 1996 to head IDEO, Tokyo. Fukasawa helped to win three major awards in 1991 for the patient-support device for the Baxter Healthcare artificial heart pump, and his stacking chair created for Metro Furniture can be seen in the permanent collection of the San Francisco Museum of Modern Art. 5.1

Jakob Gebert was born in Freiburg in Breisgau, Germany. He worked until 1989 as a social worker and in community service. He then trained in architecture until 1994, and studied interior, product and building design at the Basle Academy of Design. In 1994 he founded his own studio in Weil am Rhein. 2.46

Edward Geluk graduated in 1979 from the Art Academy of the EKI Euschede. He has been an independent architect and designer based in Amsterdam since 1987. 1.80

Anna Gili was born in Orvieto in 1960 and studied at the Istituto Superiore delle Industrie Artistiche, Florence, graduating in 1984. She has designed objects for Alessi; tiles for Inax, Tokyo; ceramic pots for Richard Ginori; carpets, tapestries and furniture for Cassina; glass vases for Salviati and Bisazza; furniture and textiles for Cappellini; and furniture for Interflex and Play Line. In 1992 she was the cultural co-ordinator of the exhibition 'Nuovo Bel Design', and in 1994 the curator of the exhibition and conference 'Primordi', which was held in the Triennale Building in Milan. Gili was the curator of the exhibition 'Mutamenti' under the patronage of the Milan City Council (1995) and since 1990 has taught industrial design at the Accademia di Belle Arti in Milan. 3.43

Ginbande was founded in Frankfurt by Uwe Fischer and Klaus-Achim Heine in 1985. Fischer and Heine both studied at the Hochschule für Gestaltung, Offenbach, specializing in industrial design and visual communication, respectively. Ginbande works on corporate identities for public and private companies, and its experimental two- and three-dimensional pieces are regularly shown and published. 1.55

Maurizio Giordano formed an architectural practice, Pro-Lab, in 1991 along with three other designers. He works mainly in domestic, industrial and furniture design in the Lombardia and Triveneto district of Italy. He is also involved in the restoration of historical sites in the Liguria hinterland, and since 1992 has been responsible for the Architecture Department of the Spaziosuono Architecture and Contemporary Music Association. 1.97

Paolo Giordano was born in Naples in 1954 and studied architecture in Milan. Today he lives in Milan and India and works as a designer and a photographer, producing his own collection of furniture in limited edition in India. 1.6

Stefano Giovannoni was born in La Spezia, Italy, in 1954 and graduated from the Faculty of Architecture at the University of Florence in 1978. From 1978 to 1990 he lectured and carried out research at Florence University and also taught at the Domus Academy in Milan and at the Institute of Design in Reggio Emilia. He is the founding member of King-Kong Production, which is concerned with avant-garde research in design, interiors, fashion and architecture. Clients include Alessi, Cappellini, Arredaesse and Tisca France. In 1991 he designed the Italian Pavilion at 'Les Capitales Européennes de Nouveau Design' exhibition, which was held at the Centre Georges Pompidou in Paris. 1.77; 2.11; 5.101

Gaspar Glusberg was born in 1959 and graduated in architecture from the Buenos Aires National University, where today he is Assistant Professor in the School of Architecture. Glusberg is a member of the Design Department at the Centre of Art and Communication, Buenos Aires, as well as being Director of the Design Department of Modulor SpA. In 1986 he started a programme of collaborative work with Andrea Branzi. He has taken part in many collective shows, including 'Identity and Differences' in the Public Spaces at the Milan Triennale in 1996, and also held a one-man exhibition at the Art Museum of São Paulo, Brazil, in 1992, entitled 'Light and Space Poetry'. 2.78

Natanel Gluska was born in Israel in 1957 but now lives and works in Zurich. He has studied in Israel, The Hague and at the Rietveld Academy, Amsterdam (1985 to 1989). He has exhibited work in The Netherlands and Switzerland. 1.67–69

Didier Gomez is an interior architect. He opened his agency in 1985 and has worked on numerous headquarters, offices, and shops for clients such as Yves Saint-Laurent, Jean-Paul Gaultier, Cartier and Rolex. He has also designed private residences, factories and office blocks. Since his association with the architect Jean-Jacques Ory, he has become involved with larger-scale projects and has also created First Time, which is involved in the creation of product designs for companies such as Ligne Roset, Artelano and Habitat. 1.116; 2.58

Marco Gorini is the founder of the company Strato, which specializes in the design of kitchens. He has worked in fashion styling and techniques and master building. 5.92

Ingrid Gossner and **Reinhard Paulus** were born in 1958 and 1953, respectively. They both have a bachelor's degree in design, Gossner having first studied jewellery design and Paulus industrial design. They worked closely together from 1978 to 1991 when Gossner opened her own jewellery and product design studio in Cologne. Paulus worked for Jürgen Lange for four years before opening his own design studio in Cologne. 5.75

Ramon Benedito Graells was born in Barcelona in 1945. He graduated from the Elisava School and concentrates on the design of technical equipment. He is also engaged in teaching and recently completed a research project with the Transatlantic Group. He was President of the ADI-FAD from 1988 to 1989. Clients include Amat, Carlsberg, Rank Xerox and Roca Radiadores and his work has been exhibited in Berlin, Milan, New York, Stuttgart, Stockholm, Tokyo and São Paulo. 5.91

Tobias Grau was born in Hamburg in 1957. He studied design in New York at the Parsons School of Design, after which he worked in the Design and Development office of Knoll International in Pennsylvania. He founded Tobias Grau KG in Hamburg in 1984, producing light designs for his own collection. Graudesign was set up four years later and under this name he redesigns hotels and showrooms and was responsible for the corporate identity of 40 branches of the jeans shop Werdin. He also

produces series of furniture and product designs for various clients. He received the *ID* magazine Award, New York, in 1993. 2.67

Konstantin Grcic is a German furniture designer, working freelance in London and Munich. He was born in 1965, trained as a cabinet-maker and continued his education at the John Makepeace School for Craftsmen and the Royal College of Art, London. 5.68

Bruno Gregori was born in 1954 and received a diploma at Milan's Accademia di Brera in 1977. From 1978 to 1989 he was a member of Studio Alchimia, after which he designed textiles, products and graphics for companies such as Swatch, Mobelstoffe and the TDK Corporation. Since 1990 he has been consultant designer for TDK and in 1992 joined Atelier Mendini. 5.32

David Grimshaw founded his own company, Grimshaw Design Associates, in 1991. He produces furniture designs for Allermuir, Viaduct, Davison Highley and Berry & Sons. Recent projects include the Abbey Road Studios, Harrods Restaurants, Brussels Airport and corporate designs for clients such as British Telecom and Rank Leisure. He has lectured at Manchester College of Art and at Manchester Metropolitan University, where he recently supervised the furniture entries for the RSA Design Awards competition. 1.101

Roberto Grossi founded the architectural company Pro-Lab in 1991 along with three other designers, and is active in architecture, furniture and lighting design. Since 1992 he has been a senior member of the Architecture Department of the Spaziosuono Architecture and Contemporary Music Association. 1.97

Zaha Hadid was born in Baghdad. Today her London-based architectural firm encompasses all fields of design, ranging from the urban scale through to products, interiors and furniture. Hadid studied at the Architectural Association from 1972, receiving the Diploma Prize in 1977. She then became a member of the Office for Metropolitan Architecture, began teaching at the AA with Rem Koolhaas and Elia Zenghelis and led her own studio at the AA until 1987. Since the formation of her independent company, projects have included furniture and interiors for Bitar, London (1985), designs for buildings in Japan, the Exhibition Pavilion for Video Art in Groningen (1982), and the Vitra Fire Station (1993). Since 1989 large-scale studies have been completed for harbour developments in Hamburg, Bordeaux and Cologne leading to the prize-winning Düsseldorf art and media centre project. Hadid's work is in the permanent collections of the Museum of Modern Art, New York, and the Deutsches Architektur Museum, Frankfurt. 3.65

Andreas Hagn was born in Austria in 1964. He studied architecture at the Technical University in Vienna and in 1993 founded his own company, di'[sain]. 2.61

Koji Hamai was born in Japan in 1964 and graduated from the Bunka Fashion College. He believes strongly in the importance of the textile in fashion design. He initially joined Miyashin Corporation in Hachioji, where he acquired his knowledge of textile production. In 1986 he moved to the Issey Miyake Design Studio, staying until 1991, when he left to work as a freelance fashion designer. He has received many awards in Japan, such as the Grand-Prix at the International Textile Design Contest (1991). 4.11, 12

Sven Heestermann was born in Zwolle in The Netherlands. He trained at various design schools and today has his own practice, Zolo, in Arnhem. 5.82

Klaus-Achim Heine see Ginbande

Jochen Henkels was born in 1956 in Solingen, Germany. He studied at the Solingen Workshop for Wood and Metal, and then studied industrial design at Wuppertal University. From 1986 to 1989 he trained under Dieter Rams at the Hochschule für Bildende Künste in Hamburg. He has worked as a freelance designer since 1989. 5.47, 98

Osiris Hertman is an industrial and interior designer. After serving an internship with Ulf Moritz, he graduated from the Department of Man and Living at the Eindhoven Academy of Industrial Design. 3.60

Akamine Hidetoshi is a Japanese architect who lives and works in Warsaw, Poland. 2.5

Yoshiki Hishinuma, born in Sendai, Japan, in 1958, is a fashion and textile designer. He has presented collections since 1984, showing in Japan and Europe. He exhibited work at Expo '92, Seville, and was costume director of Universiade '95, Fukuoka. Recent exhibitions include 'Japanese Design 80' at the Seoul Museum of Modern Art, and 'The History of Jeans' at the Musée de la Mode du Costume, Paris. 4.1–10

Thierry Hodel and **Regis Vogel** founded their furniture design studio, Fou du Roi, in 1992. Hodel studied at the Lycée du Bâtiment in Illkirch, obtaining a degree in interior architecture. He spent six months in the studio of Michel Gomez and a further six months with J. Michel Gaillot, during which time he took a diploma in applied arts. He has since taken a master's degree in this subject. Regis Vogel also studied interior architecture in Illkirch and went on to take first a diploma and later a master's degree in applied arts. He too worked in architectural practices before co-founding Fou du Roi. 1.109

Jeff Hoefer is a CAD Sculptor for Lunar Design. He has worked on a variety of projects, ranging from medical products to exhibition design. Hoefer has a degree in Fine Arts from the State University of New York at Oswego. 5.17

Ben Hoek studied architecture and worked for eight years in an architect's office before specializing in furniture design and opening his studio in 1996. He received an award for best Dutch furniture design in 1995 and collaborates with the furniture company Spectrum. 1.91

David Huycke was born in 1967. He lives and works in Sint-Miklaas, Belgium, where he has his own metalsmith workshop. He studied at Sint-Lucas, Antwerp. 3.47

Niels Hvass was born in 1958. He studied at the Danish Design School and today has his own design studio. 1.38

Massimo Iosa Ghini was born in Borgo Tossignano, Italy, in 1959 and graduated in architecture from Milan Polytechnic. He worked with Ettore Sottsass and Memphis in 1986. In 1987 he launched his first furniture collection, Dinamic, for Moroso, which received awards worldwide. Interior design projects include the planning of the fashion store chain Fiorucci and the planning and design of the Renault Italy showrooms. Since 1992 he has held various major retrospectives, including one at the Steininger Gallery, Munich, and a second on drawings, canvases and design objects at the Axis Building, Japan. Also in 1992 he was invited to take part in the 'Busstop' exhibition. In 1994 Iosa Ghini began his collaboration with Ferrari, designing exhibition showrooms and factory interiors, and the following year was selected to design the corporate identity of Omnital, part of the Olivetti

Group. Iosa Ghini has worked for leading furniture and product manufacturers, including Moroso, Fiam, Poltrona, Swatch and Silhouette. 3.62

Setsu Ito was born in Yamaguchi, Japan, in 1964 and obtained his master's degree in product design at the University of Tsukuba. He has undertaken design research projects for the TDK Corporation, NEC Electric Co. and Nissan Motor Co., and in 1989 worked for Studio Alchimia in Milan. Since 1989 he has collaborated with Angelo Mangiarotti and has also become consultant designer for the TDK Corporation, with Bruno Gregori. 5.32

Camille Jacobs was born in 1963 in Brussels, Belgium. She studied at the Institute of Fine Arts, St Luc, Ghent, and at the Royal Academy of Fine Arts, Antwerp. She has exhibited her glass work in Belgium, The Netherlands, France and Japan and in 1993 was commissioned to design the stained-glass window for the entry hall of the Spijker School, Hoogstraten. 3.26

Hans Jakobsen has been a cabinet-maker since 1986. He studied at the Danish Design School and worked independently before joining Nanna Ditzel's drawing office in 1991. 1.30, 108, 121

Hella Jongerius studied at the Eindhoven Academy of Industrial Design and spent periods as an apprentice with Xinta Tinta fashion fabrics in Barcelona and with Catherine Laget in Paris, training in styling. She has exhibited at Le Vent du Nord in Paris, at Droog Design in Milan and in the show 'Mutant Materials in Contemporary Design' at the Museum of Modern Art, New York. 2.19

Carsten Jorgensen was born in Denmark in 1948. From 1965 to 1969 he studied at the School of Art, Copenhagen, after which he became a designer at Royal Copenhagen. After a period as a lecturer at the School of Art, he co-founded the Experimental School of Fine Arts Atelier 12 in Copenhagen and taught there until 1978, whilst at the same time starting to work for Bodum. In 1983 he moved to Switzerland. Several of his products have been selected by museums in Europe and the USA. 3.50; 5.51

Caprica Joseph was born in 1979. She attends the L.E. Rabouin Career Magnet High Schoo, New Orleans, and is also a student at YA/YA (Young Aspirations/Young Artists), where she is a guild member. 1.7

Alfred Kainz trained as a sculptor and stone mason. Since 1983 he has taken part in numerous competitions and art exhibitions in Germany, France and the USA. He produces one-off and limited batch pieces of furniture using unusual material combinations. He has his own showroom in Mallersdorf and since 1993 has had his own stand at the Cologne Furniture Fair in the Avant Garde Design Centre. 3.27, 28

Nazanin Kamali was born in Iran. She moved to London and graduated in furniture design from the Royal College of Art in 1991. After working as a freelance designer for several years, she was asked to join Aero as an in-house designer. She now also manages the company's image and undertakes research and product development. 2.52

Brian Kane graduated from the University of Bridgeport, Connecticut, in 1970 with a degree in industrial design. He has worked for several design studios in the USA and for architect Silvio Coppola in Milan, and has collaborated with Mobil Italia and Bernini SpA. In 1977 Kane joined the Metropolitan Furniture Corporation, becoming a partner three years later. He retained the position of vice-president until 1989, when he left to establish his own practice, Kane Design Studio, in San Francisco. The firm is currently involved in the design and development of products for clients such as Metropolitan Furniture Corp., Steelcase, Tuohy Furniture Company and LFI/Landscape Forms. 1.64

Peter Karpf was born in 1940 in Copenhagen. He worked as a carpenter before entering the Academy of Arts and Crafts in 1961 to study furniture design. Since this time he has developed many furniture and lighting products. In 1989 he wrote an architectural manifesto and formed the Alfabetica Group. 1.84

Masamichi Katayama was born in Okayama Prefecture, Japan, in 1966 and was employed by Koji Okamoto Design Office and Design Value before founding H. Design Associates Inc. in 1993. He is active in architecture and furniture, product and interior design. 1.66

Masafumi Katsukawa is a Japanese designer working in Milan. He graduated from the Kyoto Institute of Technology in 1983 and since moving to Italy has collaborated with Studio Arosio, Studiodada and Sottsass Associati. He is currently a freelance designer and consultant for Lumen Center Italia. 2.73; 5.59

Eleanor Kearney was educated at Camberwell College of Arts and Crafts, London and received an award from the Worshipful Company of Pewterers in 1993. She has exhibited in Jeddah, San Francisco, Dublin, London and New York, and lectures on product design at Evesham College and on art and design at Kingsway College, London. 3.54

Larry Kerila is the senior mechanical engineer for Lunar Design. He was born in Pennsylvania in 1960 and graduated from Pennsylvania State University in 1982. 5.18

Takeshi Kimura was born in Tokyo in 1961. He graduated from the Department of Design for Industrial Art and Engineering at the Musashino College of Art and started work in the Kimura Glass Co. Ltd. He has won various craft competitions in Japan and in 1994 held a one-man show at the Gallery Miharudo, Tokyo. 3.36

Perry A. King and **Santiago Miranda** have been working together in Milan since 1976 on industrial, interior, interface and graphic design. In addition to working with some of the main office furniture and lighting companies in Italy, King and Miranda have designed for manufacturers in the electromechanical and office equipment industries. Their interior design projects are to be found in Milan, Rome, Paris, London, Madrid and Tokyo, and they designed the exterior public lighting system for Seville Expo '92. 2.86; 5.21

Toshiyuki Kita was born in Osaka in 1942. He has been working in environmental product design in Milan and Japan since 1969, and is also involved in traditional Japanese craft design. In 1987 he took part in the celebration of the tenth anniversary of the Centre Georges Pompidou, and in 1990 was awarded the Delta de Oro in Spain. In 1991 Kita designed the interiors and a chair for the revolving theatre for Seville Expo '92. His work is in the permanent collections of the Museum of Modern Art, New York (*Wink* chair, *Kick* table), and the Design Museum, London. 1.71

Morten Kjeldstrup and **Allan Östgaard** are Danish furniture and industrial designers. Their studio works on furniture, clothing, graphic and architectural design, as well as merchandise concepts. In 1994 they received the Swedish Design Award for their chair *Mammut*. 1.33

Klok Design was formed by Lydia Kümel (born in 1947) and Koen Ooms (born in 1964) in 1988. It is concerned mainly with the renovation of shops, offices, hospitals and private homes, but also with the design of furniture, carpets and jewellery. Its work has been exhibited throughout Belgium. 2.2, 66

Kazuyo Komoda was born in Tokyo and studied at the Musashino University of Art. She started her career in industrial and interior design in 1982 and since 1989 has worked in Milan. She is currently a freelance designer and has worked for Denis Santachiara. Her work has been exhibited throughout Europe and Japan as well as being published widely. Clients include Domodinamica, Proggetti and Bernini. 5.29

Thomas Krause was born in Copenhagen. He has degrees in industrial design from Denmark's Design School and from the Royal College of Industrial Design. He works independently for IKEA, Tuborg/Carlsberg and Post and Telegraph, Denmark, and Lego. 5.64

Larry Kuba is Design Director of Herbst, LaZar and Bell. His work in engineering and plastic processing has earned him two IDEA awards and two IF awards at the Hanover Fair. He has a Bachelor of Science Industrial Design Award from the University of Bridgeport and is a member of the Industrial Designers Society of America. 5.13

Axel Kufus was born in Essen in 1958. He served a carpentry and joinery apprenticeship, then worked in wood and bronze workshops in Bischofsheim from 1979 to 1982. In 1985 he studied industrial design at the Hochschule der Künste, Berlin, and since 1986 he has been a partner in the Crelle Workshop. Kufus has worked with Jasper Morrison and Andreas Brandolini for Utilism International, and since 1989 has collaborated with Jonas Milder in New York. From 1990 he developed serial furniture pieces for Atoll, Cappellini and Moorman and in 1992 was responsible for the conception and interior design of projects for Hans Hansen, Hamburg; the Academy of Arts, Berlin and the Museum Fredericianum in Kassel. 1.114

Masayuki Kurokawa was born in Nagoya, Japan, in 1937 and graduated in architecture from Nagoya Institute of Technology in 1961. In 1967 he completed a doctorate at the Graduate School of Architecture, Waseda University, Tokyo, and founded Masayuki Kurokawa Architect and Associates. Major architectural works include the Kita Hotel (1991); the Tamaki Factory for the Miwa Lock Co. Ltd, the Sodegaura Tower, Chiba-Minamisode, and the Paloma Head Office. Many of his product designs can be seen in the permanent design collection of the Metropolitan Museum of Art, New York, including the *Grand Blue* underwater rebreathing apparatus, which in 1994 won him the Good Design Award. In 1995 he took part in the exhibition 'Mutant Materials in Contemporary Design' at the Museum of Modern Art, New York. 3.48

Tsutomu Kurokawa was born in Aichi Prefecture, Japan, in 1962. He was employed as Chief Designer by Super Potart Co., before forming his own company, H. Design, in 1993. He is active in architecture, furniture, product and interior design. 1.66; 5.74

David Laituri is a senior designer for Lunar Design. He graduated from the Ohio State University, Columbus, in 1984 with a bachelor of science degree. He has received a number of awards from the Industrial Designers Society of America, including gold awards for his designs of the Chevy Beretta engine environment, the

Cadillac Northstar V-8 engine and the Apple Computer PowerBook DuoDock and charger system. 5.17

Lawrence Laske was born in Chicago in 1963 and studied at both the Northern Illinois University and the University of Illinois, Champaign-Urbana. After graduation he travelled to Italy to study urban scenography at the Domus Academy under Andrea Branzi and received a master's degree in design. Following a year spent with Sottsass Associati, Laske exhibited two lamps in the last Memphis show (1987). In 1988 he moved back to the USA and worked with Emilio Ambasz Design Group before founding Laske Design Consultancy. Projects include boutiques in Japan, consulting work for Armani Exchange and product development for Alessi, Artemide and Dansk. In 1991 Philippe Starck selected one of Laske's designs to be produced by OWO in Paris, and from 1991 to 1992 Laske operated his consultancy in Paris. In 1993 the Knoll Group introduced his *Cactus Collection* which received the ID Design Review honourable mention. His work is in the permanent collection of the Musée des Arts Décoratifs, Montreal. 5.104

Kristiina Lassus was born in 1966 in Helsinki. She studied at the University of Industrial Arts, Helsinki, and the National College of Arts, Crafts and Design in Stockholm. In 1995 she was awarded a master's degree in interior architecture and furniture design. She has worked in several architectural design studios in Finland and from 1992 to 1993 carried out research into corporate identity and product development issues for Finnish furniture manufacturers. She has designs in production for both Alessi and Zanotta. 5.94

Giovanni Lauda was born in Naples in 1956. Since 1994 he has been responsible for the 'Design Culture' option of the Industrial Design Master Course at the Domus Academy. Professionally he is involved in interior, exhibition and industrial design, working for companies such as Artas and Play Line. Between 1989 and 1992 Lauda was a member of the Morozzi and Partners Design offices, where he collaborated with Alessi, Edra, Formica, Ideal Standard, Mitsubishi, Nissan and Uchino. He has exhibited his work in Italy, Japan and France. 1.56

Jennifer Lee was born in 1956 in Aberdeenshire, Scotland, and attended the Edinburgh College of Art and the Royal College of Art, London. She has held one-person exhibitions at the Victoria and Albert Museum and the Crafts Council, London, and has shown her work in numerous group exhibitions, most recently at the Design im Wandel, 'Product Fetish Ritual' show at the Ubersee Museum, Bremen. Examples of her work can be seen in many permanent UK collections, in the Los Angeles County Museum of Art and in the Röhss Museum of Arts and Crafts, Gothenburg, Sweden. 3.59

Jürgen Lehl was born in 1944 in Poland. He worked in France from 1962 to 1969 and moved to Japan in 1971. He founded Jürgen Lehl Co. two years later and designs women's and men's clothing, accessories and jewellery. 3.56

Rainer Lehn was born in 1961. He studied at the University of Darmstadt and received practical training at the Pakistan Design Institute in Karachi. In 1988 he received second prize in the Laffon Package Design competition and in 1990 won an honourable mention from the Design Centre Nordrhein Westfalen for his *Coat Hanger No. 1*. 5.99

Diego Lemme was born in Rome in 1965. He has had his own workshop since 1989 and designs objects in wood. 5.78

Laurene Leon was born in 1964 in New Jersey, USA. She obtained degrees from the School of Visual Arts in 1986 and the Pratt Institute in 1993. She then joined Boym Design Studio and has designed products, exhibitions, graphics and interiors for Swatch, Steelcase Design Partnership, and the Cooper-Hewitt Museum as well as Alessi and Authentics. She received the ID Magazine Annual Design Award in 1990, 1993 and 1994 and the IDSA first prize with Constantin Boym in 1990 for Edible Pencils. In 1993 Leon was made Designer in Residence at the Cooper-Hewitt Museum and since autumn 1994 has been the Junior Year Studio Teacher in the Product Design Department at the Parsons School of Design. She is the founding member of the Association of Women Industrial Designers (AWID). 5.85

Lievore y Asociados was created in 1977 by Alberto Lievore (born in Buenos Aires in 1948) who is now a partner with Jeanette Altherr and Manel Molina. The company is active in all areas of design, but best known for its furniture. Clients include Perobell, Kron, Simeyco, Andreu and Divano. The company is increasingly recognized for its interior projects, including exhibition design and corporate image schemes. 2.63

Claus Lippe trained at the School of Art in Munster and later studied industrial design at the Universität-Gesamthochschule, Essen. Since 1986 he has worked as an independent designer, collaborating with various firms concerned with furniture manufacture. His most recent projects include a standing workplace for the office of the future, and he has also diversified into the design and production of tableware items. 5.71

Piero Lissoni was born in 1956 and took his degree in architecture at Milan Polytechnic. He worked for G14 Studio, Molteni and Lema before forming his own company with Nicoletta Canesi in 1984, which is involved in product, graphic, interior and industrial design as well as architectural projects. Since 1986 he has worked with Boffi Cucine as art director, creating corporate images and sales outlets, and in 1987 he started his collaboration with Porro, Living, Matteograssi and Iren Uffici. He worked in Japan in the early 1990s for the company Takashimaya. Since 1994 he has worked as art director for Lema and in 1995 became the art director for Cappellini and started his collaboration with Cassina and Nemo. In 1996 Lissoni was appointed art director for Units, the new Boffi and Cappellini kitchen company, and opened two showrooms in Paris for Matteograssi and Boffi. He was awarded the Compasso d'Oro in 1991 for the *Esprit* kitchen designed for Boffi. 1.119, 123, 124

Josep Lluscà was born in Barcelona in 1948. He studied industrial design at the Escola Eina, where he is now professor, and at the Ecole des Arts et Métiers, Montreal. He was vice-president of ADI-FAD (Industrial Designers' Association) from 1985 to 1987, and was one of the founding members of the ADP (Association of Professional Designers). He is also a member of the Design Council of the Catalonian Government. He has been the recipient of several major awards, including the 1990 National Design Award and two prizes from the ID Design Award in Furniture (1993). He also received the AEPD Award of Design in 1995 from the Spanish Association of Professionals for a series of emergency lights he designed for Daisalux. 1.89, 99; 3.51; 5.52

Roberto Lucci and **Paolo Orlandini** began their partnership in 1968. Lucci was born in Milan in 1942 and studied design at the Institute of Design in Chicago and at the Corso Superiore di Disegno Industriale in Venice. Orlandini was born in Grosseto in 1941 and graduated from Milan Polytechnic, where he studied architecture. They have collaborated for many years with Marco Zanuso Snr and Richard Sapper. Their designs can be seen in the permanent collections of the Museum of Modern Art, New York, the Centre National d'Art Contemporain at the Louvre, Paris, and the Museum of Contemporary Art, Chicago. Lucci and Orlandini have been the recipients of many design awards, including the Compasso d'Oro six times between 1979 and 1991, and the Industrial Design Distinction Award in New York in 1996. 1.96

Stefano Maffei has a degree in architecture from Milan Polytechnic. He graduated in industrial design in the same year as E. Manzini, with whom he often collaborates, and is active in architecture, interior and product design. 1.29, 40

Vico Magistretti was born in Milan in 1920 and graduated with a degree in architecture in 1945. Since 1967 he has been a member of the Academy of San Luca in Rome. As well as teaching at the Domus Academy in Milan, he is an honorary member of the Royal College of Art in London, where he is a visiting professor. He has been the recipient of numerous major awards, including the Gold Medal at the Milan Triennale in 1951, the Compasso d'Oro in 1967 and 1979, and the Gold Medal of the Society of International Artists and Designers in 1986. His buildings are primarily found in Italy, but his furniture, lamps and other designs are known internationally. Magistretti has worked for companies such as Alias, Artemide, Cassina, de Padova, Fiat, Knoll International and Rosenthal. His work can be seen in the most important design collections worldwide. 1.54, 70, 112

Erik Magnussen was educated at the Danish School of Arts and Crafts. He has his own design studio and is a partner of Eleven Design, which is active in furniture, product and industrial design. Clients include Bing and Grondahl, Royal Copenhagen and Stelton, and his work is exhibited at museums worldwide. Magnussen has also worked as a lecturer at the Royal Danish Academy of Fine Arts. 3.49

Hans Maier-Aichen was born in Stuttgart in 1940. He studied interior design at the Academy of Applied Arts in Wuppertal and fine art at the State University of Fine Arts, Munich. He has taught at the Art Institute of Chicago, the Academy of Fine Arts, Münster, and the National Academy of Fine Arts, Karlsruhe. He joined Artipresent GmbH in 1974 as Managing Director and created the Authentics trademark in 1980. From 1978 to 1985 Maier-Aichen was the consultant for cultural affairs in the European Community, Brussels. 3.53, 58

David Malina graduated from the Art Center College, Pasadena in 1996 and is currently working as a student intern at Lunar Design. 5.90

Angelo Mangiarotti was born in Milan in 1921 and studied architecture at Milan Polytechnic. Before opening his design office in 1955, he was visiting professor at the Design Institute of the Illinois Institute of Technology in Chicago. His architectural schemes include an industrial building near Como (1962); Certosa and Rogorado station in Milan (1989), offices and exhibition buildings in Carrara (1993) and an industrial building in Giussano (1993). His awards include a medal and honorary diploma at the Third World Architectural Biennial in Sofia in 1986 and the ADI Prize Compasso d'Oro in recognition of his career. 1.100

Amos Marchant and **Lyndon Anderson** founded Blue in 1994. They specialize in the design of furniture, artefacts and lighting using a wide knowledge of materials, production processes and technology. They studied furniture and product design at Kingston University and took master's degrees in Design Studies at Central Saint Martin's College of Art and Design. In 1996 Lyndon Anderson took up a position at Leeds University. 1.82

Enzo Mari was born in Novara in 1932 and studied at the Accademia di Belle Arti in Milan. In 1963 he co-ordinated the Italian group Nuove Tendenze and in 1965 was responsible for the exhibition of optical, kinetic and programmed art at the Biennale in Zagreb. He has also taken part in several Biennali in Venice and in the Milan Triennale. In 1972 he participated in 'Italy: The New Domestic Landscape' at the Museum of Modern Art, New York. Mari is involved in graphic and industrial design, publishing and the preparation of exhibitions. He has recently been occupied with town planning and teaching. He has been awarded the Compasso d'Oro on three occasions and was President of the Association for Industrial Design from 1976 to 1979. His work can be found in the collections of various museums, including the Stedelijk Museum, Amsterdam, the Musée des Arts Décoratifs, Paris, and the Kunstmuseum, Düsseldorf. 1.44

Javier Mariscal was born in Valencia in 1950. He trained as an artist and graphic designer at the Escuela Elisava, Barcelona, and collaborated on the Memphis collection in 1981. Early works included the 'Bar Cel Ona' logo. He has designed lights, with Pepe Cortes, for Bd Ediciones de Diseño, textiles for Marieta and carpets for Nani Marquina, as well as collections of furniture and china for Alessi, Akaba and Rosenthal. More recently he has produced a cartoon series on 'Cobi', the mascot for the 1992 Olympic Games in Barcelona, which he designed in 1988, and he has worked with Alfredo Arribas on the interior of the Torres de Avila bar in Barcelona. In 1994 he invented and co-ordinated the corporate identity for the post-production company Frame Store (UK). Studio Mariscal is currently collaborating with Canal Plus (Spain) and Colossal Pictures (San Francisco) in the development of an animated cartoon project, *Mondo Loco*, based on Mariscal's early cartoon characters 'Los Garris'. 2.33

Michael Marriott was born in 1963. He received a master's degree in furniture design from the Royal College of Art, London, and is now a freelance designer and maker of furniture put together from *objets trouvés*. 5.66

Jonathan Marshall graduated in 1992 from the Product Design Department of Ravensbourne College of Design and Communication in Kent. He worked for two years as a designer for Absolute Design Consultants in London and from 1994 to 1996 worked on a master's degree in Industrial Design at the Royal College of Art. 5.41

Andrew Martin was born in Sydney, Australia, in 1962. He studied architecture at the Architectural Association School of Architecture in London and at NSWIT in Sydney. He is currently working in both architecture and design in Europe and in Japan. 1.59; 2.82

Luciana Martins and **Gerson de Oliveira** (born in 1967 and 1970, respectively) studied cinema at the Art and Communication School of São Paulo University. They have exhibited their work in Brazil and in 1996 at the 'Brasil Faz Design' exhibition in Milan. In the same year they received the Museu de Casa Brasileira Award in the residential furniture category. 1.15

Kubo Masahiko is a young Japanese designer currently working with Studio de Lucchi in Milan. 3.63

Josep Massana and **Josep Tremoleda** were born in Barcelona in 1947 and 1946, respectively. They are both industrial designers and members of ADI-FAD (Industrial Designers' Association), ADP and BEDA. In 1973 they founded Mobles 114, which was initially a retail outlet but by 1981 had developed into a manufacturing enterprise dealing with contemporary furniture and lighting. In 1978 they won international acclaim for their lamp *Gira* and received several design awards and selections of ADI-FAD and SIDI. From 1989 to 1990 Josep Tremoleda was President of ADI-FAD. 5.70

Ingo Maurer was born in 1932 on the Island of Reichenau, Lake Constance, Germany, and trained in typography and graphic design. In 1960 he emigrated to the USA and worked as a freelance designer in New York and San Francisco before returning to Europe in 1963. He founded Design M in Munich in 1966, and since then his lighting designs have achieved world recognition. He has exhibited widely, in shows that include 'Ingo Maurer: Making Light', at the Museum Villa Stuck, Munich, and 'Licht Licht' at the Stedelijk Museum in Amsterdam, and his work is in the permanent collections of many museums, including the Museum of Modern Art, New York. 2.17, 18, 30

Mario Mazzer was born in 1955 and educated in Milan at the Polytechnic Design School, where he graduated with a degree in architecture in 1978. In 1980 he founded his own practice in industrial and architectural design. He has collaborated with companies such as Acerbis, Busnelli, Morphos and Zanotta. 1.39

Robert McCaffrey joined IDEO (Boston) in 1993. He has 17 years of design experience in all phases of product development and has worked for such companies as Digital Equipment Corporation, Datasec Corporation and Wang Laboratories. 5.35, 36

Steve McGugan was born in Vancouver in 1960 and studied product design at the Art Center College of Design from 1979 to 1981. He has worked as an in-house designer for Bang and Olufsen and David Lewis Industrial Design. In 1988 he formed his own design consultancy in Copenhagen, working in all areas of product design. He has received the Danish Design Competition award for the best plastic product in production. His work is displayed in the permanent collection of the Museum of Modern Art, New York. 5.10, 14

Alberto Meda was born in Como, Italy, in 1945 and graduated with a degree in mechanical engineering from Milan Polytechnic in 1969. He worked at Magneti Marelli as assistant to the production manager, and at Kartell as executive producer before starting a freelance practice collaborating with Gaggia, Kartell, Centrokappa, Lucifero, Cinelli, FontanaArte, Luceplan, Anslado, Mondedison, Mandarina Duck and Carlo Erba. He was awarded the Compasso d'Oro in 1989 for his *Lola* lamp and the Design Plus in 1992 for his *Titania* lamp. In 1994 he won the European Design Prize for his work with Luceplan and the Compasso d'Oro for the *Metropolis* series of lamps, again for Luceplan. In 1995 his chair *LightLight* was chosen for the Vitra exhibition '100 Masterpieces' at the Design Museum, London. 1.79

Megalit, founded in 1979, is a small lighting company producing about ten new product lines each year. Its innovative designs include work with fibre optics, inductional lamps and metal-halide xenon lamps. Megalit has received many awards, including three from the French Ministry of Culture, and numerous VIA Labels of Innovation. Its designs are available through Artemide. 2.85

Eva-Maria Melchers was born in Germany in 1956 and graduated in management and marketing from the Academy of St Gallen in Switzerland. She married the founder of C. Melchers GmbH & Co., one of the largest dealers in raw precious stones, and in 1990 founded the company Eva-Maria Melchers – Design in Precious Materials to revitalize the art of making decorative interior design products and unique art objects from precious stones. The designers with whom she collaborates include Alessandro Mendini, Garouste and Bonetti, Massimo Iosa Ghini and Marcello Panza. 5.67

Gianni Menguzzato, Claudio Nascimben and Michele Villis opened Studioquadrifoglio in 1981. The company is involved in the concept design and prototype development of industrial design pieces, which are then produced by mass-market manufacturers. They are concerned with the development of new materials and the use of recycled products and have worked for companies such as Casmania by Frezza, Gruppo Landi, Martinello SpA and Euro 3 Plast. Their architectural work is based mainly in the area around Vicenza. 1.81

Mario Mengotti was born in 1947 and graduated from the Institute of Arts. He worked as an architectural consultant for 15 years and in 1985 became manager of the design department at Prandina srl. He has been a partner of the company since 1987. 2.48

Metz.Schlett.Kindler was founded by Guido Metz, Matthias Schlett and Michael Kindler, three product designers from the University of Darmstadt. The company is active in public design and tableware and aims to redefine traditional household objects, working for innovative manufacturers such as Authentics, Alessi and WMF. In 1992 and 1995 three of its projects won the exhibition at the Braun Design Prize, and the *Die Enyklopen* cutlery was awarded the Sabattini Prize. 3.33, 34; 5.96, 97, 100

Miguel Milá was born in 1931 and studied at the Academy of Architecture in Barcelona. He started work in the studio of Federico Correa and Alfonso Mila, and after eight years founded his own company in 1958. He is involved in industrial and interior design. 2.80

Enric Miralles was born in 1955 and studied at the Faculty of Architecture in Milan. From 1973 to 1985 he worked with Pinon-Viaplana, during which time he won various competition prizes, two of which were constructed: Placa dels Paisos, Catalans, and the Park in Besos, Barcelona. In 1984 he formed his own practice, working with Carme Pinos until 1989. Miralles was the Fullbright Visiting Scholar at Columbia University, New York, from 1980 to 1981, has been Professor of the Master Class in the Städelschule of Frankfurt, and held the Kenzo Tange Chair at Harvard University. Recent projects include a boarding school in Morella, Spain, and a park-cemetry in Igualada, Barcelona. 1.98

Ulf Moritz graduated in 1960 from Krefeld Textilingenieurschule and worked as a textile designer for Weverij de Ploeg before setting up his own design studio in 1970. His work includes collection co-ordination, corporate identity, art direction, exhibition stands and architectural projects. He has collaborated with Felice Rossi, Montis, Ruckstuhl, Interlübke and Interline Nova. The textile collection Ulf Moritz by Sahco Hesslein was established in 1986. Moritz's work is represented in the Stedelijk Museum, Amsterdam, the Cooper-Hewitt Museum, New York, and the Textielmuseum, Tilburg. Since 1971 he has been a professor at the Eindhoven Academy of Industrial Design. 4.32–37; 5.106

Jasper Morrison was born in London in 1959. He studied at the Kingston School of Art, Surrey, and at the Royal College of Art, and won a Berlin scholarship in 1984. In 1986 he established his own design office in London. He designs for SCP, Cappellini, Alias and Vitra, amongst others, and lectures at the Hochschule der Künste, Berlin and Saarbrücken, the Istituto Europeo di Disegno, Milan, and the Royal College of Art, London. He has exhibited widely in Europe and the UK, most notably for Vitra in Milan, at the Kunstmuseum in Düsseldorf and at Galerie Néotù, Paris. 1.60

Ann Morsing and **Beban Nord** are the founder members of Box Architects and Box Möbler. Morsing was born in Uppsala, Sweden, in 1956. She studied art in San Francisco and later took an art and craft course in the Department of Interior Architecture at the Konstfackskolan, Stockholm. Beban Nord was born in Stockholm in 1956. He studied art history and fine art before studying at the Konstfackskolan. Together they received the Forum Närmiljö Prize for the best home furniture and the Golden Chair nomination for their interior design of an advertising agency. 1.115

Benny Mosimann was born in Baden, Switzerland. He took an interior architecture and product design course at the arts and crafts school in Zurich. He served an apprenticeship with the architecture and design studio Keller and Bachmann and has since worked with Devico Design and Greutmann Bolzern Design, Zurich, and Franco Clivio in Erlenbach. He received a diploma in product design in 1990 and is currently undertaking a graphic design course at the Arts and Crafts School in Basle. 1.5

Pascal Mourgue was born in 1943 in Neuilly-sur-Seine, Paris, and is a graduate of the Ecole Nationale Supérieure des Arts Décoratifs. Since 1969 he has been designing furniture, carpets, tableware and even trimarans. He has exhibited his work widely within Europe and in 1984 was elected 'Designer of the Year' by the Salon du Meuble de Paris. He received the Grand Prix de la Création de la Ville de Paris in 1992. Mourgue's work can be seen in the permanent collection of the Musée des Arts Décoratifs in Paris. 1.78, 103

Carlo Nason was born in Murano, Italy. His glasswork can be seen in the permanent collections of the Museum of Modern Art, New York, and the Corning Museum of Glass, New York. 2.54

Mikala Naur was born in Copenhagen in 1957. She trained as a goldsmith and has had her own studio since 1983, designing both jewellery and decorative objects for the home. She has held many exhibitions in Denmark. 2.44; 3.30

Mark Nichols joined IDEO (Boston) in 1993 as an industrial designer. Prior to this he worked for Motorola in its Land Mobile Group. He received a degree in industrial design from the Cleveland Institute of Art. Nichols received the *Business Week* magazine IDEA award for design excellence in 1994. 5.6, 35, 36

Guido Niest was born in Ciudad Ojeda, Venezuela, in 1958. In 1979 he moved to Europe, where he studied economics at the university in Munich and later industrial design at the Fachhoschschule München, where he specialized in product design. He worked as a designer for the WMF Metalwares Company of Geislingen and for the Design Centre for the German Railways before moving to Italy, where he spent nine years in the product development department of the Sabattini silversmithery. In 1987 he founded a studio, Canaima, and in 1995 formed his own company, Sabrina Creative Production. In 1996 he presented the Guido Niest Atelier Collection. His pieces can be seen in the permanent collection of the Musée des Arts Décoratifs in Montreal, Canada. 3.32

Anne Nilsson was born in 1953. She trained at the Dickinson College in Pennsylvania, the National College of Arts, Crafts and Design, Stockholm, and the California College of Arts and Craft, where she specialized in glass design. She worked for Höganäs Keramik before moving to Orrefors Glasbruk in 1982. She has won the Excellent Swedish Design Award in 1985 and 1986, and from 1992 to 1995, and the Design Plus Award in Frankfurt, Germany. Her work can be seen in the collections of the National Museum, Stockholm, the Röhss Museum of Arts and Crafts, Gothenburg, and the Corning Museum, New York. Nilsson has held various one-woman shows, the latest being 'Sorbet' at the Orrefors Crystal Gallery, Los Angeles. 3.57

Ninaber/Peters/Krouwel Industrial Design was established in 1985 by Bruno Ninaber van Eyben, Wolfram Peters and Peter Krouwel with the aim of producing a wide variety of line-assembly and mass-produced products for the consumer and professional market. Ninaber graduated from Maastricht Art Academy in 1971, Peters and Krouwel from the Delft Technical University in 1978. Their designs can be seen in the permanent collections of the Museum of Modern Art, New York, the Stedelijk Museum, Amsterdam, and the Design Museum, London, among others. In 1990 nine of their products received a Gute Industrieform recognition. 5.56

Katsuhiko Ogino was born in 1944 and graduated from the Musashino University of Art in 1966. From then until 1969 he was a lecturer at the Japan Design School after which he established various practices – Mono-Pro Kogei (1972), Humpty Dumpty Ltd (1976) and Time Studio Ltd (1978). In 1986 he was made a member of the Craft Centre Japan, of which he is now director. 2.15

Gianni Orsini was born in Amsterdam in 1970. After graduating from Delft University of Technology he was asked to join Ninaber/Peters/Krouwel, where he has worked since 1995. 5.16

Oval Design was formed in 1995 by Job Smeets and Hugo Timmermans who both studied at the Eindhoven Academy of Industrial Design. It consists of two divisions: OVAL Research and Development and OVAL Products. Smeets and Timmermans designed the Droog Design exhibition 'New Plastic Treat' at the Milan Furniture Fair in 1996 when they marketed their second product, the *Bumperlights Nina* and *Rosie*. Oval is currently working on a furniture collection. 2.13

David Pacchini is a project manager and senior mechanical engineer for Herbst, LaZar and Bell, and is responsible for the design of electro-mechanical and biomedical products, and mechanical pressure vessels. He holds a BSME and an MSME from the University of Michigan, Ann Arbor, and is a member of the Engineering Society of Detroit. 5.53

Paola Palma and **Carlo Vannicola** are architects and designers, but spend most of their time teaching furniture, interior and industrial design in Florence. They are the founding members of the Made Useful Art and Design group, which is involved in design research, and are also consultants for the fashion exhibition 'Firenze Pronto Moda', for which they design exhibition stands and advertising. Their expertise covers furniture design, with clients such as Zeritalia, BRF and Oliko; jewellery design for Flavio Mancini; carpets (Sisal Collezioni); and industrial design. Palma and Vannicola also collaborated with Gae Aulenti and B. Ballestrero in the design of the entrance and reception areas of the Florence Railway Station, for which they created the *Gap* and *Novella* lamps. 1.27

Marcello Panza was born in Naples in 1956. He studied architecture at the University of Naples and in 1983 he founded the interior and design company Studio Minimo. In 1984 he started to work for Driade Follies, Anthologie Quartett and Arcade. He has been teaching at the Istituto Superiore di Disegno in Naples since 1990. 3.8

Stefan Patte was born in 1963 in Coesfeld near Münster, Germany. He served an apprenticeship as a locksmith and following a move to Munich worked with a blacksmith, a stucco worker and in film, and from 1985 to 1989 assisted a technical specialist in a power plant. In 1989 he rented his own studio and designed installations for private rooms and shop fittings. He founded Objektiv Design Ltd with a partner, which later became Fürst and Patte Design and then Stefan Patte Design Ltd. His growing interest in alternative energy sources resulted in the fomation of SolArt, which exhibited for the first time in Cologne in 1996. 1.12, 83; 2.64

Lluis Pau was born in Girona, Spain in 1950 and studied at the EINA design school in Barcelona. In 1973 he started work for Martorell Bohigas Mackay, then joined Studio IDP, working on interior architecture, design and exhibitions. 1.102

Ricardo Paul was born in New Orleans in 1979. He is a senior at the L.E. Rabouin Career Magnet High School, where he is currently taking a course in commercial art. He is also a student with YA/YA (Young Aspirations/Young Artists). 1.9

Gentelle Pedescleaux attends the L.E. Rabouin Career Magnet High School, New Orleans, and is also a student at YA/YA (Young Aspirations/Young Artists). She was born in 1981 and plans to become a commercial artist whilst maintaining her interests in the performing arts. 1.8

Christophe Pillet was born in 1959. He has a diploma in Decorative Arts from Nice and a master's degree from the Domus Academy. From 1986–1989 he worked with Martine Bedin in Milan and later with Philippe Starck. Since 1993 he has worked independently in furniture, product and interior design. In 1994 he was elected Designer of the Year. 1.61; 2.56

Giancarlo Piretti was born in Bologna in 1940. He studied and later taught interior design at the Institute of Art in Bologna, after which he worked for 12 years as a furniture designer for Castelli SpA, where he developed designs such as *Plia*, *Platone* and *Alky*. In 1988 he independently launched the Piretti Collection, an office seating system that included more than 50 different chair models, which is now produced and marketed worldwide. He is currently working on another seating programme, the Tosion Collection. 1.90

Paolo Piva was born in Adria, Italy, in 1950. He studied at the University Institute of Architecture and the International University of Art in Venice, specializing in industrial design and the visual arts. His design work has been mainly in the architectural field. In 1980 he was invited by the Kuwaiti government to design the Kuwait Embassy in Qatar. He was awarded the Compasso d'Oro in 1987 and in 1990 won first prize for his design of a public area in the centre of Vienna. Piva is a Professor of Design at the Hochschule für Angewandte Kunst in Vienna. 2.57

Christian Ploderer was born in 1956 and studied at the Fine Art College in Vienna, where he took a masterclass in industrial design under Professor Hans Hollein. He opened his first studio, Ploderer and Rollig, in 1979 and concentrated mainly on interior, product and graphic design. From 1987 he started to work for Vest Leuchten, specializing in the field of lighting design and planning. In 1992 he founded Ploderer and Partner. Ploderer received the State Prize for Design in 1987 and since 1993 has been a member of the Executive Committee of Austrian Design. 2.16, 24, 53

Andrea Ponsi was born in 1949 in Viareggio, Italy, and holds degrees in architecture from the University of Florence, the Architectural Association in London and the University of Pennsylvania. In the early 1970s he focused on the relationship between architecture and ecology and participated in the design of experimental communities in California. After returning to Italy in 1988, he concentrated on interior architecture and product design, establishing Andrea Ponsi Design, a studio dedicated to the production of interior furnishings. He has taught at the University of California at Berkeley, the California College of Arts and Crafts, and the University of Toronto, and since 1990 has been a visiting professor at Syracuse University. 1.92; 5.60

Gio Ponti (1891–1979) was born in Milan, and completed his training as an architect in 1921. In 1923 he became artistic director of Richard Ginori. He founded *Domus* magazine in 1928. His work included residential buildings, public buildings and utensils; and he also worked as a painter and stage-set designer. In 1930 he built several buildings in Milan in the 'New Style', including the tower of the Corso Venezia, the Rai and Ferrania Palaces and the tower in Sempione Park. In 1956 he designed a multi-storey building to house the Italian firm of Pirelli, and drew up the plans for well-known housing developments in Europe, the Middle East, Canada, the USA and South America. 2.34

Tim Power is an architect living and working in Milan. Before forming his own practice he worked for Sottsass Associati. Current projects include furniture and product design, and illustrations and interiors for various international firms. Clients include Rosenthal, FontanaArte, Quattrifolio and Zeritalia. Since 1994 he was been teaching at the Istituto Europeo di Disegno in Torino/Milan. 1.43

Sergio Prandina was born in 1947 and graduated from the Technical Commercial Institute. He founded Prandina srl in 1975, manufacturing furniture and lamps. Since 1981 he has specialized solely in the production of lamps. 2.48

Kuno Prey was born in 1958 in San Candido in the Dolomites. After completing his art and design education, he opened his own design studio. Prey is a design consultant for numerous international companies. In 1993 he became Professor of Industrial Design at the Hochschule für Architektur und Bauwesen, Weimar, in the Faculty of Art and Design. 1.93; 5.80

Paul Priestman see Priestman Goode

Priestman Goode is a product and industrial design practice, which was founded in London in 1986. Its designs cover a broad range of products, including audio equipment and televisions, stationery, sporting goods, domestic appliances, furniture and yacht interiors. It has been awarded design prizes and won major international competitions for its work in the Far East, Europe and the USA. 5.48

David Privitera joined IDEO Product Development in 1990. Previously he was a principal mechanical engineer for Wang Laboratories. He has a BSME from Worcester Polytechnic Institute, Massachusetts. 5.6, 36

Timothy Proulx joined IDEO (Boston) as a staff engineer in 1991. He has worked as a designer for such companies as Wang Laboratories, Fitch Richardson & Smith and Agfa Corporation. He is currently taking a BSME at the University of Lowell, Massachusetts. 5.36

Enrico Quell has a degree in industrial design and since 1981 has worked in professional studios gaining experience in both industrial design and graphics. In 1984 he began to work as an industrial design consultant for Olivetti in Milan, and in 1990 he founded his own industrial design studio with Fabrizio Galli. 5.78

Harald Quintus-Bosz joined IDEO (Boston) in 1994, before which he worked at XRE Corporation designing medical x-ray imaging equipment for angiography. He graduated from Stanford University with a master's degree in mechanical engineering, focusing on the design of microprocessor-driven products. He also holds an SSME from the Massachusetts Institute of Technology. 5.36

Karim Rashid received a Bachelor of Industrial Design degree in 1982 from Carleton University in Ottawa, Canada. He completed his graduate studies in Italy, then moved to Milan for a one-year scholarship at the studio of Rodolfo Bonetto. On his return to Canada he worked for several years with KAN Industrial Designers. He is currently a full-time Associate Professor in Industrial Design at the University of Arts in Philadelphia. Since 1992 he has been principal designer for Karim Rashid Industrial Design in New York, designing products, lighting, tableware and furniture. He has won many awards, including 'ID 40' Leading Edge Designers by *ID* magazine (1996) and the Good Design Award/Permanent collection (32 objects for Nambe Mills) in 1995. His work has been exhibited at the Museum of Modern Art, New York, the Chicago Athenaeum, and the Design Museum, London. 3.40

Prospero Rasulo was born in 1953 in Stigliano, Matera, Italy, and graduated from the Milan Academy of Fine Arts. In 1980 he opened a studio dedicated to printing, sculpture and stage decoration. He collaborated with Alchimia and Alessandro Mendini, and during the same period worked with the Occhiomagico studio, designing scenery for videos, photographs and exhibitions. From 1986 to 1988 he organized 'Sexy Design', 'Sexy Mental', 'The Imprudent Image' and 'Living with Art'. In 1987 he founded the design, art and architecture gallery Osido with Gianni Veneziano. Osido subsequently became the trademark for a collection of furniture and art objects called Oxido Zoo. Since then Rasulo has begun to create mass-produced lines, working with companies such as Foscarini, Poltranova, Metals and BRF. 1.49

Fabio Reggiani is an industrial designer in charge of product design for the Reggiani Group. He has developed techniques that have resulted in lower energy consumption. He was selected for the Compasso d'Oro in 1991 and received the Roscoe Award the following year for the *Eidos* series. His work is exhibited in the Permanent Hall of Innovations at the Leonardo da Vinci National Museum of Science and Technology, Milan. 2.83

Jochen Reichenberg and **Volker Weiss** both trained as joiners/cabinet-makers. They started their collaboration in 1986/87, developing a range of garden furniture. In 1990 they designed a tower of drawers in aluminium and ebony that was to earn them the National Manu-Factum (the highest award in the field of trades and crafts) the following year. This success persuaded them to form their own studio. They presented a line of furniture for the first time at the Cologne Furniture Fair in 1992 and have shown every year since. 1.126, 7

Ann Richards, who trained initially as a biologist, takes an experimental approach to weave design. She studied woven textiles at the Surrey College of Art and Design, and has since exhibited widely in the UK and in Japan. In 1989 she won first prize at the International Textile Design Contest in Tokyo. Her work is in a number of public collections, including the Fashion Foundation, Tokyo, and the Crafts Council, London. 4.23–25

Paolo Rizzato was born in Milan in 1941 and graduated in architecture from Milan Polytechnic. He founded Luceplan in 1978 with Riccardo Sargatti, and from 1985 to 1987 he designed for Busnelli and Molteni and was also involved with interior architecture, planning and exhibitions, and interior design for private residences. Today he works as a freelance designer. He has collaborated with many leading manufacturers and has exhibited his work worldwide. Examples can be seen in the permanent collection of the Museum of Modern Art in New York. In 1990 he was invited to Japan to represent Italian design in the exhibition 'Creativitalia' in Tokyo. He has been awarded the Compasso d'Oro on three occasions: in 1981 for his lamp *D7*, in 1989 for the *Lola* lamp series produced for Luceplan and in 1995 for the *Metropoli* lamp series, again for Luceplan. 1.26

Daniel Rode has a degree in architecture and design from L'Ecole Boulle, Paris. Following his graduation he travelled throughout Africa, China and Hong Kong and designed fashion accessories and bags. Today he lives and works in Paris, where he has his own architectural practice and designs furniture for companies such as Ycami, Magis, Néotù, Thonet, Protis and Sony. Rode has recently been commissioned to design the next fashion exhibition for the Lux and Haute Couture Industry in Avenue Montaigne. 1.10, 51

Mark Rogers is the founding member of BUT, UK, an emerging design house whose products are now being manufactured by major retailers and contract furniture companies in Europe, the USA and the Far East. Its work has been exhibited in Japan, Cologne, Brussels and New York. 5.79

Vibeke Rohland studied art history at Copenhagen University and worked at the Willumben Museum of Art. From 1982 to 1986 she attended the Textile Department of the Copenhagen School of Decorative Arts. In 1987 she started work for Eliakim, Creation de Tissue in Paris, where she was responsible for the handpainting of textiles for Parisian haute couture and produced a textile collection for the Japanese market. Since 1991 she has been working freelance for designers such as Esprit and Agnès B. Exhibitions have included 'Textile Manifestation' at the Museum of Decorative Arts, Denmark (1988), a solo exhibition at Esprit, Copenhagen (1995), 'Dansk design aktuelt' – a selection of the best design in Denmark – (1992) and a solo show at the Boras Art Museum (1996). In 1995 Rohland was invited to design pattern interiors and accessories for the Danish State Railways. 4.30

Hannes Rohringer was born in 1956 in Seewalchen, Austria, and studied at the School of Applied Arts in Vienna from 1989 to 1996, specializing in product desgin. He worked as an interior architect before founding his own company in 1989. Clients include Miele, Porsche Design, Molto Luce and M-Group. He has exhibited his work in Austria and Germany. 3.10

Heinz Röntgen worked as a designer and consultant for textile and embroidery manufacturers and for weaving mills specializing in fashion fabrics before founding his own company, nya nordiska, in 1964. Today he concentrates exclusively on interior furnishing fabrics. He has received numerous awards in Germany and Switzerland, and in 1996 took part in the XIX Milan Triennale. 4.27–29

Gary Rooney studied at the St Helens College of Art and Design, followed by a degree in textile design at Huddersfield Polytechnic, and a master's degree in knitted textiles at the Royal College of Art, London. He is currently Research Fellow at Winchester School of Art, specializing in developing CAD knitting and constructed fabrics. Since the early 1990s he has been involved in forecasting and fabric development for such companies as ICE Fibres, Ford Ghia SpA and Romeo Gigli. His freelance work sells to Italy, France, Germany and the USA to designers such as Jean-Paul Gaultier and Faliero Sarti. Rooney is currently working on a solo show entitled 'Pleats' at the Winchester Southern Arts Gallery. 4.21, 22

Alex Ross graduated from the Art Center College, Pasadena, in 1995, and currently works as a student intern at Lunar Design. 5.18, 19

Mario Rossi Scola has collaborated with Michele de Lucchi since 1990, designing furniture and industrial objects for clients such as Consonni International Furniture, Matsushita Lighting, AV Mazzega, Rossana Kitchen Systems and Produzione Privata furniture and domestic items. He has exhibited his work in Italy and The Netherlands. 1.95

Michael Rowe was born in 1948 in High Wycombe, England. He graduated from the Royal College of Art, London, in 1972 and set up his own metalworking studio the same year. He became head of the Department of Metalwork and Jewellery at the RCA in 1984. Rowe's work is in the British Crafts Council, the municipal galleries of Birmingham and Leeds, the Victoria and Albert Museum, London, the Karlsruhe Museum, Germany, the Art Gallery of Western Australia, Perth, the Stedelijk Museum, Amsterdam and the Vestlandske Kunstindustrimuseum, Bergen, Norway. 3.4–7

Mario Ruiz Rubio is the founder of Costa Design and the Shareholder Associate and Industrial Design Department Manager of Artimana SL. He studied industrial design at the Elisava School, Barcelona, and has taken courses in plastic piece design and computer technology. He was Professor at the Elisava School from 1994 to 1996 and is currently Design Master lecturer at the Engineering High University of Barcelona. 5.30, 31, 33, 34

Jeff Salazar was born in San Francisco Bay, California. He graduated from the Art Center College of Design, Pasadena, in 1994 with a bachelor's degree in industrial design. He joined Lunar Design the same year and has since received many awards for his work, most recently the grand prize for his design in the 1995 Absolut Competition. 5.18

Kasper Salto is a young Danish designer, currently designing for Botium. 1.63

Andrea Salvetti received an art diploma in 1984, after which she decided to study architecture in Florence. She left her studies before graduating to start work in an architectural office whilst at the same time designing fashion accessories. She has shown these items and later interior design schemes at various national competitions. Salvetti has her own workshop at Chaitri, where she produces furniture and one-off pieces. She is currently working on a series of lamps for a Tuscan business and plans to complete her university course. 1.17

Júlio Sannazzaro was born in 1966 and studied art at the Santa Marcelina University, Brazil. He trained at the Nucleo de Arte, organized by Isnael dos Santos, where he attended drawing, interior design, sculpture and fine art courses. He has exhibited his work in numerous shows in Brazil and was selected to participate in the 'Brasil Faz Design' exhibition, Milan, in 1996. 2.51

Pete Sans was born in Barcelona, and worked in the studio of Pratmarso before moving to Ulm to study industrial design. Before completion of his course, he returned to Barcelona, where he opened a graphic design studio, produced an 'underground magazine', *Papel Especial*, and directed the Nikon Gallery and School. In 1979 he began his collaboration with Snark Design for whom he produced several award-winning designs such as *Lamparaprima*. He took part in the Spanish Design Exhibition organized on the occasion of Europalia-Brussels (1986) and in the fifth Arango International Design Competition Award, Miami (1986). He was awarded the Delta de Oro prize in 1988 for his *Ciqueta* armchair, produced by Bd Ediciones de Diseño. 1.46

Denis Santachiara was born in Reggio-Emilia, Italy, and now lives and works in Milan. He collaborates with major European manufacturers such as Oceano Oltreluce, Artemide, Kartell, Vitra, Yamagiwa, Domodinamica and Zerodisegno. His work has been exhibited in private and public galleries, and he has taken part in the Venice Biennale and Documenta Kassel, as well as the Milan Triennale in 1982, 1984, 1986 and 1988. 1.16; 3.25

Richard Sapper was born in 1932 in Munich. After studying philosophy, anatomy, graphics and engineering and obtaining a degree in economics he started work in the styling department of Mercedes-Benz in Stuttgart. In 1956 he worked in Italy, first for Gio Ponti and later with Marco Zanuso. From 1970 to 1976 Sapper worked as consultant to Fiat and Pirelli and since 1980 he has been the product design consultant of the IBM Corporation. Professor of Industrial Design at the Kunstakademie in Stuttgart since 1986, he has also taught in Beijing, Vienna, Barcelona and Buenos Aires, and at Yale University and the Domus Academy. Exhibitions include 'Italy: the New Domestic Landscape' with Zanuso in 1980 (the Museum of Modern Art, New York) and one-man shows at the Museums of Applied Arts in Cologne and Hamburg. He has been an Honorary Member of the Royal Society of Arts since 1988. 3.52; 5.50

Louise Sass was born in Copenhagen in 1965. She graduated from the Danish Design School and from 1992 to 1993 worked in Tokyo as a surface designer. Since 1993 she has worked independently, with many of her designs being produced by Kvadrat. She received the Art and Crafts Award, first prize, in 1991, and her work is represented in the collections of the Museum of Decorative Arts in Copenhagen and in the Danish State Art Foundation. 4.39

William Sawaya was born in Beirut in 1948 and graduated in 1973 from the National Academy of Arts. Before moving to Italy in 1978 he worked in the USA and France. In 1984 he founded Sawaya and Moroni with Paolo Moroni, where he is artistic director and project manager. He has taken part in collective exhibitions and one-man shows in Italy, Germany, France, Switzerland and Japan, and his work can be found in the permanent collections of the Israel Museum, Jerusalem; the Chicago Athenaeum; the Museum für Gestaltung, Basle; the Westerburg Museum, Bremen; the Kunsthal Museum, Rotterdam; and the Design Centre, Malmö. 1.128

Carlo Scarpa (1906–1978) was born in Venice, and studied at the Academy of Fine Arts, where he later taught. He set up his own architecture practice in 1927. He is best known for his work for the Venini glassworks and for interior design. He designed premises for the Paul Klee exhibition in Venice during the 24th Biennale in 1949, and the art book pavilion at the 26th festival in 1951. In 1956 he started work on the restoration of the Castelvecchio Museum in Verona and designed the 'Pavillon del Veneto' for the exhibition 'Italia G1' in Turin. In 1967 he designed what is considered to be his most important work, the 'Brion' tomb in San Vito d'Altivola. 2.36

Patrizia Scarzella is an architect and a journalist. She worked on *Domus* from 1980 to 1986 and has collaborated with leading Italian design firms both as product researcher and designer. She has curated numerous design shows and installations, including 'Shiro Kuramata, Executed Design' at the Museo di Milano; 'Italian Inspiration' at the Kunstmuseum, Düsseldorf, and 'From Japan to Japan, – Japan's Shibori Textile Art'. From 1985 to 1995 she was Zanotta's corporate image and communications consultant. 1.62

Winfried Scheuer was born in Calw, Germany, in 1952. He worked as a trainee in the styling department of Mercedes-Benz in Sindelfingen before studying at the Royal College of Art, London, from 1979 to 1981. He has worked in London as a self-employed industrial designer since 1986 and has exhibited his work at Documenta Kassel and the Luci Exhibition, Memphis, Milan. He is visiting lecturer at the Royal College of Art, London, and the Hochschule der Künste, Berlin. 5.81, 107

Wulf Schneider was born in 1943 and studied furniture construction and interior design at the Free College of Art and the State Academy of Visual Arts in Stuttgart. He has held management positions with a number of architectural firms and in 1976 he founded the Office for Design Concepts. His activities include environmental design, interior design, consultancy for industrial and furniture companies, design and development of buildings and furniture, and writing. He has received national and international awards and since 1991 has been Professor of Design at Munich Technical College. 1.113

Reto Schoepfer was born in Zurich in 1958. He trained and worked as a precision mechanic, and in 1990 he began his studies at the Academy of Design, Zurich, graduating with an Equipment Design Diploma. Today he has his own design workshop in Rüschlikon and also teaches at the Zurich School of Design. 2.72

Gary Schultz is responsible for Alias three-dimensional computer modelling, rendering design development and animation at IDEO. A graduate in industrial design of the Art Center College of Design, Pasadena, he joined IDEO (San Francisco) in 1994. Schultz has won awards from professional organizations and his work has been published in *ID* magazine, *Wired*, *Mountain Biking* magazine and *Computer Graphics World*. 5.1

Christian Schwamkrug was born in Düsseldorf, Germany, in 1957. He received a diploma in industrial design from the University of Wuppertal, after which he worked on a freelance basis for several design studios. He has been a designer for Porsche Design, Zell am See, Austria, since 1987. 5.9

Lloyd Schwan was born in Chicago in 1955. He trained as a sculptor at the Art Institute of Chicago and the Minneapolis College of Art and Design. In 1984 he set up a design studio with Lyn Godley, Godley-Schwan, specializing in lighting, furniture and interior design. 1.41, 88

Christof Schwarz was born in 1965 in Hamburg. From 1988 to 1993 he studied industrial design at the College of Art and Design in Hamburg and received a scholarship the following year to study at the Institute of Technology, Chicago. Since 1990 Schwarz has run his own design office and in 1996 opened Hafenatelier in Hamburg. He has exhibited his work in Germany and in 1994 was awarded first prize from the International Talent Forum for Crafts and Trades. 5.58

Frederick Scott served an apprenticeship as a cabinet- and chair-maker. In 1963 he won a scholarship to the Royal College of Art, London, to study furniture design and from there embarked on a freelance career working with manufacturers in the UK and abroad. In 1982 he won the Design Council's award for the *Supporto* chair. He has taught at numerous design colleges, including the Royal College of Art. 1.104

Pietro Silva was born in Milan in 1964 and received a doctorate in architecture from Milan Polytechnic. He has taken part in many exhibitions, including 'Progetto Europa 93' by Arflex and the 13th international biennale competition in Kortrijk, Belgium. From 1992 to 1995 he was the assistant professor in the Department of Architecture at Milan Polytechnic. In 1996 he took over the consultancy for remodelling the design store/gallery Tevere. 1.47; 5.77

Borek Sípek was born in Prague in 1949. After taking a furniture design course at the School for Arts and Crafts in Prague he moved to Germany in 1968, where he studied architecture in Hamburg and took a philosophy course in Stuttgart. Before moving to Amsterdam in 1983 he taught design theory at the University of Essen. Since starting his own architecture and design studio in 1983 he has held numerous solo exhibitions, including shows at the Musée des Arts Décoratifs, Paris; the Stedelijk Museum, Amsterdam; the Vitra Design Museum, Weil am Rhein; and the Umeleckoprumyslové Muzeum, Prague. He received La Croix Chevalier dans l'Ordre des Arts et des Lettres from the French government in 1991 and the Prins Bernard Fonds Prize for Architecture and Applied Arts in 1993. Recent works include interior design projects such as the offices for Art Factory, a computer animation company in Prague (1995), and the conversion of a warehouse to showroom/art gallery in Amsterdam for the Steltman Gallery (1995). 3.16–24

Paolo Sironi was born in 1964. He founded his own interior design company in Lissone, Italy, in 1986 and also teaches at the technical school, where he is an expert in specialized equipment. He has also designed stage sets and has worked in the technological workshop for the Scala in Milan. 2.22

Penny Smith trained in the UK, where she took a bachelor of arts degree in Furniture Design in 1969. She emigrated to Tasmania in 1970 and established her first pottery shop three years later, followed by a further studio that deals more specifically with semi-industrial processes. She is currently Head of the Ceramics Studio and the Ceramic Research Unit at the Tasmanian School of Art, University of Tasmania. She is artist-in-residence at Banff, Canada, and at the Arabia tableware factory in Helsinki. She has taken part in many solo and group exhibitions. 2.6; 3.9

Michael and **Mark Sodeau** studied product design at Central Saint Martin's College of Art and Design and nautical engineering at the City University, respectively. Michael met Nick Crosbie whilst they were students and they set up Inflate in 1995. Mark joined Inflate after completing his university course. Since its first inflatable collection was launched at '100% Design' in London, the company has had considerable success both in the UK and abroad. 3.31; 5.72, 108

Frédéric Sofia was born in France in 1967. He graduated from the Institute of Technology, Lyons in 1988 and has worked on several engineering projects for various industrial companies. Since 1993 he has been a full-time designer and has created a range of lights and objects for Wombat. He is also currently working on a hotel room interior, a panel for SNCF and various furniture designs. 2.3, 21

Ettore Sottsass was born in 1917 in Innsbruck. He completed his architectural studies in 1939 at the University of Turin and since 1947 has been working as a designer in Milan. In 1958 he became the chief consultant for design at Olivetti and was responsible for a number of innovative design concepts in information electronics. During this period Sottsass became involved in experimental projects, starting with the radical architecture of the 1960s. This work was followed up with the Memphis Group, which initiated the New Design of the 1980s. In 1980 he founded Sottsass Associati and his clients include major manufacturers such as Alessi, Cassina, Mitusbishi, Olivetti, Seiko, Zanotta, Esprit and Knoll. Among his architectural projects are interior furnishings for Esprit; the 'Zibibbo' bar in the Il Palazzo hotel, Japan; the Daniel Wolf apartment block in Colorado; and a hotel and shopping mall in Kuala Lumpur. 3.1–3

Jasper Startup was born in London in 1961 and qualified as a furniture designer in 1983 from Middlesex Polytechnic. He received a master of arts degree in 1994 following an industrial design course at Central Saint Martin's College of Art and Design. He has worked as a freelance designer since 1983, producing designs for companies such as Tangerine and Paul Priestman Associates. He has been design tutor at both Kingston University and Central Saint Martin's and from 1995 on the Foundation Studies course at the Chelsea College of Art and Design. Since 1996 he has taken on a seminar lectureship on design and environmentalism at Central Saint Martin's. 1.65; 5.49

Scott Stropkay is the Industrial Design Manager at IDEO Product Development. He joined the Boston branch in 1992, before which he worked for the industrial design firm Design Bridge. He has ten years of experience as a designer and has worked on a variety of products for the consumer, medical and business markets. Stropkay has a degree in Industrial and Graphic Design from the Cleveland Institute of Art. 5.6, 35, 36

Reiko Sudo was born in Ibaraki Prefecture, Japan, and educated at the Musashino University of Art. From 1975 to 1977 she assisted Professor Tanaka in the Textile Department. Before co-founding Nuno Corporation in 1984, she worked as a freelance textile designer and has since designed for the International Wool Secretariat, Paris, and for the clothing company Threads, Tokyo. At present she is the Director of Nuno Corporation and a lecturer at the Musashino University of Art. Her work can be seen in the permanent collections of the Museum of Modern Art and the Cooper-Hewitt Museum, New York; the Museum of Art, Rhode Island School of Design; the Philadelphia Museum of Art; the Museum of Applied Arts, Helsinki; and the Musée des Arts Décoratifs, Montreal. She has received many prizes for her work, including the Roscoe Award in 1993 and 1994. 4.15–19

Mitsumasa Sugasawa was born in Tokyo in 1940. Since 1973 he has worked for Tendo Co. Ltd, Japan. 1.85

Shinichi Sumikawa was born in Tokyo in 1962 and graduated from Chiba University Industrial Design Department in 1984. Before establishing his own design studio in Tokyo he worked for Sony both in Japan and the USA. His work can be seen in the permanent collection of the National Technology of Science Museum, Ottawa, Canada. 5.89

Mitsushige Sumimoto was born in Ono City, Hyogo, in 1955 and graduated from Kobe University Department of Civil Engineering in 1978. He joined Design EMI Associates in 1982, becoming Managing Director in 1987. 5.39

Yoshitaka Sumimoto was born in Ono City, Hyogo, in 1953 and graduated from Kobe University Department of Civil Engineering in 1978. He established Design EMI Associates in 1980 and became the Managing Director in 1985 when he was awarded the Good Design Prize for products used in light industry. He has designed for Silky and Mitsubishi, Japan. 5.37, 38

Svitalia Design was founded in 1986 by Susann Guempel and Urs Kamber. They have studios in Agra, Switzerland and Milan. Susann Guempel was born in 1956 in Germany and studied textile design in Basle. Urs Kamber was born in 1948 in Switzerland and studied architecture in Zurich, interior design in Basle and industrial design in Milan. The practice is involved in product design, interior decoration, interior architecture for industrial projects and private commissions. Svitalia has manufactured under its own name since 1989. 1.42

Mitsuru Takami was born in Osaka in 1964 and attended the Kyoto Institute of Technology. In 1988 he joined the Design Department, Television Sector, of Matsushita Electric Co. Ltd. 5.3

Hayden Taylor has a bachelor of arts degree in industrial design engineering from the University of Teeside, England. He joined IDEO in 1993, before which he was a freelance designer working on CAD development, production engineering and theme park design. Whilst at IDEO he has worked on consumer and medical products for clients such as Polaroid, Baxter, Spaceball Technologies and Lifeline. 5.36

Magdalena Thaler was born in Dornbirn, Austria. She studied at the Academy of Applied Arts in Vienna under Paolo Piva and later at the Royal College of Art, London, and the University of Industrial Arts, Helsinki. In 1996 she received the Design Plus Award at the international fair 'Ambiente' in Frankfurt. 5.73

Shozo Toyohisa is a lighting designer who lives and works in Kanagawa, Japan. His work can be seen in the collection of the Museum of Modern Art, New York. 2.87

Oscar Tusquets Blanca was born in Barcelona in 1941. He attended the Escuela Técnica Superior de Arquitectura, Barcelona, and in 1964 established Studio Per with Lluis Clotet, collaborating on nearly all their projects until 1984. He has been a guest professor and lecturer at universities in Germany, France and the USA, and his work has been exhibited worldwide. 1.98

Patricia Urquiola Hidalgo was born in 1961 in Oviedo, Spain, and trained as an architect at Madrid Polytechnic and at Milan Polytechnic, graduating in 1989. Since then she has been assistant lecturer of industrial design at Milan Polytechnic. In 1992 she established a partnership with Emanuela Ramerino and Marta de Rienzo, which deals mainly with interior design and landscape architecture. Since 1995 she has been collaborating with Vico Magistretti on furniture designs for Edizione De Padova. 1.70

Alan Vale joined IDEO (Boston) in 1993. He graduated from Worcester Polytechnic Institute with a degree in Mechanical Engineering. Whilst at college he co-invented a new configuation of an internal combustion engine and is currently applying for a patent. 5.6

Luk van der Hallen is an artist and designer. He lectures in the Department of Audio-Visual Arts at the Catholic University of Limburg and at the Eindhoven Academy of Industrial Design. His artistic output consists mainly of paintings, drawings and installations using paper and packaging. As a designer he edits small series of interior products, ranging from furniture and tableware to rugs and jewellery. He has his own studio and is the organizer of the Industrial Design Educational Meeting, an international workshop for students and professors in industrial design. 3.11–13

Jos van der Meulen lives and works in Rotterdam. Every design he makes has to do with recycling. He is self taught and before becoming a designer worked as a gardener. 5.65

Edward van Vliet was born in 1965. He trained at the Academy of Arts in Utrecht and later at the Eindhoven Academy of Industrial Design, where he received a degree in interior and industrial design. He has worked in design studios in The Netherlands, Italy and France involved with interior, industrial, graphic and textile design. Projects to date include textile and carpet design; domestic and commercial interior design projects; and exhibition, lighting and furniture designs. At the 1996 Salone Internazionale del Mobile & Euroluce, Van Vliet presented the first collection designed for his new company Equilibrium. 1.24, 25; 2.33, 37

Venini was created in 1921 by the Milan lawyer Paolo Venini, who had a great passion for glass. Many famous artists, designers and architects have created objects for Venini. 2.35

Raffaele Venturi was born in Modena, Italy. He has worked in the F. Bortolani Studio since 1989, designing products for Driade, Aleph, Atlantide and Ravarini Castoldi & Co. 1.48

Maria Verstappen and **Erwin Driessens** (born in 1964 and 1963, respectively) both studied at the State Academy of Fine Arts, Amsterdam, and the Academy of Fine Arts, Maastricht. They have held numerous joint and solo exhibitions in The Netherlands. 5.55

Marlies von Soden was born in 1948 in Hamburg. Since 1974 she has been involved in furniture, costume and theatre/film accessory design, and since the mid 1980s has become involved in the creation of unique lighting objects. She has exhibited her work throughout Germany. 2.27

Lois Walpole trained as a sculptor and later studied basket-making. She is based in London and for the past 14 years has been involved with the design of one-off pieces and *objets d'art* using post-consumer waste products. 5.62

Rene Wansdronk was born in 1959 and trained at the University of Delft. He founded Wansdronk Architektuur in 1983 and Abracadabra Design in 1992. He works on interior design and architecture projects, and produces product designs from furniture to prefabricated kiosks and from drum kits to roofing tiles. 1.19

Karsten Weigel received an industrial design diploma in 1995. He lives and works in Kiel, Hamburg and Berlin. 1.37

David Weissburg has been with IDEO (Boston) since 1991. Prior to this he worked for the Consumer Products Division at Polaroid, participating in all aspects of high volume product design. He has an MSME from the Massachusetts Institute of Technology. 5.35

Hannes Wettstein was born in Ascona, Switzerland, in 1958 and is involved in furniture, lighting, product and interior design and architecture. He has worked with Baleri Italia since 1985 and with other manufacturers such as Revox, Kleis, Belux, Ventura, Oluce Italia, Philips and Ritzenhoff. Today he is a partner in 9-D Design, Zurich, which he co-founded in 1992. 2.70, 77

Weyers and Borms are self-taught designers. They were born in the 1960s. 4.31

Köbi Wiesendanger studied at the Kunstgewerbeschule in Zurich. He was art director at Young and Rubicam, and co-founder of both TBWA Italia and Avant de Dormir. 1.36

Theo Williams was born in Oxford, UK, in 1967 and studied in Bristol and Manchester, graduating in industrial design in 1990. He works as a freelance designer in Milan and London. He has collaborated with Aldo Cibic on a project for Fiat cars and with Marco Zanuso on lighting and furniture, and recently a milk glass for the Ritzenhoff Collection. Williams is also a design consultant to Technogym Italia, designing the complete *XT* line of cardio fitness equipment. In 1993 he was retained by Nava Design as in-house graphic and product design consultant. In 1995 he was awarded the Première Design Plus Award for his 'service' mouse pad, and in 1996 was presented with the Design Plus Award for his *Disk Containers* and desk and pocket diary *Uno & Uno*, produced by Nava Design. 5.26

Herman Wittocx was born in Belgium in 1949 and has been working as a freelance designer since 1979. He has exhibited in Belgium, Switzerland, Germany, The Netherlands, France and, most recently, at the International Contemporary Furniture Fair in New York. 1.120

Gil Wong, an industrial designer, joined Lunar Design in 1987. Born in Hong Kong in 1962, he graduated with an industrial design degree from San Jose State University. He has received numerous national and international design awards and patents. 5.17, 19

Terence Woodgate was born in London in 1953. He studied at Westminster and Middlesex Colleges and in the mid-1980s spent two years at what is now known as the London Guildhall University. His work consists mainly of furniture, lighting and product design. His clients include Cappellini, Casas, Concord Lighting, Punt Mobles, SCP, Teunen and Teunen and Victoria Design. He has won two major design awards: the British Design Award 1992, and the German Design Award 'Die Besten der Besten Design Innovationen 1992'. His work is exhibited in the collection of the Museo de las Artes Decorativas, Barcelona, and in the review collection of the Design Museum, London. In 1994 he set up a studio in Portugal, where he now works. 5.28

Yamada Design Studio is the in-house design group of Yamada Lighting, Japan. 2.81

Max Yoshimoto holds a bachelor's degree in industrial design from San Jose State University and is vice-president of industrial design at Lunar Design. Before joining Lunar he was principal of his own firm, where he specialized in industrial design for electronics and medical technology companies. He has received a number of awards from the Industrial Designers Society of America, *International Design* magazine and *Appliance Manufacturer* magazine. 5.18, 19

Marco Zanuso was born in 1954 in Milan and studied architecture at the University of Florence. He became assistant to the Professor of Industrial Design at Milan Polytechnic in 1980, and in the same year set up his own practice, which specializes in architectural, industrial and exhibition design. In 1981 he became one of the founding members of the lighting trademark Oceano Oltreluce. His clients include de Padova, Néotù, Artelano, Ultima Edizione, Memphis and Giotto International Ltd; he has also realized various architectural projects throughout Europe and interior design schemes in Milan. Recent exhibitions include the 'Design Miroir du Siècle', Gran Palais, Paris (1993), and 'Fantasy Objects', Galleria Frau, New York (1993). 1.118, 122

[Zed] is a team of designers, theorists and constructors of various nationalities. The headquarters acts as a co-ordinator and consultant, uniting project-oriented talents. In order to emphasize the product rather than the design and also to act as a platform for newcomers, the names of the contributors are not made public. 2.71

Marcello Ziliani was born in Brescia in 1963 and studied at Milan Polytechnic. He started working for and is now owner of the company Studio Zetass, which is concerned with product design, engineering, architecture, furnishings, graphic design, corporate identity and design co-ordination, and he has received five Compasso d'Oro awards. International companies such as Flos-Arteluce, Vanini and Interflex have manufactured his work. Ziliani is chairman of the 'ABC – incontri sul progetto' association which he founded along with Paolo Deganello, Paolo Lomazzi, Roberto Marcatti, Vanni Pasca, Paolo Pedrizzetti, Ambrogio Rossari and Marco Zanini to organize design events. 2.49, 84

suppliers

Acerbis International SpA, via Brusaporto 31, Seriate 24068, Bergamo, Italy. *Outlets* Australia: Space, 111 Flinders Street, Sydney, NSW 02010. Denmark: Interstudio, 12 Pakhusm, 2100 Copenhagen. France: Helven Francis, Château le Mouchet, 26260 Chavannes. Germany: Offenhauser Hermann, 61 Bergastrasse, 69259 Wilhelmsfield; Weiss and Weiss, Von Merveldt Strasse 12, D-48336 Sassenberg. Japan: Renda Valentino (AG Far East), Piazza Roma 84, Mariano Comense 22066, Italy. The Netherlands: Van't Hul Ronald, 320 Ginnekenweg, 4835 Breda. Spain: Carrasco Igncio, 9 Plaza Conde Valle Suchil, 28015 Madrid. UK: Environment, 120 High Street, Leeds LS25 5AQ. USA: I.L. Euro Ivan Luini, 315 Hudson Street, New York, NY 10013.

Activa, 8 Berkley Road, London NW1 8YR, UK.

Adele C., Piazza Vittorio Veneto 4, I–20036 Meda (MI), Italy.

Aero Ltd, Unit 4, Glenville Mews, Kimber Road, London SW18, UK. *Outlets* Belgium: Visa Versa, 40 Langestraat, 9160 Loreren. USA: Niels Ole Hansen Inc., PO Box 10087, San Rafael, CA 94912.

Afro City, Corso Porta Buova 46, 20121 Milan, Italy.

Ajeto, Lindava 167, 47158 Czech Republic.

Alessi SpA, via Privata Alessi 6, 28023 Crusinallo, Novara, Italy. *Outlets* Denmark: Gense AS, 17 Maglebjergvejm, 1800 Lyngby. Finland: Casabella OY, 24 Yliopistonakatu, 20100 Turku. France: Société Métallurgique Lagostina, 62 rue Blaise Pascal, 93600 Aulnay-sous-Bois. Germany: Van der Borg GmbH, Sandbahn 6, 4240 Emmerich. Japan: Italia Shoji Co. Ltd, 5–4 Kojimachi, 1–chome, Chiyoda-ku, Tokyo 102. The Netherlands: Interhal BV, 8 Zoutverkoperstraat, 3330 CA Zwijndrecht. Sweden: Espresso Import, 10E Furasen, 42177V Frolunda. Switzerland: Guido Mayer SA, 9 rue du Port Franc, 1003 Lausanne. UK: Penhallow Marketing Ltd, 3 Vicarage Road, Sheffield S9 3RH. USA: The Markuse Corporation, 10 Wheeling Avenue, Woburn, MA 01801.

Alias srl, via dei Videtti 2, Grumello D. Monte 24064, Bergamo, Italy. *Outlets* France: Roger von Bary, 24 rue Laffitte, Paris 75009. Germany: Taubert 40 Nerostrasse, Wiesbaden 65183; Franzbecker, Postfach 1367-31865 Lavenau; Karo-Amalienstrasse 69, 80799 Munich. Japan: Interdecor, 2-9-6 Higashi, Shibuya-ku, Tokyo 150. The Netherlands: Eikelenboom, 54 Keienbergweg, Amsterdam 1101 GC. Spain: Idea International, 5/7 Ap. de Correos C/Ripolles, Prat de Llobregat 8820. Switzerland: Quadrat, Muesmattstr 15, A–3012 Berne; Segura Ch. Des Croix Rouge 3, 1007 Lausanne. UK: Coexistence, 323 City Road, London EC1V 1LJ. USA: Luminaire, 7300 SW45 Street, Miami, FL 33155.

Nick Allen, 3 Shelgate Road, London SW1W 1BD, UK. *Outlets* Germany: Galerie Artificial, 19 Bucher Strasse, Nuremberg D–90419. The Netherlands: Cortina, 334 Houtmankade, 1013 RR Amsterdam.

Allermuir Ltd, Branch Road, Lower Darwin, Lancashire, BB3 0PR, UK.

Antonio Almerich SL, 41 Ciudad de Liria, Paterna 46980, Valencia, Spain.

American Power Conversion, 755 Middlesex Turnpike, Billerica, MA 01821, USA.

Antonangeli Illuminazione srl, via E. de Amicis 42, Cinisello Balsemo 20092, Milan, Italy. *Outlets* Benelux: Danver Light, 63 Tabaksves, 2000 Antwerp, Belgium. Canada: Artemide Canada Ltd, 9200 Place Picasso, Québec-St Léonard. France: C & D Diffusion, 23 Que de Savoie, 75700 Sallanches. Germany: Dr. Arch. Salvo Causarano, 2 Katharinenstrasse, 59348 Ludinghausen. Spain: Dimmer scv, 61–20A c/Jesus, 46007 Valencia.

Apple Computer for Bandai Co. Ltd of Japan, 2730 Valley Green Drive, San Jose, CA 95014, USA.

Jan Armgardt, 164 Luitpoldstrasse, Ludwigshafen 67063, Germany.

Art & Design, 1 Molenstraat 1, Maasmechelen B–3630, Belgium.

Art Andersen & Copenhagen, 3 Gammel Kongevej, Copenhagen V, DK–1610, Denmark.

Arte srl, via Nazario Sauro 34, Arosio 22060, Como, Italy.

Artelano, 4 rue Schoelcher, Paris 75014, France. *Outlets* Belgium: Lydia Maughan, 75 Avenue de L'Université, Brussels 1050. Germany: Harald Noede KG, 3 Oderveg, Zirenberg 3501. UK: Walter International, 42 High Street, Daventry, Northants NN1 1HU. USA: Luminaire, 7300 South West 45th Street, Miami, FL 33155.

Arteluce (Division of Gruppo Flos SpA), via Angelo Faini 2, Bovezzo, Brescia 25073, Italy. *Outlets* Belgium: Flos SA, Gossetlaan 50, 1720 Groot Bijgaarden. France: France Flos srl, 5 rue de Bicêtre, 94240 L'Hay Les Roses. Germany: Deutschland Flos GmbH, Am Probsthof 94, 5300 Bonn 1. Japan: Flos Co. Ltd, PMC Building, 1–23–5 Higashi-Azabu, Minato-ku, Tokyo 106. Spain: Flos SA, c/Bovedillas 16, San Just Desvern, 08960 Barcelona. Switzerland: Flos SA, 75 Blvd St-Georges, 1025 Geneva. UK: Flos Ltd, 31 Lisson Grove, London NW1 6VB. USA: Flos Inc., 200 McKay Road, Huntington Station, New York, NY 11746.

Artemide SpA, via Bergamo 18, 20010 Pregnana Milanese, Italy. *Outlets* Australia: Ornare, 14 Ormond Avenue, 5072 Magil. Austria: Vertreter Design Agentur R. Greinecker, Herbeckstrasse 27, 1183 Vienna. Belgium/The Netherlands/ Luxembourg: Horas SA, Beemstraat 25, 1601 Ruisbroek. Canada: Artemide Ltd, 9200 Place Picasso, Montréal (St Léonard), Québec H1P 3JB. Cyprus: HC Furniture and Art Ltd, 24 Pindarou Str., PO Box 586, Nicosia. Denmark/Finland/Sweden/ Norway: Renzo d'Este, H.E. Teglersvej 5, 2920 Charlottenlund. France: Artemide E.u.r.l., 6–8 rue Basfroi, 75011 Paris. Germany: Artemide GmbH, Itterpark 5, D-4010 Hilden. Hong Kong: Artemide Ltd, 102–103 Ruttonjiee Centre, Duddel Street. Japan: Artemide Inc., 4–5–18 Higashi Nippori, Arakawa-ku, Tokyo 106. Korea: Kunyang Trading, Kangnam-Gu, Yeoksam-Dong 721-39, PO Box 7594, Seoul 135–080. New Zealand: ECC Lighting Ltd, 39 Nugent Street, PO Box 291, Auckland. Singapore: Concept Lighting Pte Ltd, 356 Alexandra Road, 0315 Singapore. Spain: Artemide SA, C/Ripolles 5 y 7, 08820 Prat de Llobregat, Barcelona. Switzerland: Artemide Illuminazione AG, via Trevano 72, 6900 Lugano. UK: Artemide GB Ltd, 323 City Road, London EC1V 1LJ. USA: Artemide Inc., National Sales and Customer Service Center, 1980 New Highway, Farmingdale, NY 11735.

Artimeta BV, Postbox 2504, Heerlen 6401 DA, The Netherlands.

Art-line Wohndecor GmbH, Am Gewerbehof 1 Nr. 7–9/50170 Kerpen, Germany. *Outlet* Switzerland: Art-line Suisse, Verkaugsburo, Lager Werkstatt, Willikerhus A, CH–8618 Oetweil am See.

Asahi Glass Co. Ltd, 2–1–2 Marunouchi, Chiyoda-ku, Tokyo, Japan.

Jane Atfield, No Sign of Design, 244 Grays Inn Road, London WC1X 8JR, UK.

Authentics artipresent GmbH, 30 Max-Eyth-Strasse, Holzgerlingen 71088, Germany. *Outlets* Denmark: Niels Blom-Andersen, 28 Dyrehavevej, Klampenborg 2930. France: Jean-Marie Ritterbeck, 1 Allée Taine, Pontault-Combault 77380. Italy: Modo & Modo srl, 21 via Bressan, 20126 Milan. Japan: Fujii Corp. Ltd, 8 Ichibancho, Chiyoda-ku, Tokyo 102. The Netherlands: Steve Top, 5 Welgelegen Staat, Brussels 1050, Belgium. Spain: Fisura SA, Carretera Leon Astorg Trobajo del Camino, Leon 24198.

Avant de Dormir, via Turati 3, 20121 Milan, Italy.

Ave Design Corporation, via Olmetto 10, 20123 Milan, Italy.

AV Mazzega srl, via Vivarini 3, Murano Venezia, Italy.

Gijs Bakker, 518 Keizersgracht, Amsterdam 1017 EK, The Netherlands.

Baleri Italia, via S. Bernardino 39, Lallio 24040, Bergamo, Italy. *Outlets* France: Francis Helven, 21 Côte des Chapeliers, Valence 2000. Germany: Walter Schiedermeier, Marienbergerweg 12, Cologne 5000. Japan: Casatec Ltd, 9–6 Higashi, 2-chome Shibuya-ku, Tokyo 150. The Netherlands: Kreymborg, 66 avenue Molière, Brussels 1180, Belgium. Scandinavia: Lysygn, 1 Horseager, Greve 2670, Denmark. UK: Viaduct Furniture, 10 Spring Place, London NW5 3BH. USA: I.C.F. Inc., 305 East 63rd Street, New York, NY 10021.

Bär & Knell Design, 7 Untere Turmgasse, Bad Wimpen 74206, Germany. *Outlets* Cyprus: Cocoon Furniture, PO Box 1126, Limasol. Italy: Delafabro SNC, Mobili di Casa, via dei Ponti 7, 330967 Spilimbergo; AGF srl, via Madonna Dena Neve, 24 Bergamo; Marmi & Graniti, Zantedeschi, via A. de Gaspari, 37015 Domegliara; Dilmos s.a.s, Piazza San Marco, 20121 Milan. South Africa: Innovation Furniture Contracts, 179 Loop Street, Cape Town 8001. Switzerland: Interni, Emmentalstrasse 240, 3414 Oberburg; Kluge AG, Dufourstrasse 138, 8008 Zurich. UK: Space, 28 All Saints Road, London W11 1HG.

Barigo, 3030 Postfach, VS–Schwienningen 78019, Germany.

Baroni & Associati, Corso di Porta Romana 122, 20122 Milan, Italy.

Bd Ediciones de Diseño, 291 Mallorca, Barcelona 08037, Spain. *Outlets* Belgium: Espaces and Lignes, rue Ulens Straat 55, 1210 Brussels. Denmark: Gubi Design, Gronnegade 10 Pistolstraede, 1107 Copenhagen. France: Clipper Conseil, 18 rue du Rhin, 18180 Montigny-le-Bx. Germany: IMD, Flöthbruchstrasse 11, D–47877 Willich–2 Anrath. Greece: Collection Artefacto, Tsimiski 72, 546–22 Thessalonki. Italy: Bruno Arnabodi, via Canonica 54, 20154 Milan. Japan: Kenchiku Shiryo Kenkyusha, Dai 2 Ohiani Bld, 2F 1–41–6 (Tokyo 171) 81121 Nishi Ikebukuro Tosh. The Netherlands: Heneka & Goldschmidt 1E Constantun Hugensstraat 102-104, Amsterdam 1054 BZ. Philippines: Domani International, Inc., Store No. 7 N.W.H. 63 Esperanza Cor., Makati. Portugal: Altamira Mobilario SA, Rua Viriato 23 1 E, 1050 Lisbon. Switzerland: IMD Inter Marketing, Eebrunnestrasse 26, CH 5212 Hausen (AG). Taiwan: M. Jose Luis Cuevas, 97–3 Si-tun Rd. Sec. 2. Taichung-Taiwan R.O. Thailand: Elitis Co. Ltd, 44/6 Soi Thonglor 1, Sukumvit 55, 10110 Bangkok. USA: Current, 1201 Western Avenue, Seattle, WA 98101.

Bent Krogh A/S, Gronlandsvej 5, Skanderborg 8660, Denmark. *Outlets* France: Bivex, 65 rue Pascal, Paris 75013. Germany: Möbex, 46 Parkstrasse, Diez 65582. Japan: Toshiaki Takigami, 103 Sakamoto Mansion, Tokyo 151, 4–40–5 Honmachi. The Netherlands: Brainbow BV, Postbus 8360, Veenendaal 3900 AV. Norway: Per-Roy Winge, Postboks 921, Moss 1500, Bergersborg. Sweden: BO Bertilsson Förs AB, Box 54, Kinna 51121. UK: Zon International Ltd, PO Box 329, Edgware, Middlesex HA8 6MH. USA: Soho Contract Group Inc., 216 Route 206, Suite No. 22, Somerville, NJ 08876.

Belux AG, Bremgartnerstrasse 109, Wohlen 5610, Switzerland. *Outlets* Australia: Création Baumann, 87 King William Street, Fitzroy, Victoria 3065. Benelux: Belux Benelux BV, Hettenheuvelweg 14, NL–1101 BN Amsterdam. Canada: Création Baumann, 302 King Street East, Toronto, Ontario M5A 1K6. Czech Republic: Sirius Light, Masarykovo Nabrezi 20, CR 110 00 Prague 1. Denmark: Belux Denmark, Birkewaenget 21, 3520 Farum. France: Technopolis 4, ZAC de Mercières, 60200 Compiègnes. Germany: Nils Holger Moorman, Kirchplatz, 83229 Aschau im Chiemgau. Italy: Belux Italia, Piamide s.a.s, via Feltre 148, I–32100 Belluno. Japan: Création Baumann Japan Ltd, Tokyo Design Centre, 5–25–19 Higashi-Gotanda, Shinagawa-ku, Tokyo 141. UK: Belux United Kingdom, Lumino Ltd, Lovet Road, Harlow, Essex CM19 5TB. USA: Ernest Stöcklin, 135 Fort Lee Road, Leonia, NJ 07605.

Bieffe SpA, via Pelosa 78, 75030 Caselle di Selvazzano, Italy.

Bigelli Marmi, via Arceviese 26, 60019 Senigállia (AN), Italy.

Bisazza SpA, 36041 Alte-Vicenza, Italy.

Bodum (Schweiz) AG, Kantonsstrasse CH–6234, Triengen, Switzerland. *Outlets* Australia: Gibsons & Paterson (WA) Pty, Gibpat House, Herdsman Business Park, 40 Hasler Road, Osborne Park, WA 6017. Austria: Bodum (Österreich), Franz Quantsschnig, A–9072 Ludmannsdorf 38. Canada: Danesco Inc., 18111 Trans-Canada Highway, Kirkland (Montréal), Québec H9J 3K1. Denmark: Bodum (Danmark) A/S, Vibe Allé 4, DK–2980 Kokkedal. France: Bodum (France) SA, Z.A. de Courtaboeuf, 18 Avenue du Québec, Bât N3 – B.P. 703, F–91961 Les Ulis Cedex. Germany: Peter Bodum GmbH, Postfach 1164, D–24559 Kaltenkirchen. Italy: Bodum (Italia) srl, via Perugino 13, I–20093 Cologno Monzese, Milan. The Netherlands: Bodum (Nederland) BV, Satijnbloem 14, NL–3068 JP Rotterdam. New Zealand: Peter Gower Ltd, PO Box 37–411, 7 Windsor Street, NZ–Parnell, Auckland. Singapore: Lexim (Singapore) Pte Ltd, 112 Killiney Road, Singapore 0923. Spain: Bodum España SA, P.A.E. Neisa Norte,

Avenida Valdelaparra, 27 Nave 15, Edf. III, E–28100 Alcobendas, Madrid. Sweden: Bodum Stenius AB, Box 748, S–13124 Nacka. UK: Bodum (UK) Ltd, Bourton Industrial Park, Bourton-on-the-Water, Cheltenham, Gloucestershire, GL54 2LZ. USA: Bodum Inc., 2920 Wolff Street, Racine, WI 53404.

Bohner, Bachmayer, Lippert, 71 Falkerstrasse, Stuttgart 70176, Germany.

Renata Bonfanti Snc, 52 via Piana d'Oriente, Mussolente 36065, Vicenza, Italy. *Outlets* France: MG Diffusion srl, rue du Faubourg St Honoré 184, 75008 Paris. UK: Interdesign UK Ltd, Unit M, 30c Chelsea Harbour, Design Centre, London SW10 0QL.

Botium, Bella Centre, Copenhagen 2300, Denmark.

Box Möbler AB, Repslagarg 17B, Stockholm 11846, Sweden.

Boym Design Studio, 56 West 11th, New York, NY 10011, USA.

Breuer/Tornado Corporation, 7401 W. Lawrence Avenue, Chicago, IL 60656, USA.

Brüel & Kjaer A/S, 307 Skodsborgbej, Naerum 2850, Denmark.

BUT, 81 Lothair Road North, London N4 1ER, UK.

CAD Woven Textiles, 94 Balfron Tower, St Leonards Road, London E14 0QT, UK.

Canon Inc., 3–30–2, Shimomaniko 146, Tokyo, Japan. *Outlets* Australia: 1 Thomas Holt Drive, North Ryde, Sydney, NSW 2113. Belgium: Bessenveldstraat 7, 1831 Diegem. Finland: Kornetintie 3, 00380 Helsinki. France: Centre d'Affaires Paris-Nord, 93154 Le Blanc-Mesnil Cedex. Germany: Hellersbergstrasse 2–4, W–4040 Neuss. Italy: via Mecenate 90, 20138 Milan. Japan: 11–28, Mita 3–chome, Minato-ku, Tokyo 108. The Netherlands: Bovenkerkerweg 59–61, 1185 Je Amstelveen. Spain: Calle Joaquin Costa, No. 41, 28002 Madrid. Sweden: Stensätravägen 13, S–127 88 Skärholmen. Switzerland: Industriestrasse 9, 5432 Neuenhof AG. UK: Canon House, Manor Road, Wallington, Surrey SM6 0AJ. USA: One Canon Plaza, Lake Success, New York, NY 11042.

Cappellini Arte, via Marconi 35, 22060 Arosio, Italy. *Outlets* Austria: Wolfgang Bischof OHG, Judenplatz 6, 1010 Vienna. Belgium: Rika Andries,

Turnhoutsebaan 144b, 2200 Borgerhout. France: Cerutti Giuseppe, Loc. Gran Chemin 1, 11020 Saint Christophe. Germany: Novus, Gartenstrasse 26, 7959 Achstetten Bronnen 3. Greece: Aveope SA, 40 M. Botsari, G–151–21 Pefki. The Netherlands: Hansje Kalff Meubelagenturen, Puttensestraat 8, 1181 Je Amstelveen. Portugal: Galante Interior Design, Rua Borges, Carneiro 49/55, P–1200, Lisbon. Spain: Santa & Cole, Blames 71, E–8440 Cardedeu, Barcelona. Sweden: Mobile Box AB, Nybrogatan 11, 11439 Stockholm. Switzerland: Yves Humbrecht Diffusion, Mon Repos 3, 1066 Epalinges. UK: SCP Ltd, 135–139 Curtain Road, London EC2. USA/Canada: I.L. Euro Inc., 9000 Broadway 902, New York, NY.

Carnegie, 110 N. Centre Avenue, Rockville Centre, New York, NY 11570, USA. *Outlet* Switzerland: Création Baumann, Weberei und Farbrei AG, CH–4901 Langenthal.

Casa Artiach SA, 8 Trabajo, Zaragoza 50008, Zaragoza, Spain.

Casas, Poligono Santa Rita Dinamica 1, Castellbisbal 08755, Barcelona, Spain. *Outlets* Austria: Josef Schlenkert, Franziskanerplatz 8, Langenlois. Belgium: Quattro Benelux, Ltenaken 11, Hoegaarden 3320. Denmark: Ingterstudio, Lüdersvej 4, Frihaven 2100, Copenhagen. Finland: Artek, Hiekkakiventie 3, 00710 Helsinki. France: Sedec, PC D'Activité de la Slagne 70, 06120 Mandelieu Cedex. Germany: Design Focus GmbH, Postfach 2101, 5042 Erfstadt. Japan: Aichi Co. Ltd, 27–25 Tsutsui, 3–chome, Higashi-ku, Nagoya. Portugal: Intr. Mobiliario, Rua David de Sousa, 10 2a Esqu, Lisbon. Singapore: Nobel des & Centrs Pte, 134 Joo Seng Road, 1336. Switzerland: Vias AG, Leutschenbachstr 46, Zurich 8050. Taiwan: Enform, 2 F1–1, No. 62, Fu Shing Road, Taipei. UK: Acanthus, The Studio, Old Scriven, North Yorkshire, HG5 9DY. USA: I.C.F., 10 Maple Street, Norwood, NJ 07648–2004.

Cassina SpA, via Busnelli 1, Meda 20036, Milan, Italy. *Outlets* Japan: Cassina Japan Inc., 2–9–6 Higashi, Shibuya-ku, Tokyo 150. The Netherlands: Mobica, 50 Gossetlaan, Groot-Bijgaarden 1720, Belgium. USA: Cassina Usa Inc., 200 McKay Road, Huntington, New York, NY 11746.

Ceccotti Aviero SpA, viale Sicilia 4, Cascina 56021, Pisa, Italy. *Outlets* Germany: Idea Design Agentur, Jurgen Brandt, 16 Peter Schlemihl Strasse, 81337 Munich. Japan: Takayuki Araki Banri Co. Ltd, 1–5–22 Higashigaoka Meguro KU, Tokyo 152. Spain: Indefil – Juan Torrent, 11 Gibarna sl Tres Torres, Barcelona 08017.

Ceramica Il Coccio, via della Lora 35, Barberino di Mugello (GI) 50031, Italy.

Sophie Chandler, 257 Kennington Lane, London SE11 5QU, UK.

Peter Christian, Christian Stuart Partnership, 51 Arthur Court, Charlotte Despard Avenue, London SW11 5JA, UK.

Consolidated & Technical, 8A Maude Road, London SE5 8NY, UK.

Anne Crowther, 21 All Saints Road, Bradford, West Yorkshire, BD7 3AY, UK.

Custom Plastics, 11112 South Western, Oklahoma City, OK 73170, USA.

David Design, 25 Stortorget, Malmö 21134, Sweden. *Outlets* France: Günter Pommerenchu, 3 rue de l'Arrivée, Paris 75015. Germany: Ingrid Strube, Nordwohlde 117, 27211 Bassum; Creative Collection, Nadege Commandoux, Brüsselerstrasse 16, 50674 Cologne. Italy:

Hoffmann, via Belzoni 4, Cadoneghe 35010. Japan: T.Form, 15–34 Kozu-cho, 3–chome, Chuo-ku, Osaka 542. Scandinavia: T.W.O., 68 Artillerigaton, Stockholm, Sweden. UK: SCP Ltd, 135–139 Curtain Road, London EC2A 3BX.

Michele de Lucchi, via Pallavicino 31, 20145 Milan, Italy.

De Padova, Corso Venezia 14, 20121 Milan, Italy. *Outlets* Belgium: Rika Andreas, 144 Thurnhoutsebaan, Antwerp 02140. Denmark: Paustian, 2 Kalkchaenderiloe Chskaj, Copenhagen 02100. Germany: Andrea Frandschek, 11 Wiedersbacherstrasse, Nuremberg 90449. Japan: Interdecor, 2–6–9 Higashi, Shibuya-ku, Tokyo. The Netherlands: Hansje Kalff, 8 de Boog, MN Schagen 1714. Spain: Gibarna SL (Indefil), 11.1 Tres Torres, Barcelona 08017. UK: Aram Design Limited, 3 Kean Street, Covent Garden, London WC1B 4AJ. USA: Luminaire, 7300 45 Street, Miami, FL 33155.

Design Gallery Milano, via Manzoni 46, 20121 Milan, Italy.

Design in the Round, 502 Nelson Road, Mt Nelson, Tasmania, Australia.

DesignTex, 200 Varick Street, New York, NY 10014, USA. *Outlets* Australia: Mirabilis Textiles, 3/58 Garden Street, South Yarra, Victoria 3141. Canada: DesignTex Fabrics, 22 Wilcox Court, Whitby, Ontario LIN 9A2. Hong Kong: Springs Textiles, 1/F Decca Industrial Building, 12 Kut Shing Street, Chalwan. Japan: Fujie Textiles, No. 7–12 4-chome, Sendagaya, Shimuya-ku, Tokyo 151. Philippines: Ergonomic Systems, 2634 Rockefeller Street, Makati Metro, Manila. Singapore: Businessworld Services, 5 Temasek Boulevard No. 04–02/03, Suntec City Tower, Singapore 0103. Taiwan: Springs Textiles Taiwan, 10th F2, No. 7–57, Sec. 2, Tun Hwa S. Road, Taipei. Thailand: Modernform Group, 81–16 Srinakarindr Road, Bangkok 10250. UK: Tyndale Solutions, 15 St Mark's Rise, London E8 2NL.

Designvertrieb, 2 Petersburger Platz, Berlin 10249, Germany.

Gabriele de Vecchi, via Lombardini 20, Milan 20143, Italy.

Di'[sain] Hagn & Kubala OEG, Zieglergasse 69, A–1070 Vienna, Austria. *Outlet* France: Axis, Impasse Rohry, Villejuif 94800.

Disibeint Electronics, 91 Segle XX, Barcelona 08032, Spain.

DMD-Developing Manufacturing Distribution, Partweg 14, 2271 AJ Voorburg, The Netherlands. *Outlets* Italy: Dovetusai, via Sannio 24, 20137 Milan. The Netherlands: Mobach, 5 Portengen, Kockengen 3628. Scandinavia: Dawson, 158 Postboks, Copenhagen 1005, Denmark. UK: Space, 28 All Saints Road, London W11 1HG. USA: Moss Ltd, 146 Greene Street, New York, NY 10012.

Driade SpA (Aleph), via Padana Inferiore 12, 29012 Fossadello di Caorso, Piacenza, Italy. *Outlets* France: Arturo Del Punta, 7 rue Simon Le France, 75004 Paris. Germany: Stefan Müller, Bereiteranger 7, 8000 Munich 90. Japan: Ambiente International Inc., Sumitomo Semei Building, 3–1–30 Minami-Aoyama, Minato-ku, Tokyo. The Netherlands/Belgium: Espaces & Lignes, 55 rue Ulensm, Brussels. Scandinavia: Design Distribution, Doebelnsgatan 36D 1, 11352 Stockholm, Sweden. Spain: Sellex, 84 Donosti Ibilbidea Poligono 2, Astigarraga 20115. UK: Viaduct Furniture Ltd, Spring House, 10 Spring Place, London NW5 3BH.

Erwin Driessens, Maria Verstappen, Sarphatistraat 410, 1018 GW Amsterdam, The Netherlands.

Droog Design, 518 Keizersgracht, Amsterdam 1017 ER, The Netherlands.

Edda Design, 26–36 Avda Montliriol, Sant Fost. Camp 08105, Barcelona, Spain.

Edizioni Galleria Colombari, via Solferino 24, Milan 20121, Italy.

Edra, PO Box 28, 56030 Perignano (PI), Italy.

Electronica Escuder SL, S/N Partida Sobrevejla, Benicarlo 12580, Castellon, Spain.

Emform, Urwald Strasse 8, 26342 Bockhorn, Germany.

Equilibrium (division of Studio Edward van Vliet), WG Plein 61–62, 1054 RB Amsterdam, The Netherlands.

F. Fabbian & Fratelli Snc, via S. Brigida 50, Resana 31020, Treviso, Italy. *Outlets* Japan: F. Fabbian Lighting Asia Ltd, Mita Kokusai Building, 1–4–28 Mita, Minato-ku. New Zealand: F. Fabbian Lighting NZ Ltd, 5 Cleveland Road, Parnell, Auckland.

Farallon Computing Inc., 2470 Mariner Square Loop, Almeda, CA 94501, USA.

Faraone, via Montenapoleone 7/A, Milan I–20121, Italy.

Feldmann & Schultchen, 53c Peutestrasse, Hamburg D–20539, Germany.

Fermob, ZI St Didier BP 8, 01140 Thoissey, France.

Fiam Italia SpA, Chiara del Vecchio, Conseil, 38 Vitruvio, Milan 20124, Italy. *Outlets* France: Guy Favali, 15 rue Reynaud de Trets, Marseilles 13010. Germany: Klaus Beckord, 21 Lehmkuhlstrasse, Bad Salzuflen 32108. Japan: Italprogram, 43/a E. Bertini, Forlì 47100, Italy. The Netherlands: Mobica BV, m 38/a Industrieweg, Ma Ijsselstein 3401. Spain: Gibarna, 11 Tres Torres, Barcelona 08017. Switzerland: Humbrecht Diffusion, CP 4277, Morges 1110. UK: Bianchi Furniture Traders, Manley House, 2 High View, Hitchin, Herts SG5 2HL. USA: Forma & Design, Shore Point, One Selleck Street, Norwalk, CT 06855.

Diana Firth, 91a Westend Road, Auckland 1002, New Zealand.

Siggi Fischer, 14 Wittenstein Strasse 144, Wuppertal 42285, Germany.

Flos SpA, via Angelo Faini 2, Bovezzo 25073, Brescia, Italy. *Outlets* Austria: Giovanni Marelli, via Oberdam 5, 20036 Meda (MI), Italy. France: Flos SARL, rue de Bicêtre 5, 94240 L'Hay Les Roses. Germany: Graf Bethusy HUC, Vertriebs GmbH, Laerchenstrasse 24, 82152 Krailling. Spain: On Off SL, Tudona 19, San Just Desvern, 08960 Barcelona. Scandinavia: Interstudio A/S, Pakhus 12, Dampfaergevej 10, 2100 Copenhagen, Denmark. Slovenia/Croatia: Guido Vittori, Stradone della Mainizza 130, 34170 Gorizia, Italy. Switzerland: P.M. Trembley, 75 Boulevard St Georges, 1205 Geneva. UK: MC Innes Cook, 31 Lisson Grove, London NW1 6UV. USA: Flos Inc., 200 McKay Road, Huntingdon Station, New York, NY 11746.

Foscarini Murano SpA, Fondamenta Manin No. 1, 31041 Murano (Venezia), Italy. *Outlets* Canada: Agences Volt., 68 rue Alie Dollard Des Ormeaux, Québec H9A 1H1. France/The Netherlands: Horas International, 22 rue Copernic Copernicusstraat, B–1180 Brussels, Belgium. Germany: Altalinea GmbH, Sandhof 6, 41469 Neuss-Norf. UK: Catalytico Ltd, 25 Montpelier Street, London SW7 1HF. Taiwan: H.N. Lin Enterprise Co. Ltd, 32 Chin Shan S. Rd, Sec 1. Taipei, ROC. USA: Italiana Luce USA Inc., 400 Long Beach Boulevard, Stratford, CT 06497.

Fou du Roi, 7 rue de Sarrebourg, Strasbourg, France.

Susie Freeman, 71 Sheffield Terrace, London W8 7NB, UK.

Frezza srl, via Ferret, 11/9, 31020 Vidor-Treviso, Italy.

John Frietas, 191 Taunton R8, Bridgwater, Somerset, UK.

Michal Fronek and Jan Nemecek, Libensky Ostrov 7555, Prague 8, Czech Republic 18000.

Fürst & Patte, 30 Hellabrunnerstrasse, Munich 81543, Germany.

Fusital srl, via Comcordia 16, Renate 20055, Milan, Italy. *Outlets* Austria: Valli & Valli GmbH, Mayrwiesstrasse 12, 05300 Hallwang, Salzburg. Belgium: Vali & Valli NV, Koningin Astridlaan 2, 02550 Kontich/Antwerp. Germany: Valli & Valli GmbH & Co., KG, Industriestrasse 1, 74206 Bad Wimpfen. UK: Valli & Valli Ltd, 8 Lichfield Road, Tamworth, Staffordshire B79. USA: Valli & Valli (USA) Inc., PO Box 245, 1540 Highland Avenue, Duarte, CA 91009–0245.

Global Village Communication, 1144 East Argues Avenue, Sunnyvale, CA 94086, USA.

Natanel Gluska, Renggerstrasse 85, 8038 Zurich, Switzerland.

GN Netcom A/S, 4 Bispevej, Copenhagen NV, 2400, Denmark.

Goods, Prinsengracht 218, 1016 HD Amsterdam, The Netherlands. *Outlets* Denmark: Dawson, PO Box 158, 1005 Copenhagen. Germany: Details, Martinsfeld 17, 50676 Cologne. Italy: Dovetusai, via Sannio 24, 20137 Milan. Sweden: Biondi, Eriksgatan 6, 72460 Vasteras.

Goto, Massimo Lunardon Glass Collection, via Mottarello 6, 36060 Molvena (VI), Italy.

T. Grau KG GmbH & Co., 18 Borselstrasse, Hamburg 22765, Germany.

Hafenatelier, (Christof Schwarz) 6 Neustädter Neuerweg, Hamburg 20459, Germany.

Halifax srl, via Furlanelli 96, Giussano 20034, Milan, Italy.

Hamai Factory Inc., Tachibana Building 7F, 2–11–20 Sangenchaya, Setagaya-ku, Tokyo 154, Japan.

H–Design Associates Inc., No. 303, 2–31–21 Jingumae, Shibuya-ku 150, Tokyo, Japan.

Jochen Henkels, 15 Gaupstrasse, Hamburg 22765, Germany.

Hewlett Packard Company, 3000 Hanover, Palo Alto, CA 94304, USA.

Hishinuma Institute Co. Ltd, 5–41–2 Jingumae, Shibuya-ku, Tokyo 150, Japan.

Holmes Product Corporation, 233 Furtune Boulevard, Milford, MA 01757, USA.

Horm srl, via Crocera di Corva 25, Azzano Decimo 33082, Italy. *Outlets* Denmark: Don Batchelor, 25 Vidnaesdal, Holte 2840. France: SEDEC, Parc d'Activités de L.S., Mandelieu 06212. Germany: Andreas Jaek, 3 Neue Strasse, Oldenburg 26122. Japan: Actus, 2–19–15 Shinjuku, Shinjuku-ku, Tokyo 160. The Netherlands: Kos BV, Rokerijweg, Huizen 1270 AH. Spain: Aranzadi Hnos, 35

c/Gorriti, Pamplona 31004. UK: Purves & Purves, 83 Tottenham Court Road, London W1P 9HD. USA: Luminaire Inc., 7300 SW 45 Street, Miami, FL 33155.

David Huycke, 160 Bekelstraat, Sint-Niklaas 9100, Belgium.

I & I, via Giordano Bruno 12, Milan 20154, Italy.

IKEA, Box 702, 34381 Älmhult, Sweden.

Inflate, 5 Old Street, London EC1V 9HL, UK.

Ingenieria de Control SA, C/. Morgades 48 I.I., Vic 08500, Barcelona, Spain.

Inredningsform AB, PO Box 5055, Malmö S–20071, Sweden. *Outlets* France: Transat SARL, 53 Route de Fournes, Erquingham Le Sec, F–59320. Germany: Treforma 17, Glockengiesserwass 17, Hamburg D–20095. Hungary: Nordhouse Ltd, 36–3 Diosaruk, Budapest H1125. Japan: Toshiaki Takigami, Skauidto Mansion 103, 4–40–5 Honcho, Shibuya-ku, Tokyo 151. Spain: Scaridesa, 8 Pasaje de Dona Carlota, Madrid E–28002. USA: Liurn Co., 290 Townsend Street, San Francisco, CA 94107.

Interlübke Gebr. Lübke GmbH & Co., KG, 145 Ringstrasse, Rheda-WiedenbrÅck 33378, Germany.

Itachair SpA, via Fornaci 45, Rovereto 38068, Trento, Italy.

I Tre srl, via della Industrie 16/c, 30030 Salzano, VE, Italy.

Camille Jacobs, 143 Middle Harbour Road, East Lindfield 2070, Sydney, NSW, Australia.

Hans Jakobsen, 41 Braenshoy 2700, Denmark.

Kartell SpA, via dell Industrie 1, 20082 Noviglio, Milan, Italy. *Outlets* Australia: Plastex, 85 Fairbank Road, 3168 Clayton, Victoria. Austria: Eugen Leopold, Fielderstrasse 2–4, 4020 Linz. Belgium: Tradix SA, 90–02 rue du Mail, 1050 Brussels. Denmark: Collection Creative Danas Plads 15, 2000 Frederiksberg. France: C & D Diffusion SARL, 3 avenue du Bois Vert, 77240 Vert-Saint-Denis. Germany: Gotthilf Riexinger, Vorstadt 7, 7034 Gärtringen. Hong Kong: William Artists International Ltd, 232 Aberdeen Main Road, 3/F Shing Dao, Aberdeen. Japan: Interdecor Inc., 2–9–6 Higashi, Shibuya-ku, Tokyo 150. The Netherlands: Modular Systems, Bosboom Toussaintstraat 24, 1054 Amsterdam. Portugal: Grup Dimensao SA, Av. Eng. Arantes E Oliveira 5, 1900 Lisbon. Spain: Jordi Rotger, Zaragoza 62, 8008 Barcelona. Sweden: Claes Brechensbauer, Möbelagentur, Kyrkoköpinge Pl. 26, 23191 Trelleborg. Switzerland: Gatto Diffusion, 30 rue des Chavannes, 2016 Cortaillod. UK: Environment, 120 High Street, South Milford, Leeds, West Yorkshire LS25 5AQ. USA: I.L. Euro Inc., 900 Broadway 902, New York, NY 10003.

Masafumi Katsukawa, via Marchesi de Taddei 18, 20146 Milan, Italy.

Eleanor Kearney, Unit 10, Cockpit Work Shops, Cockpit Yard, Northington Street, London WC1N 2NP, UK.

Kimura Glass Co. Ltd, 3–10–7, Yushima, Bunkyo-ku 113, Tokyo, Japan.

Knoll Textiles, 105 Wooster Street, New York, NY 10012, USA.

Koziol GmbH, 90 W.V. Siemens Strasse, Erbach 64711, Germany. *Outlets* Belgium: Zet BVBA, 98 Noorderlaan, Antwerp 2030. France: Vesa, 14 Allée des Fongeres, Paris 93340. Italy: Anteprima srl,

via Fonseca Pimentel 11/7, 20127 Milan. Japan: Shimada Internati Ing., 15F Canal Tower, Tokyo 103. The Netherlands: Copi, 24B Stadhouderskade, Amsterdam 1054 ES. Scandinavia: Lisbeth Dahl, 8B Harmsdorthsvej, Frederiksberg 1874, Denmark. Spain: Pilma Disseny SA, 20 Valencia, Barcelona 08015. Switzerland: Samei AG, 16 Oberdorf Strasse, Wädenswil 8820. UK: Environment, 120 High Street, Leeds LS25 5AQ. USA: Robert Greenfield Ltd, 225 Fifth Avenue, New York, NY 10010.

Thomas Krause, 8 Bassett Road, London W10 6JJ, UK.

Lammhults Möbel AB, Box 26, S–360 30 Lammhult. *Outlets* Australia: Mid Design, Shed 8, Cowper Street, Victoria Dock, Melbourne, Victoria 3000. Denmark: Collection Creative, St Kongensgade 36–38, DK 1264 Copenhagen K. Finland: Nomart Oy, Merikasarminkatu 6, SF–00160 Helsingfors. France: Agence Frédéric Cabantous SARL., 30 rue de L'Eglise, F–94300 Vincennes. Germany: Lammhults Möbel, Käthe-Niederkirchner-Strasse 10, Prenzlauer Berg, D–10407 Berlin. Italy: Francesco Pessina, Rapsel SpA, via Volta 13, I–20019 Settimo Milanese (MI). Japan: Royal Furniture Collection, Sweden Centre Building, 1st Floor, 6–11–9 Roppongi, Minato-ku, Tokyo 106. The Netherlands/Belgium: Agencies for Design, 't Diepe 10, NL–5404 KB Uden. Norway: Berg Studio, Nobelsgt 18, N–0268 Oslo. Switzerland: Pur Handelsagentur, Südstrasse 24a, CH–4900 Langenthal. Spain: Oken, Strauss S/N Pol. Ind. Can Jardf, E–0891 Rubi. USA: OCF, International Contract Furnishings Inc., 10 Maple Street, Norwood, NJ 07648.

Lawrence Laske, 1000 Springhaven Drive, Libertyville, IL 60048, USA.

Jennifer Lee, 16 Talfourd Road, London SE15 5NY, UK. *Outlets* USA: James Graham and Sons, 1014 Madison Avenue, New York, NY 10021.

Jürgen Lehl Co. Ltd, Kiuosumi 3–1–7, Koto-ku, Tokyo 135, Japan.

Lifeline Systems Inc., 640 Memorial Drive, Cambridge, MA 02139, USA.

Living Divani srl, Strada del Cavolto 15, Anzano D. Parco 22040, Como 22100, Italy.

Loewe Opta GmbH, 11 Industriestrasse, Kronach 96317, Germany. *Outlets* France: Loewe Opta France SA, 16–18 rue des Oliviers, Thiasis F–94657 Cedex. Italy: General Trading Trust SpA, via Ponte a Giogoli 125, Sesto Fiorentino I–50019. The Netherlands: Loewe Opta Benelux NV/SA, 44 Lt. Lippenslaan, Antwerp B–2140, Belgium. Spain: Gaplasa SA, 25 Conde de Torroja, Madrid E–29022. UK: LINN Products Ltd, Floors Road, Waterfoot, Glasgow, Scotland.

Logitech, 6505 Kaiser Drive, Fremont, CA 94555, USA.

Luceplan SpA, via E. T. Moneta 44/46, 20161 Milan, Italy. *Outlets* Austria: Lindmaier Möbel & Leuchten, Silbergasse 6, 1190 Vienna. Australia/Singapore: Ke-Zu Pty Ltd, 95 Beattie Street, Balmain, NSW 2041. Belgium: Sisterco SA/NV, Altenaken 11, 3320 Hoegaarden. Brazil: Broadway Ind Coms S, Rua des Crisandalias 104, Jardim das Acacias, São Paulo, CEP 04704–020. Denmark: Finn Sloth APS, Heilsmindevej 1 2920 Charlottenlund. France: Arelux, Zac Paris Nord II, 13 rue de la Perdrix, 93290 Tremblay-en-France. Germany: Agentur Holger Werner GmbH, Nachtigallenweg 1c, D–61462 Koenigstein/TS (postal districts 1,4,5,6); Doris Schmidt Agentur für Licht und Möbeldesign, Johannesweg 1, D–33803 Steinhagen (postal districts 2,3); Robert Karl Karo, Amalienstrasse 69, D–80799 Munich. Hong Kong: Artemide Ltd, 102–103 Ruttonjee Centre, 11

Duddell Street, Central Hong Kong. Japan: Casa Luce Inc., 3–16–12 Sotokanda, Chiyoda-ku, Tokyo 101. The Netherlands: Simon Eikelenboom BV, Keomembergweg 54, 1101 GC Amsterdam ZO. Spain: Rotger, C/Nou 8, 00870 Garraf, Barcelona. Sweden: Annell Lluis & Forum AB, Surbrunnsgatan 14, 11421 Stockholm. Switzerland: Andome Engros, Eigentalstrasse 17, 8425 Oberembrach. USA: Luceplan, 900 Broadway No. 902, New York, NY 10003.

Lunar Design, 237 Hamilton Avenue, Palo Alto, CA 94301, USA

Luzon GmbH & Co., 53 Muenchner Strasse, Hohenschaeftlarm 82069, Germany.

Magis srl, 15 Magnadola, Motta di Livenza 31045, Reeviso, Italy.

Michael Marriott, Units No. 4 & 6, Ellsworth Street, Bethnal Green, London E2 AEX, UK.

Jonathan Marshall, 58A Ormiston Grove, London W12 0JS, UK.

Andrew Martin, 22 rue du FBG Monmartre, Paris 75009, France.

Matsushita Communication Industrial Co. Ltd, 600 Yokohama 226, Kanagawa, Japan.

Matsushita Electric Industrial Co. Ltd, 1–4 Matsuo-cho, Kadoma City 571, Osaka, Japan. *Outlets* Canada: Matsushita Electric of Canada Ltd, 1475 The Queensway, Toronto, M8Z IT3 Ontario. France: Panasonic France SA, 932–938 Avenue de Président Wilson, 1a Plaine Saint Denis 270, Cedex. Germany: Panasonic Deutschland, 22525 Winsbergring, Hamburg 54. Hong Kong: Shun Hing Electronic Trading Co. Ltd, New East Ocean Centre 14th–15th Floors, 9 Science Museum, Kowloon. Italy: Panasonic Italia SpA, via Lucini 19, 20125 Milan. Scandinavia: Panasonic Svenska AB, Fitta Backe 3, Norsborg 145, 84 Stockholm, Sweden. Spain: Panasonic Sales Spain SA, 20–30 Plantas 4, Josep Taradellas, 5Y608029 Barcelona. UK: Panasonic House, Willoughby Road, Bracknell, Berkshire RG12 8FP. USA: Matsushita Electric Corporation of America, 1 Panasonic Way, Secacus, NJ 07094.

Matsushita-Kotobuki Electronics Industries Ltd, Office Equipment Division, 247 Fukutake, Saijo City 793, Ehime, Japan. *Outlet* USA: Panasonic Company, Division of Matsushita Electric Company, 1 Panasonic Way, Secacus, NJ 07094.

Ingo Maurer GmbH, 47 Kaiserstrasse, 80801 Munich, Germany. *Outlets* France: Altras SARL, 24 rue Lafitte, 75009 Paris. Japan: Studio Noi Co. Ltd, Rangee Aoyama Building, No. 710, 1–4–1 Kita-Aoyama, Minato-ku, Tokyo 107. The Netherlands: Inter Collections BV, 2 Bosrand Schiedam 3121 XA. Scandinavia: Mr Finn Sloth, 1 Heilsmindevej, Charlottenlund, Denmark 2920. Spain: Santa & Cole, 71 Balmes, 08440 Carcedeu, Barcelona.

MDF srl, via Wittgens 3, 20123 Milan, Italy.

Megalit, Z.I. du Breuil, B.P. 55, 18400 Saint Florent sur Cher, France. *Outlets* Germany: Alleinvertrieb, Artemide GmbH, Itterpark 5, 40724 Hilden. Italy: Artemide SpA, via Bergamo 18, 20010 Pregnana Milanese (Mi). UK: Artemide GB Ltd, 323 City Road, London EC1V 1LJ.

Eva-Maria Melchers, 39–40 Schlachte, Bremen 28195, Germany. *Outlets* Italy: Edizioni Galleria Colombari, via Solferino 37, 20121 Milan; Antonia Jannone, Disegni di Architettura, Corso Garibaldi 125, 20121 Milan. France: Galerie Néotù, 25 rue du Renard, 75004 Paris. UK: David Gill, Decorative and Fine Arts, 60 Fulham Road, London SW3 6HH. USA: Galerie Néotù, 133 Greene Street, New York, NY 10012.

Mobles 114, 114 Enric Granados, Barcelona 08008, Spain. *Outlets* Austria: Josef Schlenkert, 8 Franziskanerplatz, Langenlis 3550. Denmark: Casa Lab, Mosebakken 19, DK–2830 Virum, Copenhagen. Germany: Elmar Flototto Handelsagentur, Haupstrasse 70, 33397 Rietberg. Italy: Dessie srl, via di Moriano 831, I–55100 Lucca. Portugal: Altamire Mobiliario, Rua Viriato 23, P–1000 Lisbon. The Netherlands: Quattro Benelux, 11 Altenaken, Hoegaardenm 3320, Belgium. Switzerland: Claudia Marlier, Rebbergstrasse 40, CH–8102 Oberengstringen. UK: Unit 23 Abbeville Mews, 88 Clapham Park Road, London SW4 7BX.

Modulor SA, 4070 Elpidio Gonzalez, Buenos Aires, 1407, Argentina.

Montis, 2 Steenstraat, Dongen 5107, The Netherlands. *Outlets* France: Jerome Pecknard, 20 avenue de la belle Gabrielle, Nogent sur Marne, F–94130. Germany: Montis Deutschland GmbH, 13 Adolf Kolpingstrasse, Ostercappeh 49179. Switzerland: Martin Stegmann, 24a Suedstrasse, Langenthal, CH–4900. UK: Viaduct, 1–10 Summers Street, London EC1R 5BD. USA: Montis America Inc., 7591 PO Box High Point, NC 27264.

Simon Moore (London) Ltd, Unit Z, Union Court, London SW4 6JH, UK.

Moorman Möbel Produktions und Handels GmbH, Kirchplatz, Aschau 1 ch 83229, Germany. *Outlets* Italy: Hoffmann srl, via Belzani 4, Cadoneghe 35010. Japan: Cross Sult Consultancy, 4 Hinter der Heck, Eschborn 65760, Germany. The Netherlands: Kreymborg, 63 Minervalaan, Amsterdam 1077. Switzerland: Andome Engros, 17 Eigentalstrasse, Oberembrach 8425.

Motorola, 50 E. Commerce Drive No. M1, Schaumburg 60173, Italy, USA.

Murano Due srl, via delle Industrie 16, 30030 Salzano (VE), Italy.

Naturquell SA, 2 Prager Strasse, Leingarten 74 211, Germany.

Mikala Naur, 37 GL Mont, Copenhagen 1117 K, Denmark.

Nava Design SpA, 5 M. Lutero, Milan 20126, Italy. *Outlets* France: Creatives, 6 Lauriston, Paris 75116. Germany: Marie & Weber GmbH, 1a Unterm Sand, Leimen D–69181. Japan: Interdecor/ Casatec Ltd, 2–9–6 Higashi Shibuya-ku, Tokyo 150. The Netherlands: 63 Minervalaan, Amsterdam

1077 NR. Scandinavia: Anesco Scandinavia, 26A Baldershoj, Ishoj, Copenhagen DK–2653, Denmark. Spain: Comabella, 99–101, 64 Zamora, Barcelona 08018. UK: B2B Ltd, Pattishall, Northampton NN12 8NA.

NEC Corporation, 7–1 Shiba 5-chome, Minato-ku, Tokyo 108–01, Japan.

Guido Niest A.T.E.L.I.E.R., viale Kennedy 10, Bregnano 22070, Como, Italy. *Outlet* USA: Sabrina Creative Productions, Albertine C. Niest, 4127 Wilbur Drive, Columbus, GA 31901.

Nuno Corporation, Axis B1 5–17–1 Roppongi, Minato-ku 106, Tokyo, Japan. *Outlet* USA: Nuno N.Y., D & D Building 2nd Floor, 979 Third Avenue, New York, NY 10022.

Nuova Metalmobile, Loc. Belvedere, Colle Val D'Elsa (SI), Italy.

Nya Nordiska, An den Ratswiesen, Dannenberg D–29451, Germany. *Outlets* Austria: Theodor Jandl, Boltzmanngasse 12, A–1090 Vienna. Belgium: Etienne u. Didier Peeters, Kapucinessenstraat 37, B–2000 Antwerp. Canada: Primavera, Interior Access, 160 Pears Avenue No. 111, Toronto, Ontario M5R 1T2. Finland: Runar Hagen, Ståhlbergsvägen 6 D 37, SF 00570 Helsinki. France: Nya Nordiska – France i.s., 86 rue du Cherche-Midi, F–75006 Paris. Italy: Nya Nordiska Italia srl, Piazza San Alessandro 4, I–20123 Milan. The Netherlands: G.J.M. de Rie, Dirck van Deelenstraat 1, NL–5246 HC Rosmalen. Norway: Anette Holmen, Josefines Gt. 37, N–0351 Oslo. Sweden: Erik M. Andersen, Grev Tureg 57, S–11438 Stockholm. Switzerland: H.P. Gehri, Sägegasse 2, CH–3110 Münsingen. USA: Randolph & Hein, 1 Arkansas Street, San Francisco, CA 94107.

Octo Corporation, 27 Dampfaergevej, Copenhagen 2100, Denmark.

Oggetti Latini srl, via Tadino 24, Milan 20124, Italy.

Olgoj Chorchoj, 1555 Libensky Ostrov, Prague 8, 1800 00, Czech Republic.

Olimpia Splendid SpA, via Guido Rossa, Gualtieri, Reggio Emilia 42044, Italy. *Outlets* France: Alpatec SA, BP 6, avenue du Jura, Bons en Chablais 74890. UK: Rapid Heat and Building, 423 Becontree Avenue, Dagenham BM8 3UH.

Ing. C. Olivetti & Co. SpA, 77 G. Jervis, Ivrea 10015, Turin, Italy.

Opos, via Ermenegildo Cantoni 3, Milan, Italy.

Oracle, 500 Oracle Parkway, Redwood Shores, CA 94065, USA.

Orrefors-Kosta Boda AB, Orrefors 380 40, Sweden. *Outlets* Belgium: Stenver-Engel SA, avenue Louis Lepoutre 97, B–1060 Brussels. Canada: Continental Tableware Inc., Belcroft, Gilford, Ontario LOL 1RO. Denmark: Scandi Salg Aps, Lyngbygaardsvej 38, DK–8220 Brabrand. Finland: Olle Nygard Oy, Panimokatu IG Pb 52, Fin–00581 Helsinki. France: AG Distribution, 8 rue Martel, F–75010 Paris. Germany/Austria: Mercantile, Edgar Lindenau GmbH, Robert-Koch-Strasse 4, D–82145 Planegg/Munich. Hong Kong: Scandinavia Arts Ltd, 228 Prince's Building, Central Hong Kong. Italy: Messulam SpA, via Rovigno 13, I–20125, Milan. Japan: J. Isawa & Co. Ltd, 2–8 Shibaura 4–chome, Minato-ku, Tokyo 108. The Netherlands: Bertrams BV, Gaspeldoornstraat 6, NL–5062 AC Oisterwijk. Norway: Skanform AS, Uranienborgveien I, N–0351 Oslo. Singapore: Pacific Kigyo Enterprise(S) Pte Ltd, 545 Orchard Road No. 11–01, Far East Shopping Centre. Taiwan: The Eslite Corporation, 1F, 249 Tun

Hua South Road, Section 1, Taipei. Spain: Riera Internacional SA, Vilmari 72, SP–08015 Barcelona 15. Switzerland: Royal Copenhagen (Schweiz) AG, Bachstrasse 72m, CH–5034 Suhr. UK: Dexam International Ltd, Haslemere, Surrey GU27 3QR.

Gianni Orsini, 29 Westlandseweg, Delft 2624 AB, The Netherlands.

Packard Bell, 1 Packard Bell Way, Sacramento, CA 91362, USA.

Philips International BV, Building SX, PO Box 518, 1 Glaslaan, Eindhoven 5600 MD, The Netherlands. *Outlets* France: SA Philips Industrielle et Commerciale, 51 rue Carnot, PO Box 306, 92156 Suresnes Cedex. Germany: Philips GmbH – U.B. Elektro-Hausgeräte, Hammerbrookstrasse 69, 20097 Hamburg; Postfach 10 48 49, 20033 Hamburg. Italy: Philips SpA, Piazza IV Novembre 3, PO Box 3992, 20124 Milan. Japan: Philips K.K. Kaden Division, Philips Building, 13–37 Kohnan, 2–chome Minato-ku, Tokyo 108. The Netherlands: Philips Nederland BV, Boschdijk 525, Gebouw VB–10, 5621 JG Eindhoven. Spain: Philips Iberica S.A.E., Martinez Villergas 2, Apartado 2065, Madrid 28027. Sweden: Philips Hushallsapparater AB, Kottbygatan 7, 16485 Stockholm. UK: Philips Electronics, PO Box 298, City House 420–430 London Road, Croydon CR9 3QR.

Andrea Ponsi, via Laura 18R, 50121 Florence, Italy.

Louis Poulsen & C., A/S, 11 Nyhavn, DK–1001 Copenhagen K, Denmark. *Outlets* Australia: Louis Poulsen Lightmakers Pty Ltd, 755–759 Botany Road, Roseberry, NSW 2018. Finland: Louis Poulsen OY, Kanavaranta 3 D 9 SF 00160 Helsinki. France: Louis Poulsen & Cie SARL, 128 bis avenue Jean Jaures, F–94851d Ivry sur Seine Cedex. Germany: Louis Poulsen & Co. GmbH, Postfach 1563, D–42379 Haan. Japan: Louis Poulsen Japan KK, 2–11–13 Higashiazabu, Minato-ku, Tokyo 106. The Netherlands: Louis Poulsen BV, Paredlaan 26, 2132 WS Hoofddorp. Norway: Louis Poulsen & Co., A/S, Lillakerveien 2, Boks 102, Lilleaker, N–0216 Oslo 2. Sweden: Louis Poulsen AB, Box 514, S–183 25 Taby. Switzerland: Louis Poulsen AG, Neue Winterthurerstrasse 28, CH–8304 Wallisellen-Zurich. USA: Poulsen Lighting Inc., 5407 NW 163 Street, Miami, FL 33014–6130.

P.P. Mobler, 30 Toftevej, Allerod 3450, Denmark.

Prandina srl, via Capitelvecchio 5, Bassano del Grappa 36061 (VI), Italy. *Outlets* Germany/Benelux: Prandina BV, De Koumen 86, NL–06433 KE Heerlen. The Netherlands: Lancari, Rua do Campo Alegre 1380 HAB 124, Porto. Spain: Kambi Iluminacion, Blay Net, 35a de Correos, E–08830 Sant Boi de LL, Barcelona. UK: Forma Lighting Ltd, 52 Upper Street, London 100H. USA: Current, 1201 Western Avenue, Seattle WA.

Paul Priestman, Priestman Goode, 8 Worlds End Place, Kings Road, London SW10 0HE, UK.

Produzione Privata SAS e Pintacuda, via Pallavicino 31, Milan 20145, Italy.

Punt Mobles SL, 48 Islas Balearies, Fuente del Jarro 46988, Valencia, Spain. *Outlets* Denmark: Animex International, 103 Hasselhoej, Nivaa 2990. France: Dominique Devoto, 11 rue Azais Barthes, Beziers 34500. Germany: Creativ' Collection, 16 Brüsseler, Cologne 50674; Agentur Essenko, 57 Volkartstrasse, Munich 80636. Italy: C & C Distribuzione, 1 Localita Grand Chemin, St Christophe 11020. The Netherlands: Heneka & Golschmodt, 104 Eerste Cons Huygensstrasse, Amsterdam 1054. Sweden: Arne Dahl, 7B Strandvaegen, Stockholm 114 56. UK: Neil Rogers Interiors, 88 Clapham Park Road, London SW4 7BX.

Enrico Quell and Diego Lemme, via Senofonte 7, Milan 20145, Italy.

Radice snc, via B. Marcello 4, Milan 20124, Italy.

Radius GmbH, 145 Weisser Strasse, Cologne 50999, Germany.

Karim Rashid, 145 West 27th Street, 4e, New York, NY 10001, USA.

Reggiani Illuminazione SpA, via della Misericordia 33, Vedano al Lambro, Milan 20057, Italy.

Reichenberg Weiss, Pascalstrasse 17, D–47506 Neukirchen-Vluyn, Germany. *Outlets* Belgium: Kreymborg NV, avenue Molière Laan 66, B1160 Brussels. Germany: Schröder KG, GmbH & Co., Postfach 2627, 47726 Krefeld. Italy: De Padova srl, Coro Venezia 14, Milan I–20121. Luxembourg: Domizil by Biotop, 100 rue de Bonnevoie, L–1260. The Netherlands: Quintessens, Assumburg 152, 1081 GC Amsterdam. Switzerland: Wohnbedarf AG, Basle, Aeschenvorstadt 48, CH 4010. UK: The Conran Shop, 22 Shad Thames, London; The Home, Salts Mill, Victoria Road, Saltaire, Bradford BD18 3LD.

Richard-Ginori 1735 srl, viale Giulio Richard 1, Milan 20143, Italy.

Ann Richards, 16 Albany Road, Southsea PO5 2AB, UK.

Compania Roca Radiadores SA, 211–213 Aptdo Juan Guell, Correps 30024, Barcelona 08028, Spain. *Outlet* Italy: Roca srl, via Leonardo da Vinci 24, Casarile 20080 (MI), Italy.

Vibeke Rohland, 19 Holbergsgade, Copenhagen 1057, Denmark.

Hannes Rohringer, 38 Hauptstrasse, Seewalchen 4863, Austria.

Gary Rooney, 312A Old Brompton Road, London SW5 9JH, UK.

Rosenthal AG, 43 Wittelsbacherstrasse, Selb 95100, Bavaria, Germany.

Roset SA, BP 9, Briord 10470, France. *Outlets* Germany: Roset Möbel GmbH, Postfach 1230, Gundelfingen 79191. Italy: Roset Italia srl, via Boccaccio 43, Milan 20123. Japan: Sasai, Yachiyo-cho, Takata-Gun, Hiroshima-ken, 731–03. UK: Roset (UK) Ltd, 95A High Street, Great Missenden, Bucks HP16 0AL. USA: Roset USA Corporation, 200 Lexington Avenue, New York, NY 10016.

Michael Rowe, 24 Holyport Road, Fulham, London SW6 6LZ, UK.

Sahco Hesslein & Co., Kreuzburger Strasse, 17–19 D–90471 Nuremberg, Germany. *Outlets* Belgium: Sahco Hesslein Belgique, Louizalaan 262, avenue Louise, Brussels 1050. France: Sahco Hesslein France, 17 rue du Mail, F–75002 Paris. Hong Kong: Sahco Hesslein Kong Kong, C.E.T.E.C. Ltd, 29 Wellington Street. Italy: Sahco Hesslein Italia, via Durini 7, I–20122 Milan. Japan: Sahco Hesslein Japan, Manas Trading Inc., 5F Nissan Building, 4–21–13 Himonya, Meguro-ku, Tokyo 152. Switzerland: Sahco Hesslein Switzerland, Handelsagentur Carlo SEM, Weingitrasse 2A, CH–8004 Zurich. UK: Sahco Hesslein UK Ltd, 25 Chelsea Harbour Design Centre, Chelsea Harbour, London SW10 0XE. USA: Sahco Hesslein, Bergamo Fabrics USA, 979 Third Avenue, D & D Building 17th Floor, New York, NY 10022.

Andrea Salvetti, Loc 'Alle Borracce', 55050 Chiatri Lucca, Italy.

Salviati srl, 3831 Campo S. Angelo, S. Marco, Venice 30123, Italy.

Sambonet SpA, via XXVI Aprile 62, Vercelli 13100, Italy. *Outlets* Germany: Gehle KG, 9A Wullener Feld, Witten D–58454. Japan: Shimizu Tableware Co. Ltd, 6–4–2 Kokubo, Kofu City, Yamanashi Pref. Spain: Nimbex SA, Aptdo 295, Avda de Tarragona S/N, Vilafrance del Penedes (Barcelona) 08720. UK: Tableware International Ltd, 3 Sommers Place, London SW2 2AL. USA: Sambonet USA Inc., 1180 Mc-Lester St./Suite 8, Elisabeth, NJ 07201.

Samsung Electronics Co., 84–11 21st Floor, Yonsei Jaedan Severance Building, Seoul, Chung-ku, Namdaemoon-Ro, South Korea. *Outlet* Germany: Samsung Deutschland GmbH, 38–40 Mergenthaler Allee, Eschborn D–65760.

Saporiti Italia, via Marconi 23, Besnate 21010, Varese, Italy.

Louise Sass, 12.5 Lipkesgade, Copenhagen 2100, Denmark.

Sawaya & Moroni SpA, via Manzoni 11, 20121 Milan, Italy. *Outlets* Belgium: Top Mouton, Obterrestraat 67–69, 8994 Poperinge, Proven. France: Dominique Devoto, 11 rue Azais Barthes, 34500 Beziers. Germany: Gisela Grimm, 20 Rosengartenstrasse, 70184 Stuttgart. Switzerland: H.P. Gehri, c/o Mobilform, Sägegasse 2, CH–3110 Münsingen.

Segis SpA, via Umbria-loc. Fosci 14, Poggibonsi 53036, Sienna, Italy. *Outlets* Australia: Flair-Contract and Domestic Furniture, 8 Ipswich Street, Fyshwick, ACT 2609. Canada: Italinteriors, 1028 Mainland Street, Vancouver, BC V6B 2T4. Denmark/Sweden: Rialto v/F Marziani, viale Volontari della Liberta 26, Udine, Italy. France: Signatures, 34 avenue de l'Observatoire, Paris 75014. Germany: Möbelagentur Katia Mauro, 155 Ringstrasse, Essen/Kettwig 45219. Japan: Murata Interior Design, Myojo Building, 9th Floor, 3–50–11 Sendagaya, Shibuya-ku, Tokyo. The Netherlands: Martin Adelmund, 6 Vrijheidsdans, Capelle Aan den Ijssel 2907 TG. Spain: Sellex SA, 84 Donosti Ibilbidea Poligono 26115, Astigarraga. UK: Dutch Design Centre, 105 Lancaster Road, London W11 1UG. USA: Loewenstein Inc., 1801 North Andrews Ave. Ext, Pompano Beach, FL 33061–6369.

Segno, Piazza dello Sport 9, 20015 Parabiago (Milan), Italy. *Outlets* Germany: Agenzia Biggio, Lohe 16, D–27616 Heerstedt. The Netherlands: Miracles, Pruseagracht 218, HD 01016 Amsterdam. Portugal: I Ancari, R. Don Caompo Alrgre 1380, HAB 124 Porio. Scandinavia: Arelumina, Sibyltegatan 30. S 111 43 Stockholm. Switzerland: Andome Engros, Eigenstatstrasse 17, CH–08425 Oberembrach.

Seiko Epson Milan, via Spiga, Milan, Italy.

Sharp Corporation, 22–22 Nagaike-cho, Abeno-ku, Osaka 545, Japan.

Sony Corporation, 6–7–35 Kitashinagawa, Shinagawa-ku, Tokyo, Japan. *Outlets* France: Sony France SA, 15 Floréal, 75017 Paris. Germany: Sony Europa GmbH, Hugo Eckemer-Strasse 20, 50829 Cologne. Italy: Sony Italia SpA, via Fratelli Gracchi 30, 20092 Cinisello Balsamo, Milan. Spain: Sony España SA, Calle Sabinoide Arana 42–44, 08228 Barcelona. UK: Sony UK Ltd, The Heights, Brooklands, Weybridge, Surrey KT13 0XW. USA: Sony Corporation of America, 9 West 57th Street, 43rd Floor, New York, NY 10019.

Spectrum Meubelen, Postbus 15, NL 5570 AA Bergeyk, The Netherlands.

Squeeze Design, 35 Kallang Pudding Road, Singapore 349314.

Steltman Editions, 330 Spuistraat, Amsterdam 1012 VX, The Netherlands. *Outlets* USA: Steltman Gallery, 595 Madison Avenue, New York, NY 10012.

Stelton, PO Box 59, Gl. Vartov Vej 1, DK–2900 Hellerup, Denmark. *Outlets* France: Domino, 2 impasse de la Ferme, Houdemont 54180. Germany: Stelton, 5 Theodor-Babilon Strasse, Cologne 50679. Italy: Seambe srl, via deio Gracchi 30, Milan 20146. Japan: Japan Denmark Trade Centre, World Import Mart. 5F, 3–1–3 Higashi-Ikebukuro, Toshima-ku, Tokyo 170. The Netherlands: Mobach, 5 Portengen, Kockengen 3628 EB. Scandinavia: Villeroy and Boch Scandinavia, 43A Nyhavn, Copenhagen 1051, Denmark. Spain: Ms Lidia Roqueta Soriano, 3 C/San Juan, Cuenca, 16316 Campillos, Sirra. Switzerland: Leutwiler AG, Mr Oskar Leutwiler, 50 Büttenenhalde, Lucerne. UK: Storrington Trading Forum House, Stirling Road, Chichester, West Sussex PO19 2EN. USA: Entry USA Inc., 223 East 78th Street, New York, NY 10021–1224.

Strato, via Piemonte 9, Talamona 23018, Italy. *Outlets* Belgium: Tega NV, 9 Kastelpleinstr, Antwerp 2000. Germany: Design Diffusion, 1 Schwei, Stadland 26936.

Sumikawa Design Studio, No. 602, Sangenjaya 2–2–11, Setagaya-ku, Tokyo 154, Japan.

Svitalia Design SA, Piazzetta, Agra, CH–6927 Ticino, Switzerland.

D. Swarovski & Co., Watteus 6112, Tyrol, Austria. *Outlets* France: Swarovski France SA, 15 Boulevard Poissonnière, F–75002 Paris. Germany: D. Swarovski GmbH & Co. KG, Hüttenstrasse 27, Postfach 920, D–87600 Kaufbeuren/Neugablonz. Italy: Swarovski Internazionale d'Italia, via G. Puccini 3, Milan I–20121. Japan: Swarovski Japan Ltd, Sumitomo Hamamatsucho Building, 6th Floor, 18–16 Hamamatsucho, 1–chome, Minato-ku, Tokyo 105. The Netherlands: Swarovski H.O. Benelux BV, Ijsselmeerstraat 30, NL–1784 Ma Den Helder. Spain: Swarovski Ibérica SA, Avda Pompeu Fabra 12, E–08024 Barcelona. UK: Swarovski UK Ltd, Fleming Way, Crawley, West Sussex RH10 2NL. USA: Swarovski America Ltd, 2 Slater Road, Cranston, RI 02920–4468.

Taurus, Pl. Francesc Macià, 8–9, 08029 Barcelona, Spain.

Takenaka Works Co. Ltd, 2–1–16 Miyuki-cho, Takaoka City 933, Toyama, Japan.

Technische Industrie Tacx, Rijksstraatweg 52, 2241 BW Wassenaar, The Netherlands. *Outlets* Germany: Stier, Johannesstrasse 11, D–70176 Stuttgart 1. UK: Townsend Cycles, Horizon Park, Green Fold Way, Leigh Business Park, Leigh. USA: Quantum Bicycles & Fitness Inc., 26 West 515th Street, Charles Road, Unit B, Carol Stream, IL 60188.

Tendo Co. Ltd, 810 Midarekawa, Tendo 994, Yamagata, Japan.

Teunen & Teunen, Neumann-Reichardt-Strasse 27–33, Haus 14, 22041 Hamburg, Germany.

Tevere SpA, via Ermenegildo Cantoni 3, Milan, Italy.

Gebrüder Thonet GmbH, 1 Michael-Thonet-Strasse, Frankenberg 35066, Hessen, Germany. *Outlets* Austria: Leyss Classic, Tiergartenstrasse 127, A–6020 Innsbruck. Belgium: NV Trade Centre Belgium, Jonolaan 1, B–2900 Schoten. Czech Republic: Fiala Engineering srl, Pernerova 11, CZ–186 00 Prague 8–Karlin. France: Thonet Frères 283 rue de Pressoir, BP 58, F–77350 Le Mée-sur-Seine. Ireland: O'Hagan Contract Interiors Ltd, 101 Capel Street, IR-Dublin 1. Italy: Frigerio Architetture d'Interni, Divisione FAI, C. so Italia 124, I–20033 Desio-Milan. Japan: Aidec Co. Ltd, No. 28 Mori Building, 6F, 16–13 Nishiazabu 4, Minato-ku. The Netherlands: Bitter Culemborg BV, Industrieweg 18, NL–4153 BW Beesd. Scandinavia: USM Haller, Studio APS, Esplanaden 5, DK–1263 Copenhagen, Denmark. Spain: ULM, Balmes, E–08440 Cardedeu. Switzerland: Selefgorm AG, Im Gewerbezentrum, Gustav-Maurer-Strasse 8, CH–8702 Zollikon-Zh. UK: Aram Designs Ltd, 3 Kean Street, Covent Garden, London WC2B 4AT.

Toshiba Corporation Design Centre, 1–1 Shibaura 1–chome, Minato-ku, Tokyo 105–1, Japan.

UM:Kogyo, 1051–1 Kishi-cho, Ono City 675–13, Hyogo, Japan. *Outlet* The Netherlands: De Wild, 54 DeMeeten, 4700 BD Roosendaal.

Vanlux, s/n Poligono Eitua, Berriz 48240, Vizcaya, Spain. *Outlets* Australia: Inlite Pty Ltd, 75–78 Balmain Street, 3121 Vic. Richmond. Austria: Plan Licht, Vomperbach 187 A, A–6130 Schwaz. Belgium: Hilite NV, Leopold II laan 35, 8000 Bruges. Canada: Eurofase Canada Inc., 6900 Airport Road, Unit 239B, Ontario L4V 3YB. Denmark: Pasta Lab International, Duevej 54, Copenhagen 2000. Finland: Inno Interior KY, Merikatu 1, Helsinki 00140. France: Luci France, 96 boulevard Auguste Blanqui, Paris 75013. Germany: B. Lux Deutschland GmbH, Tulbeckstrasse 55, Munich 8000. Hong Kong: Krohn Ltd, 69 Jervois Street, Mezz Floor, Hong Kong. Italy: Contempora di Zannier Luigi, Piazza Rizzolatti 4, Clauzetto 33090. Japan: Akane Inc., 5–10 Higahinakano, 5–chome, Maraho-ku, Tokyo. Singapore: X.Tra Designs Private Ltd, 236 Tanjong Katong Road. Switzerland: Dedalus, via Gismonda 17, Mendristo CH–6850. Taiwan: Pinhole International, No. 11 Lane 639 Min Sheng E. Road, 10447 Taipei. UK: Candell Ltd, Carrera House, 33 Sut. Road, Walthamstow E17 6BH. USA: Artup Corporation, 3101 Shannon Street, Santa Ana, CA 92704.

Venini SpA, Fondata Vetrai 50, Murano, Venice 30141, Italy. *Outlets* France: Collectania, 168 rue de Rivoli, Paris 75001. Germany: Graf Bethusy – Huc Vertriebs, 1 Hans-Sachs-Strasse, Krailling 8033. Hong Kong/Singapore: Lane Crawford Ltd, 28 Tong Chong Street, 8/F Somerset House, Quarry Bay, Hong Kong. Japan: Kitaichi Glass Co. Ltd, 1–6–10 Hanazono, Otaru, Hokkaido 047. Monaco: L'Art Venitien, 4 avenue de la Madone, Monaco 98000. The Netherlands: Desideri, 50 Gossetlaan, Groot-Bijgaarden 1702, Belgium. UK: Liberty Retail Ltd, Regent Street, London W1R 6AH. USA: Hampstead Lighting & Accessories, 1150 Alpha Drive, Suite 100, Alpharetta, GA 30201.

Vera Vermeersch-Gilson, Rodelikvekensstraat 23, 9000 Gent, Belgium.

Verrerie de Nonfoux, Nonfoux 1417, Switzerland. *Outlets* Germany: Ingelore Lichtenberg, 25 Cristetl Schmidt-Allee, Ahrensburg 22926. USA: Cline Quest International, 2686 Middlefield Road, Redwood City, CA 94063.

Vest Leuchten GmbH, Piaristengasse 21, Postfach 323, A–1080 Vienna, Austria.

Vezet Belgium, 59 HV Zuylenstraat, Brussels 180, Belgium.

Viceversa, via dello Stelli 2A, Bagno A Ripoli 50010, Florence, Italy. *Outlets* Hong Kong: Viceversa Int. Ltd, 306 Prince Edward Road, Kowloon City, Hong Kong.

VideoGuide Inc., 209 Burlington Road, Bedford, MA 01730, USA.

Marlies Von Soden, Wielandstrasse 46, Berlin 10625, Germany.

WBM, 1815 East Lawndale Drive, San Antonio, TS 78209, USA.

Werth Forsttechnik, 22 Reidelbach, Wadern D–66687, Germany.

Werkstatt, Alte Miliere, Chur 7000, Graublinden, Switzerland.

Herman Wittocx, 262 Gallifortlei, Antwerp 2100, Belgium.

WMF, Eberhardstrasse, Geislingen/ST 73312, Germany. *Outlets* Austria: WMF Österreich GmbH, Etrichgasse 13, Postfach 502, A–6021 Innsbruck. Belgium: WMF Belgium SA, Brussels Trade Mart BP 673, Stand Dallas 445, Atomiumsquare, B–1020 Brussels. France: WMF France Succursale, 59 rue Gutenberg, F–75015 Paris. Italy: WMF Hutschenreuther Italia SpA, via della Meccanica 24, I–37139 Verona. Singapore: WMF Flatware (Pte) Ltd, 7 Gul Avenue, Jurong Town PO Box 20, Singapore 2262. Spain: WMF Espanola SA, Avda Llano Castellano 15, E–28034 Madrid. Switzerland: WMF (Schweiz) AG, Bernstrasse 82, CH–8953 Dietikon 2 ZH. UK: WMF United Kingdom, Palmerston Business Centre, 11 Palmerston Road, Sutton, Surrey SM1 4QL. USA: WMF, 85 Price Parkway, Farmingdale L.I. USA 11735, New York.

Wogg Möbelideen, Im Grund 16, CH–5405 Baden/Dättwil, Switzerland.

Wohnobjekte und Design Alfred Kainz, Steinrainer Strasse 16, 84066 Mallersdorf, Pfaffen-Berg, Bavaria, Germany.

Wombat, 49 rue Hughes Guerin, Lyon 69008, France. *Outlets* Belgium: Modern Times, 51 Jozef Cardgnlaan, St Amands 2890. Denmark: Spotlight A/S, 103 Kongensgade, Copenhagen 1264. Germany: Gisamone Grunwald, 22 Bahnstrasse, Rechernich 53 894. Hong Kong: Leo's Collection, 6 Fung Yip, Chaiwan. The Netherlands: 40 Langestraat, Lokeren 9160. Switzerland: Julia Balatoni Vertretungen, 8 Viale Papio, Ascona 6612. USA: IMC, 888 Brickell, Miami PO Box 112 305, FL.

XO, Cide 4–Servon, Brie Comte Robert 77170, France.

Yamagiwa Corporation, 1–5–10 Chiyoda-ku, Sotokanda, Tokyo, Japan.

Young Aspirations/Young Artists (YA/YA) Inc., 628 Baronne Street, New Orleans, LA 70113, USA.

Zanotta SpA, via Vittorio Veneto 57, 20054, Nova Milanese, Milan, Italy; Giovanni Marelli, via Guglielmo Oberdan 5, PO Box 148, I–20036 Meda, Milan, Italy. *Outlets* Australia: Arredorama International Pty Ltd, 1 Ross Street, Glebe, NSW 2037. Austria: Prodomo, 35–37 Flachgasse, 1060, Vienna. Belgium: Zaira Mis, 35 Boulevard Saint Michel, 1040 Brussels. France: Giuseppe Cerutti, Località Grand Chemin 1, I–11020 St Christophe (A0), Italy. Germany: Fulvio Folci, 14 Dahlienweg, 4000 Düsseldorf 30. Japan: Nova Oshima Co. Ltd, Sakakura Building, Akasaka, Minato-ku, Tokyo. The Netherlands: Hansje Kalff, 8 Puttensestraat, 1181 Je Amstelveen. Norway/Denmark/ Sweden: Poul Vigsø, Bagøvaenget 20, Skaerbaek, Fredericia 7000, Denmark. Spain: Angel Pujol, Av. República Argentina 218, 08023 Barcelona; Fernandez Casimiro, Urbanizacion Soto de Llanera, Casa No. 5, 33192 Pruvia, Oviedo. Switzerland: Peter Kaufmann, 123 Rychenbergstrasse, 400 Winterthur. UK: The Architectural Trading Co. Ltd, 219–229 Shaftesbury Avenue, London WC2H 8AR. USA: International Contract Furnishings, 305 East 63rd Street, New York, NY 10021.

238 acquisitions

Acquisitions by design collections in 1996.

Dates given in parentheses refer to the dates of the designs (from 1960 to the present day).

Australia

Powerhouse Museum, Haymarket, New South Wales

Gordon Andrews screen print on cotton, *Jungle* (1965–70), printed by Donald Clark
Mark Edgoose container, *Two Stack* (1995)
Patrick Hall tallboy, *Cityscape* (1991)
Mark Heidenreich/Stephen Bowers vase, *Chintz Vase with Cockatoos* (1989)
Karl Millar pepper grinder, *Bulbous* (1996)
Marc Newson watch, *Seaslug* (1993), manufactured by Ikepod Watch Co.
Beatrice Schlabowsky lidded barrel (1995)
Gerry Wedd screen print on cotton, *Credibility Strip* (1988), manufactured by Mambo Graphics Pty Ltd

Canada

Musée des Arts Décoratifs de Montréal

Ron Arad bookshelf, *Book-worm* (1993), manufactured by Kartell
Wendell Castle armchair, *Molar* (c. 1960), manufactured by Northern Plastics Company
Marzio Cecchi lamp, *Lumaca* (1977), manufactured by Studio Most
Antonio Citterio storage unit, *Mobil* (1993), manufactured by Kartell
Antonio Citterio/Glen Oliver low folding table, *Battista* (1991), manufactured by Kartell
Antonio Citterio/Glen Oliver low folding table, *Leopoldo* (1991), manufactured by Kartell
Antonio Citterio/Glen Oliver low trolley, *Gastone* (1991), manufactured by Kartell
Morison S. Cousins kitchen timer, *On the Dot* (1995), manufactured by Tupperware US, Inc.
Riccardo Dalisi bench, *Mariposa* (1989), manufactured by Zanotta
Roseline Delisle vase, *Quadruple 9,95* (1995)
Roseline Delisle vase, *Triptyque 11,95* (1995)
Roseline Delisle vase, *Triptyque 12,95* (1995)
Roseline Delisle vase, *Triptyque 16,95* (1995)
De Pas, D'Urbino & Lomazzi armchair, *Joe* (1970), manufactured by Poltronova
Bernhard Dessecker ceiling/wall lamp, *Lampeduso* (c. 1994), manufactured by Ingo Maurer GmbH
Guido Drocco/Franco Mello coat/hatstand, *Cactus* (1986), manufactured by Gufram srl
Jean-Paul Gaultier perfume bottle (1993), manufactured by Pochet Ducourval for Beauté Prestige International
Laura Handler/Dennis Decker/Magalhaes/ Amanda Hong goblet, *Gallery Glass* (1992), manufactured by Metrokane Inc.
Vicke Lindstrand vase, *Negresse* (1960s), manufactured by Kosa Glasbruk
John Lonczak lamp, *Cool Cat* (1991), manufactured by Form Farm Inc.
Bert Long textile, *Home Sweet Home* (c. 1990), manufactured by The Fabric Workshop
Enzo Mari container, *Java* (1968), manufactured by Bruno Danese srl
Ingo Maurer lighting system, *YaYaho* (1985), manufactured by Ingo Maurer GmbH
Ingo Maurer and Team table lamp, *Los Minimalos Uno* (c. 1994), manufactured by Ingo Maurer GmbH
Sergio Mazza mobile bar, *Bacco* (1968), manufactured by Artemide
A. Meda/Franca Raggi/Denis Santachiara floor lamp, *On Off* (1989), manufactured by Luce Plan
Alessandro Mendini textile (1993), manufactured by Design Gallery Milano 'Museum Market'
Verner Panton/Christophe Walch watch, *Click-clock* (1995), manufactured by Crival Products, Denmark

Jorge Pensi armchair, *Toledo* (1988), manufactured by Amat SA
Gaetano Pesce bucket, *Babel* (1995), manufactured by Fish Design
Gaetano Pesce clock, *Watch Me* (1995), manufactured by Fish Design
Gaetano Pesce lamp, *Moonshine* (1995), manufactured by Fish Design
Gaetano Pesce mirror, *Kalos* (1995), manufactured by Fish Design
Gaetano Pesce picture frame, *My Frame* (1995), manufactured by Fish Design
Gaetano Pesce tables, *Triple Play* (1995), manufactured by Fish Design
Gaetano Pesce tray, *Try Tray* (1995), manufactured by Fish Design
Gaetano Pesce vases, *Amazonia* (1995), manufactured by Fish Design
Jean Rancourt table Lamp, *Frobisher Bay* (c. 1985)
Astrid Sampe textile, *Versailles* (c. 1975), manufactured by Almedahls AB
Tobia Scarpa wall/ceiling lamp (1973), manufactured by Flos
Roland Simmons standard lamp, *Lumalight* (1994), manufactured by Interfold
Ettore Sottsass vase, *Mizar* (1982), manufactured by Compagnia for Memphis Milano
Philippe Starck table, *Miss Balu* (1989), manufactured by Kartell
Philippe Starck chair, *Dr Glob* (c. 1990–91), manufactured by Kartell
Philippe Starck chair, *Miss Global* (c. 1990–91), manufactured by Kartell
Philippe Starck chair, *Super Glob* (c. 1990–91), manufactured by Kartell
Philippe Starck stool, *Hi Glob* (c. 1990–91), manufactured by Kartell
Philippe Starck stool, *Bubu 1er* (c. 1992), manufactured by OWO
David Taylor scent bottle (1995)
Masanori Umeda vase, *Orinoco* (1995), manufactured by Memphis Milano srl
Andreas van Onck stepladder, *Tiramisù* (1990), manufactured by Kartell
Robert Venturi textile, *Large Equal* (c. 1990), manufactured by Fabric Workshop
Bashir Zivari stools, *Kin-der-Link* (1986), manufactured by Skools Inc.

Denmark

Museum of Decorative Art, Copenhagen

Nanna Ditzel two *Butterfly* chairs (1990)
Frank Gehry chair, *Little Beaver* (1990)
Knud Holscher thermos (1989)
Alev Siesbye dinner set, *Sirius Blue* (1990), manufactured by Royal Copenhagen
Torben Skov chair *Hølven* (1994)
Philippe Starck lemon squeezer, *Juicy Salif* (1988)
Mats Theselius chair, *Fåtölj* (1990)

France

Musée des Arts Décoratifs, Paris

César lamp, *Expansion* (1975)
César pencil case (1976), manufactured by Blanchet
Sydney Cash sculpture object (1994)
Claude Champy vase (1994)
Jorge Ferrari Hardoy, Juan Kurchan, Antoni Bonet armchair *Hardoy Chair* (1995), manufactured by Airborne
Brita Flander glass (1994), manufactured by Marimekko

Meike Groot vase (1995)
Olivier Mourgue chaise-longue, *Djinn* (1963), manufactured by Airborne (1993)
Denis Santachiara doormat, *Zerbino* (1991), manufactured by Domodinamica
Borek Šípek plates, *Albertine* from the *Follies* set (1989), manufactured by Driade
Ettore Sottsass vase, *Moneciga* (c. 1977), manufactured by Vistosi, Italy
Ettore Sottsass vase, *Joséphine* (1994), manufactured by de Sèvres
Jean-Michel Wilmotte seat (1983), manufactured by Mobilier International
Jean-Michel Wilmotte two low tables (1983), manufactured by Mobilier International

Germany

Kunstmuseum Düsseldorf im Ehrenhof

TV set, manufactured by Brionvega
Franco Clivio door handle (1994), manufactured by FSB Franz Schneider
Luigi Colani chair (1970), manufactured by Fritz Hansen
Raymond Loewy container furniture (1967)
Sergio Mazza chair, *Toga* (1968), manufactured by Artemide
Jasper Morrison door handle (1991), manufactured by FSB Franz Schneider
Dieter Rams sofa, *Modell 620* (1969), manufactured by Wiese Vitsoe
Philippe Starck chair, *Lord Yo* (1993), manufactured by Aleph
Philippe Starck chair, *Miss Balu* (1993), manufactured by Aleph
Philippe Starck door handle (1992), manufactured by FSB Franz Schneider

Vitra Design Museum, Weil am Rhein

H. Bätzner table, *Bofinger*
Mario Bellini two armchairs, *Le Bambole*
Michele de Lucchi lamp, *Oceanic*
Frank Gehry desk, *Experimental Edges*
Stefan Lindfors lamp, *Scaragoo*
Marc Newson chairs, *Bucky*
Gaetano Pesce stool and chair, *543 Broadway*
Gaetano Pesce armchair, *Feltri*
Gaetano Pesce chairs, *3 Greene Street*
Ettore Sottsass table lamp, *Valigia*
Philippe Starck stackable chair, *Dr Glob*
Superstudio table, *Quaderna 2600*

The Netherlands

Museum Boymans-Van Beuningen, Rotterdam

Andrea Branzi sauce boat with spoon, *Labrador* (1982), manufactured by Rossi e Arcandi, Monticello Conte Otto, Italy, for Memphis Milano
Konstantin Grcic computer table, *Refolo* (1995), manufactured by Atlantine/Aleph
Enzo Mari four vases and an instruction book, *Ecolo* (1995), manufactured by Officina Alessi, Crusinallo di Omegna
Richard Meitner bottle, *Porc Epic* (1996)
Issey Miyake three scarves (1995)
Barbara Nanning dish with lines from the series *Terra* (1996)
Michael Rowe container (1995)
Philippe Starck TV set, *Jim Nature* (1993), manufactured by Saba GmbH Hanover
Jan van der Vaart vase (1995)
Maarten van Severen chair, *NR2* (1992)
Frantisek Vizner bowl (1995)

Stedelijk Museum, Amsterdam

Sandra Chia/Matteo Thun cups and saucers for Illy Caffé (1993)
Vincent de Rijk bowls (1994)
Piet Hein Eek presentation case (1993)
Ineke Hans chair (1995)
Richard Hutten chair, *No Sign of Design* (1992)
Richard Hutten bench, *Crossing Italy I* (1994)
Donald Judd table and chairs (1993)
Andrea Manetti/Matteo Thun cups and saucers for Illy Caffé (1994)
Simone Meenten/Matteo Thun cups and saucers for Illy Caffé (1994)
Alberto Meda chair (1994)
Alberto Meda chaise-longue (1994)
Ulf Moritz curtain fabrics, *Uris, Laguna, Lundaris, Candidus* (1995)
Jasper Morrison chair (1988)
W. Noyons vase, *Double* (1994)
Maarten van Severen chair (1993)
Borek Sípek service, *Semaine* (1990)
Philippe Starck chair, *Lord Yo* (1994)
Pieter Sturm chair, *ISA* (1993)
Charlotte van der Waals two candlesticks (1980)
Charlotte van der Waals six folding vases (1986)
Martin Visser chair (1995)
Martin Visser chair (1993)

Norway

The Museum of Applied Art, Trondheim

Ergonomi Designgruppen coffee server, *SAS* (1987), manufactured by Dynoplast A/S
Enzo Mari, *Ecolo* (1995), manufactured by Officina Alessi
Benny Motzfeldt 188 glassware items (1958–95), manufactured by Plus Glasshytte, Randsfjord Glassverk and Hadeland Glassverk

The Museum of Applied Art of Western Norway, Bergen

Peter Raacke cutlery, *Ultima* (1982), manufactured by Norsk Stålpress
Swatch bathing cap (1995)
Swatch diving watch
Don Wallance cutlery, *Magnum* (1968), manufactured by Norsk Stålpress

The Oslo Museum of Applied Art

Black & Decker vacuum cleaner (1992)
Hans Bratterud chair, *Scandia Junior* (1960), manufactured by Hove Møbler
Sven Ivar Dysthe chair, *Prisma* (1967), manufactured by Westnofa Furniture
Sven Ivar Dysthe chair, *Akkurat* (1973), manufactured by Krosaether
Tias Eckhoff chair, *Tomi* (1983), manufactured by Teknoplast
Guzzini Italia icebucket, *Futura* (1989)
Lars Hjelle toothbrush, *Interbrush* (1971), manufactured by Jordan
Lars Hjelle dishwashing brushes (1973–80), manufactured by Jordan
Lars Hjelle toothbrushes, *Private Brand* (1973–80), manufactured by Jordan
Lars Hjelle toothbrush, *Double Action* (1985), manufactured by Colgate
Hans Jakob skiing boots, *Snow Runner* (1994), manufactured for Switzerland in the Olympic Games, in Lillehammer, Norway, 1994
Tupperware, parfait glass (1968)
Tupperware, milkshake glass (1970s)
Bendt Winge stacking chair (1970), manufactured by Nordic Products A/S

Poland

National Museum – Centre of Modern Design, Warsaw

Franciszek Aplewicz chair (1968), manufactured by Co-operative Lad
Stefania Rybus-Kujawa two bowls (1990), manufactured by Glassworks Irena
Wieslaw Sawczuk vase and bowl from the glass set *Beskidy*, manufactured by Co-operative Kamionka
Wanda Zawidzka-Manteuffel vase (1966), manufactured by Glassworks Irena
Wanda Zawidzka-Manteuffel carafe (1965–70), manufactured by Glassworks Irena

Sweden

Nationalmuseum, Stockholm

Eero Aarnio chair, *Pastilli* (1968), manufactured by Asko
Gunilla Allard stool, *Piano* (1989), manufactured by Lammhults Möbel
Mona Björk textile, *Zoom* (1987), manufactured by Borås Cotton AB
Karin Björquist service (1996), manufactured by Hackman Rörstrand
Peter Brandt footstool, *Bimbo* (1994), manufactured by Bla Station
Iittala Glasbruk glass, *Marius* (1985), manufactured by Iittala Glasbruk
Börge Lindau chair, *Gloria* (1986), manufactured by Bla Station
Börge Lindau chair, *Hövding* (1986), manufactured by Bla Station
Börge Lindau chair, *Beplus* (1987), manufactured by Bla Station
Anne Nilsson vase, *Sorbet* (1995), manufactured by Orrefors
Ingegerd Råman table service (1994), manufactured by Skrufs Glasbruk
Filippa Reuterswärd service, *Boule* (1966), manufactured by Reijmyre Glasbruk AB
Pia Törnell bench, *Sinus* (1994), manufactured by Rörstrand
Pia Törnell dish, *Sinus* (1994), manufactured by Rörstrand
Pia Törnell tray, *Plateau* (1995), manufactured by Rörstrand
Peter Opsvik stool, *Balans Vital* (1979), manufactured by Rörås
Tapio Wirkkala vase, *Ovalis* (1985), manufactured by Iittala Glasbruk

Röhsska Konstslöjdmuseet, Gothenburg

A & E Design Stockholm washing up brush (1995)
Helen Backlund hand-tufted carpet, *Nine Crosses* (1995), manufactured by Kasthalls Carpet Factory
Mona Björk printed cotton, *Dan Andersson* (1992), manufactured by Borås Wäfveri AB
Bo Bonfils cutlery (1988), manufactured by Georg Jensen
Mike Burrows bike, Lotus Sport 110 Carbon Road (1995), manufactured by Lotus GB
Kerstin Danielsson box with lid (1995)
Björn Ed bench, *Sun-carriage* (1990s)
Kicken Ericson embroidered picture, *Garden* (1994)
Anneli Ersbacken candlestick (1990s)
Bibi Forsman bowl with fruit (1995)
Mariann Gunnemark ceramic plate (1995)
Marianne Hallberg jug and basin (1995)
Lars Hellsten glass sculpture, *Blue Lagoon* (1995), manufactured by Orrefors
IKEA orange plastic chair (1970s)

Jan Klingstedt linen napkin, machine-woven damask (1995), manufactured by Horred Weaving Factory
Eva Lamby cup (1990s)
Anna Landgren bowl (1995)
Dagmar Norell vase, female figure (1974)
Gunilla Pantzar pictorial embroidery with sewn-on objects (1994)
Christina Roos jug with lid (1995)
Astrid Sampe printed fabric/polyester, *Versailles* (1970/1995), manufactured by Almedahls AB
Ylva Sandgren woven lengths, copper wire and paper strings (1995)
Gunilla Skyttla embroidered heart (1990s)
Åse Törnqvist vase (1995)
Stina Widen vase (1995)

Switzerland

Museum für Gestaltung, Zurich

Max Amsler building kit for children, *Constri* (1960), manufactured by Constri AG
Mario Bellini in collaboration with A. De Gregori, D.J. de Vries, A. Macchi Cassia, G. Pasini, S. Pasqui adding machine, *Divisumma 28* (1973), manufactured by Olivetti
Richard Fischer shaver, *Sixtant* (1967), manufactured by Braun AG
Jürgen Greubel hairdryer, *Super-Luftkissen-Trockenhaube* (1975), manufactured by Braun AG
Sonnhild Kestler silk scarves (1995), manufactured by Georg Couture
Vico Magistretti chair (1971), manufactured by Artemide SpA
Erik Magnussen salad server, *Stelton* (1975), manufactured by Stelton
Bruno Munari lamp, *Falkland* (c. 1995 re-edition of 1964 model) manufactured by Danese
Peter Schneider camera, *Nizo 2056 Sound* (1976), manufactured by Braun AG
Ettore Sottsass and Hans von Klier adding machine, *Summa 19* (1970), manufactured by Olivetti
Giotto Stoppino newspaper rack, *4626* (1971), manufactured by Kartell
Roland Ullmann shaver, *Lady-Braun Elegance* (1979), manufactured by Braun AG

UK

The Conran Foundation Collection, selected by Janice Kirkpatrick

(The selection in 1996 was predominantly graphic and packaging design)

Bill Amberg leather bag
Dalwa carbon fibre fishing rod
Nicole Farhi leather purse
Oakley Oakley Jackets sunglasses
Mike Sharp flat panel monitor, manufactured by IBM
Superdrug nail file
Tate and Style scarf

The Design Museum, London

Teaset, *Bandalasta*
Beolit radio, *707*
Bagen radio, *Freeplay*
Cossor *Melody Maker*
Ecko radio, *A33*
Kleinempfanger radio
Merconiphone radio, *P17B*
Philips radio, *2514*
Philips radio, *834A*
Wedgwood black basalt teaset

Victoria and Albert Museum, London

Ron Arad bookshelf, *Bookworm* (1995), manufactured by Kartell
Olivier Leblois cardboard armchairs (1995), manufactured by Quart de Poil
Poole Pottery *Aegean* dishes (1970s)
Pyrex table and ovenware dishes (1995)
Swatch telephone, *XK200 Twinphone* (1990)
Oiva Toikka glass beer mugs (1995)
Kati Tuominen-Niitylä earthenware jugs (1995)
Terence Woodgate modular storage system, *River* (1995), manufactured by Punt Mobles

USA

Museum of Fine Arts, Boston, Massachusetts

Nigel Coates chair, *Noah* (1988), manufactured by SCP
Nigel Coates chair, *Arc* (1994), manufactured by Theo Theo
Tom Dixon *S Chair* (1986), manufactured by Cappellini
Junko Kiramura earthenware (1995)
Shiro Kuramata chair, *How High the Moon* (1986), manufactured 1996 by Kuramata Design Office
Shiro Kuramata chair, *Miss Blanche* (1989), manufactured by Kuramata Design Office
Ingo Maurer lamp, *Lucellino* (1992), manufactured by Ingo Maurer GmbH
Barbara Nanning object from the *Unica* series (1995), manufactured by Royal Leerdam
Gaetano Pesce chair, *Pratt* (1984)
Gaetano Pesce chair, *543 Broadway* (1995), manufactured by Bernini SpA
Harvey S. Sadow plate (1981)
Philippe Starck toothbrush and stand (1990), manufactured by Fluocaril
Philippe Starck *Lola Mundo* (1995), manufactured by Driade
Philippe Starck lamp, *Rosy Angelis* (1996), manufactured by Flos
Philippe Starck lemon squeezer, *Juicy Salif* (1996), manufactured by Alessi SpA
Philippe Starck *Louis 20* (miniature)(1996), manufactured by Vitra
Philippe Starck Parmesan cheese grater, *Mister Meumeu* (1996), manufactured by Alessi SpA
Massimo Vignelli cups and saucers (1971), manufactured by Heller
Malcolm Wright bowl (1993)
Malcolm Wright vessel (1993)

The Brooklyn Museum, New York

Boris Bally wearable finger fork, *Point and Shoot* (1982)
Morison Cousins double colander (1994), manufactured by Tupperware
Morison Cousins kitchen timer, *On-the-dot* (1995), manufactured by Tupperware
Doris Hyman and Eva Zeisel plates, Waves pattern, Vivacious pattern and Iris pattern (1984)
Emily McLennan table lamp, *Steelite 5* (1994)
Roland Simmons Floor lamp, *Lumalight* (1994)
Lela and Massimo Vignelli with David Law nutcracker (1979), manufactured by Fratelli Calegaro srl

The Chicago Athenaeum – Museum of Architecture and Design, Chicago, Illinois

Anderson Design Associates Inc. baby baths, *Century* (1995)
Gino Anselmi door handle, *Cusio* (1973)
Gae Aulenti door handle, *Otto* (1983)
Mark Baldwin gas freestanding range, *Kitchenaid* (1995)

Carlo Bartoli door handle, *2010* (1980)
Mario Bellini teapot, *Cupola* (1989)
Doug Birkholz *Fiskars Press-N-Punch* (1995)
Ayse Birsel washlet, *Zoë* (1995)
Donald Booty jr flashlights, *Doubleheader Dual-beam* (1993) and *Guardlight* (1995)
Klaus Botta watches, *Titan 1* (1993) and *UNO* (1994)
Bruce Burdick and Susan K. Burdick table, *Aero* (1993)
Luigi Caramella door handles, *400* (1976) and *410* (1988)
Jerome Caruso liquid storage container (1994)
John Caruso desk lamp, *Meta* (1994)
Luigi Colani door handle, *Colani* (1989)
Joe Colombo door handle, *Paracolpi Alfa* (1989)
Gabriel Concari *Fiskars Six-Inch Protractor Plus* (1995)
Morison Cousins double colander (1994), manufactured by Tupperware
DCA Design International screwdrivers, *Irazola Premium Range* (1993)
Luigi Dominioni door handles, *Monte Carlo* (1979) and *Saint Roman* (1979)
Maurizio Duranti candlestick, *Lucifero* (1995)
Maurizio Duranti kettle, *Merlino* (1993)
Maurizio Duranti clothes hanger, *Trovatore* (1993)
ECCO Design kettle, *Revere Excel* (1995)
Georg Alexander Eisenhut suspension lamp, *Golden Gate – The Missing Link* (1994)
Fitch Inc Iomega Drives, *Zip* and *Ditto* (1994–5)
frogdesign inc. answering machine, manufactured by AT&T (1989)
frogdesign inc. personal communicator, *Envoy* (1994), manufactured by Motorola
frogdesign inc. multimedia computer system, manufactured by Packard Bell (1994)
Gai T. Gherardi and Barbara A. McReynolds, spectacles, *Regumba* (1995) and *Smokey* (1995)
John Grinkus radio (1993), manufactured by Bose
Walter Gropius teapot (1969)
Franco Guanzirolli door handle, *430* (1991)
Trisha Guild dinnerware and giftware, *Designers Guild* (1995)
Giorgio Gurioli and Francesco Scansetti, wall hanging or self-standing coat hanger, *Blos* (1995)
Dorothy Hafner teapot, *Flash* (1985)
Helix-Akantus Formgestaltung GmbH and Co. KG bottle stopper, *Pino* (1994)
Helix-Akantus Formgestaltung GmbH and Co. KG cardholder with money clip, *Clip* (1995)
Helix-Akantus Formgestaltung GmbH and Co. KG lemon squeezer, *Zitronella* (1995)

Henry Dreyfuss Associates *2-line Personal Information Center 882* (1995), manufactured by AT&T
Henry Dreyfuss Associates camera, *Spectra SE* (1995), manufactured by Polaroid
Herbst LaZar Bell Inc. vacuum cleaner, *Electrolux Canister* (1994)
Hans Hollein door handle, *1103* (1986)
Knud Holscher door handles, *D Line 112* (1972) and *115 M-Handle* (1989)
Soren Holst, door handle, *Swing* (1988)
Human Factors Industrial Design Inc. portable stereo system, *Jeep* (1995)
John Hutton stacking chair (1993)
Isao Hosoe Design office lamp, *Heron* (1994)
Isao Hosoe Design espresso coffee maker, *MACH* (1993)
Lawrence Laske tables, *Saguaro* and *Toothpick* from the *Cactus* collection (1993)
Ludwig Littmann *MultiMix M880* (1994), manufactured by Braun
Chi Wing Lo corner chests, *Eon* (1995) and *NYN* (1995)
Roberto Lucci and Paolo Orlandini chair *SoHo* (1995)
Attilio Marcolli door handle, *Desipro* (1988)
Ingo Maurer lamp, *Lucellino* (1994)
Michael McCoy table collection, *Aspen* (1995)
William McDonough textile collection (1995)
Richard Meier bowl, *Cross* (1994)
Richard Meier *Meier Medium Frame* (1984)
Richard Meier dinnerware, *Grid* (1992), *Meier White* (1992) and *Signature* (1992)
Mercatali and Pedrizzetti door handle, *Sfinge* (1982)
Tomoko Mizu centrepiece, *Leaf* (1995)
ODIN Designteam bottle openers, *Draupnir* (1993) and *Draupnir 2* (1994)
ODIN Designteam salt shaker, *Salzer* (1995)
Ole Palsby kitchen bowls (1993)
Verner Panton watches, *Verner Panton* (1994) and *Click Clock* (1995)
Dieter Rams door handle, *RGS 1* (1986)
Karim Rashid clocks, *Abaxial* (1993) and *Nambé Studio Collection* (1994)
Per Rehfeldt teapot with warmer, *Åbo* (1990)
Ben Rose upholstery/wallcover textile, *Jakago* (1994)
Aldo Rossi teapot, *Il Faro* (1994)
Ruth Adler Schnee woven upholstery, *Birds in Flight/Birds Afar* (1994)
Ruth Adler Schnee woven upholstery textile, *Threads* (1994)
Herbert H. Schultes floor lamp, *Orbis* (1992)
Massimo Scolari armchair, *Spring* (1993)
SG Hauser Design Staff shower and bath products, *In Touch* (1993–4)
Smart Design mixing bowls, *Good Grips* (1994)
Smart Design barbecue tools, *Good Grips* (1995)
Raymond Smith gas cooker hob, *Preference* (1994), manufactured by Dacor
Raymond Smith electric cooker hob, *Touch Top* (1995), manufactured by Dacor
Raymond Smith electric water dispenser, (1995)
Ettore Sottsass telephone stand (1973)
Philippe Starck *The Bathroom* (1994)
Thomas Starczewski chair, *El Toro* (1995)
Kevin Stark occasional table series, *Lauren* (1995)
Tangerine comb, *Drumm Flatliner* (1993)
Tangerine fax machine, *Goldstar* (1994)
Tangerine video recorder, *Goldstar P2000* (1994)
Mats Theselius armchair, *Theselius* (1994)
Thomson Comsumer Electronics remote control unit, *CRK 61 – The Shoe* (1993)
Thomson Comsumer Electronics televisions, *ProScan*, (1994), *Shark RCA 9-Inch*, (1994) and *13#17 series* (1994)
Thomson Comsumer Electronics video cassette recorder, *RCA VR678HF* (1995)

Alan Tye door handle, *Quaver* (1982)
Jan H. van Leirde lighting series, *Diapason* (1994)
Gerd Vieler, hat and coat hooks, *High Steel* (1993)
Gerd Vieler door handles, *High Steel Product Family 199* (1994)
Massimo Vignelli and Lella Vignelli glassware, *Whirlwind* (1994)
Massimo Vignelli and Lella Vignelli watch, *Halo* (1994)
Tassilo von Grolman cookware, *Compact GLI Range* (1992)
Tassilo von Grolman vacuum containers, *Big Mama* (1993) and *Hotel Design* (1993)
Tassilo von Grolman vacuum bottle, *Change* (1995)
A. Votteler chair, *Arno S70* (1973)
Johan Weernink boxes, *Contura* (1994)
Hannes Wettstein chronograph watches, *Ventura V-MATIC* and *V-MATIC* (1994)
Heinrich Wilke door handle, *115* (1972)
Fritz W. Wurster and Sabine Renner cutlery, *Votum* (1994)
Marco Zanini glassware, *Calypso* (1994)
Marco Zanuso door handle, *Due Z* (1983)
Zenith Electronics Corporation television remote control unit (1995)
ZIBA Design pill dispenser, *Alnamar* (1993)
ZIBA Design keyboard, *Natural* (1994), manufactured by Microsoft
ZIBA Design water filter, *Mistra* (1994)
ZIBA Design telephones, *Sprint* (1994)

Cooper-Hewitt National Design Museum, New York

Eric Chan, ECCO Design Inc. cookware, *Excel* (1993), manufactured by Revere Ware Corporation of Corning Vitro Corp.
Ursula Haupenthal chair, *Egg Chair* (1992), manufactured by Pankl Praezisionstechnik GmbH
Benny Motzfeldt pair of glass vases (1985–6)
Smart Design Inc. telephone, *Home Phone* (1994), manufactured by Cicena Inc.

Denver Art Museum, Denver, Colorado

Philip Baldwin and Monica Guggisberg glasses, *Ten Tumblers* (1987), manufactured by Lindshammer
Donald Chadwick and William Stumpf armchair, *Aeron* (1994–5), manufactured by Herman Miller Inc.
Giulio Confalonieri bowl, *Maya* (1977), manufactured by Alessi SpA
Oscar Tusquets Blanca side chair, *Gaulino* (1986), manufactured by Carlos Janes Camacho SA

Los Angeles County Museum of Art, Los Angeles, California

Rudi Baumfeld telephone stand (1970s)
Don T. Chadwick chair, *Equa* (1984), manufactured by Herman Miller Inc.
Don T. Chadwick chair, *Aeron* (1994), manufactured by Herman Miller Inc.
Jan De Swart cook's cabinet (1967)
Sir Norman Foster table, *Nomos* (1995), manufactured by Tuno

The Museum of Modern Art, New York

Junichi Arai polyester, nylon fabric (c. 1995)
Junichi Arai polyester, aluminium slit yarn (c. 1995)
Cliff Chi in-line skate tool, *Gripz* (1994), manufactured by Sonic Sports Inc.
Joe Colombo drinking glass, *Asimetrico* (1964–8), manufactured by Tiroler Glashütte – Claus Joseph Riedel KG
Shiro Kuramata chair, *Miss Blanche* (1989), manufactured by Kokuyo Co.

Lohmann GmbH and Co. KG textile, *Paraform* (c. 1995)
Sam Lucente and Robert P. Tennant portable computer, *Think Pad 701* (1995), manufactured by International Business Machines
Sir William Lyons car, *E-Type Roadster* (1963), manufactured by Jaguar Ltd
Enzo Mari container, *Java* (1969–70), manufactured by Danese Milano
Enzo Mari wastepaper basket (1971), manufactured by Danese Milano
Eiji Miyamoto scarf (1992), manufactured by Miyashin Co. Ltd
Ritva Puotila textile, *Woodnotes* (1987–91), manufactured by Woodnotes OY
N.V. Schlegel SA textile, *Isowave* (c. 1995), manufactured by N.V. Schlegel SA
Reiko Sudo fabric, *Jelly Fish* (1993), manufactured by Nuno Corporation
Reiko Sudo fabric (1994), manufactured by Nuno Corporation
Reiko Sudo fabric, *Corn Silk* (1994), manufactured by Nuno Corporation
Reiko Sudo fabric, *Rakugaci* (1994), manufactured by Nuno Corporation
Reiko Sudo fabric (1994), manufactured by Nuno Corporation
Reiko Sudo fabric, *Bubble Pack* (1995), manufactured by Nuno Corporation
Reiko Sudo fabric (c. 1995), manufactured by Nuno Corporation
Tomoyuki Sugiyama speaker, *Bubble Boy* (1986), manufactured by Inax Corporation
Toray Industries Inc. textile, *Torayca* (1995)
Toray Industries Inc. encircling net (1996)
Toray Industries Inc. tyre cord (1996)
Niklaus Troxler silkscreen (1995)
Yamazaki Vellodo Co. Ltd fabric, *Wave Process* (1995)
Koichi Yoshimura textile (1992), manufactured by S. Yoshimura Co. Ltd

Philadelphia Museum of Art, Pennsylvania

Frank O. Gehry chair, *Cross-check* (1989–91)
Rieko Sudo fabric, *Feather Flurries* (1993), manufactured by Nuno Corporation